BRAIN,
ENVIRONMENT, AND
SOCIAL PSYCHOLOGY

BRAIN, ENVIRONMENT, AND SOCIAL PSYCHOLOGY

by
J. K. Chadwick-Jones, Ph.D.
Professor of Psychology

Irmingard I. Lenzer, Ph.D.
Associate Professor

James A. Darley, Ph.D.
Associate Professor

Kenneth A. Hill, Ph.D.
Assistant Professor

Department of Psychology,
Saint Mary's University
Halifax, Nova Scotia

University Park Press
Baltimore

UNIVERSITY PARK PRESS
International Publishers in Science, Medicine, and Education
233 East Redwood Street
Baltimore, Maryland 21202

Typeset by American Graphic Arts Corporation.
Manufactured in the United States of America by
The Maple Press Company.

Publisher's note: Masculine pronouns are used exclusively
throughout this book for the sake of simplicity. They are not meant
to be preferential or discriminatory.

Library of Congress Cataloging in Publication Data

Main entry under title:

Brain, environment, and social psychology.

Includes bibliographies and index.
1. Nature and nurture.   2. Psychobiology.
3. Social psychology.   4. Environmental psychology.
I.   Chadwick-Jones, John K. [DNLM: 1.   Environment.
2.   Psychology, Social. 3.   Psychophysiology. WL103
B814]   BF341.B68   155.2'34   78-27269
ISBN 0-8391-1323-4

Contents

Acknowledgments vii

Chapter 1 INTRODUCTION
J. K. Chadwick-Jones 1

Chapter 2 BRAIN AND BEHAVIOR Recent
Topics in Human Neuropsychology
Irmingard I. Lenzer 15

Chapter 3 SEX DIFFERENCES AND
SIMILARITIES
Irmingard I. Lenzer 33

Chapter 4 SEX DIFFERENCES IN SOCIAL
BEHAVIOR
J. K. Chadwick-Jones 49

Chapter 5 SOCIAL PSYCHOLOGY
J. K. Chadwick-Jones 71

Chapter 6 LANGUAGE AND SOCIAL
BEHAVIOR
J. K. Chadwick-Jones 85

Chapter 7 SOCIAL PERCEPTION IN
CHILDHOOD
Kenneth A. Hill 107

Chapter 8 THE DEVELOPMENT OF CHILDREN'S
COMMUNICATION SKILLS
Kenneth A. Hill 127

Chapter 9 ETHOLOGY Animals and How They
"Speak" to One Another
James A. Darley 147

Chapter 10   ENVIRONMENTAL PSYCHOLOGY
              Buildings—We Shape Them; Do
              They Shape Us?
              James A. Darley 175

Chapter 11   CONCLUSION Open Questions and
              Controversies
              J. K. Chadwick-Jones 191

              Index 199

Acknowledgments

The authors wish to thank the following people for helpful and constructive comments that led to improvements in the book: Donald O. Hebb, F.R.S. (Chapters 2 and 5, and the section "Human Territoriality" of Chapter 10); Wallace E. Lambert of McGill University, Montreal, and John W. Berry of Queen's University, Ontario (Chapter 6); Karen Dion of the University of Toronto (Chapter 3); Alice Eagly of the University of Massachusetts (Chapter 3); H. R. Schaffer of Strathclyde University, Scotland and Brendan Rule, University of Alberta (Chapter 7); Stuart Dimond of Cardiff University, Wales (Chapter 2); Henry Lackner, formerly of Saint Mary's University (Chapter 2).

We were also helped by discussion with Donald Hebb at various times during the academic year 1977–78 when he came to Saint Mary's University as a visiting professor.

Thanks are due to Peter Trudgill of the University of Reading, England, for permission to reproduce five tables in Chapter 4 from his book *Sociolinguistics*.

Vicki Prosser and Shirley Buckler typed several drafts efficiently and with patience.

Occasionally the commentators' viewpoints were different from the authors', and while their criticisms led to improvements in the text, they have no responsibility for the opinions expressed herein that were and are the authors' own.

To
Araceli, Edward,
Joan, Carol

BRAIN,
ENVIRONMENT, AND
SOCIAL PSYCHOLOGY

Chapter 1
INTRODUCTION

J. K. Chadwick-Jones

The prime objective of this book is to provide a supplement to the large basic introductory text by presenting certain problems that have been the subject of very recent research. The authors intend to make topical questions easily available to beginning students, giving them a preview of issues that can be expected to attract future enquiry.

The themes are related, some are novel, and all currently form part of the science of psychology. In neuropsychology, in the development of thinking and social competence in children, in language and social behavior, and in the psychology of urban life, a variety of contemporary issues are explored. Some chapters deal with controversial, open questions concerning sex differences and the roles of men and women in society. How are these questions approached and answered by psychologists? By outlining the psychologists' questions it is hoped that students will be encouraged to ask their own questions and to discuss them.

Chapter 5 gives a view of the discipline of social psychology and shows the student the areas it covers, the methods used, and the kinds of problems studied. Chapter 10 describes many studies of animals in their natural environment; the studies have helped researchers understand more about the origins of human behavior.

When the collusive "we" is used in the text, it refers not only to the authors but to the readers as well, because we are part of a joint effort in the study of our subject—psychologists and students of psychology together.

The contents of each chapter in the book are now summarized. Some students may wish to read the chapters in this order, but others may want to read, say, the chapters on developmental psychology before the chapters on sex differences. Much will depend on the sequence of lectures in psychology courses and on the student's own preference.

CHAPTER 2: NEUROPSYCHOLOGY

Human neuropsychology is the study of brain structures and brain systems that are associated with characteristically human mental processes and behavior. Historically, most of the work in this field has been done with human patients after brain damage (incurred through disease, war injury, or accident). In recent years, however, neuro-psychology has been broadened to include data from normal humans and from animals, particularly primates, with which links with humans are most probable.

Chapter 2, first of all, provides the beginning reader in psychology with an opportunity to become aware of some of the questions that are being asked today about the mind and the brain. The questions turn out to be difficult ones, but simply asking them is salutary, for it becomes clear that psychology, whether it is defined as the science of the mind or as the science of behavior, demands an understanding of the brain as the foundation to all else.

Second, the chapter supplements discussions about the nervous system in introductory texts, which usually take the form of neuroana-tomical and neurophysiological resumés, providing the basis for sub-sequent discussions of motivation, sensation, perception, and memory. Chapter 2 has a brief account of general neuroanatomy, starting from the concept of brain function and then focusing on specific brain struc-tures and areas as they are related to functions that are peculiarly human, such as language, right- and left-handedness, and cerebral dominance. The aim is to show, ultimately, that even the most human of human experiences, the experience of the self, is open to scientific investigation using methods of human neuropsychology and building on the knowledge that these methods generate.

CHAPTER 3: SEX DIFFERENCES

The last two decades have been a period of intense interest in the study of sex differences in humans. Chapter 3 gives a brief look at some of the questions, theories, and research findings that psychologists have considered important to the understanding of what may lie behind the observed differences.

The material is organized according to the chronological develop-ment of the human individual from conception onward. Thus, at the beginning of the chapter the emphasis is on biological factors, with a sketch of how chromosomes and hormones control the development of physical sex characteristics. The limitation of the discussion to purely biological factors is only feasible, however, for the period before birth. Even for this period, cultural and environmental factors can be very important in the determination of physical sex characteristics. For example, mothers who have been persuaded to take certain sex hormones may have offspring with abnormal external genitalia. After birth, when the question of *behavioral* sex differences becomes paramount, it is essential to consider the biological and the cultural factors together.

Once the child is born, society's ways of sex typing its new member are unavoidable. Sex-typed expectations, rewards, and sanctions are built into the social and family encounters of the child, interacting with the biological groundwork. Psychological theories propose mechanisms by which the behavioral sex differences that result are established. The chapter briefly summarizes the major theories that account for the acquisition of gender identity and gender role. The three theories (besides the purely biological theory) are the social-learning theory, the cognitive-developmental theory, and the psychoanalytic theory.

Observation and study of an individual's sex-typed behavior is one thing, but the documentation of behavioral differences clearly separating men from women (and boys from girls) is quite another, That is, there is a large area of behavioral overlap that clouds the clear dichotomy of male and female. Chapter 3 focuses at some length on this area of overlap. The dichotomy is most difficult to maintain in those cases involving one form or another of hermaphroditism. Hermaphrodites are individuals of ambiguous physical sex characteristics. The way in which our society treats this biological abnormality is instructive in what it tells us about how behavioral sex differences come about. Furthermore, the question of what the early effect of hormones is on later sex-typed behavior may be partially answered.

The discussion then shifts to behaviors that have traditionally been thought to separate males from females. Aggression in particular is scrutinized. Considered by many to be positively sex-typed for males and negatively sex-typed for females, aggression, in fact, is subject to large cultural variations. It is an error to treat aggression, which is a complex behavior, or a web of similar behaviors, as if it existed invariably and uniformly across cultures and situations. The analysis of sex-typed behaviors has to take into account the many forms that such behaviors may take and the many contexts in which they may be expressed.

The chapter ends with a closer look at the concept of *role* and with an examination of the extent to which cultural stereotypes of sex-role behavior are simply reinforcing the biological undercurrents that are operative in the nature of things.

CHAPTER 4: SEX ROLES

Differences in the social behavior of the sexes have been the subject of some recent research (but not a large amount). Subtle differences appear between male and female speech, with women tending to speak more correctly than men of their same social level. This especially tends to occur in borderline social categories, for example, between lower-middle and working class. Women are conservative if it is a matter of preserving better speech forms, but they become innovative if it is a case of introducing more prestigious pronunciations into their social group.

These differences in speech suggest that women are more effective in or sensitive to speech behavior than men. We discuss some likely explanations and the supporting evidence, including the viewpoint that competence or sensitivity may be indirectly connected with the greater dependency of women in our society. Should we agree with this point of view? The question is by no means settled.

Feminist movements have encouraged a closer examination of sex differences. We illustrate this influence in the discussion of intonation in female speech. The greater expressiveness of women's speech patterns, with rapid "glides" (changes of pitch), lends itself to sex typing of a negative kind in the classic imitation of the "effeminate" voice by male impersonators. To some people such features of speech have negative connotations, indicating a "female personality" that is inferior or unstable. It is suggested, from the feminist position, that the greater dynamism of women's speech should be given a more positive interpretation.

The evidence presented shows that women seem to be more attentive to social signals from others, more sensitive to the social class significance of accent and pronunciation, and generally more alert to the social world. This evidence is, at least, consistent with the well-known tendency of females to do better on tests of verbal capacity and fluency. Moreover, in nonverbal communication, women use eye contact more than men in conversation and they look more at the faces of other people, possibly because they are more alert to signals or cues in interpersonal relationships.

Feminist movements in different countries consider Freudian theory to be an ally of male prejudice. We consider here the less common view that Freud's theories provide a better understanding of the patriarchal system. This understanding leads to some questions about the necessity for having a patriarchy. These somewhat unusual ideas constitute the most difficult part of Chapter 4, but they illustrate the persistent (and unexpected) influences of Freudian theory.

The coercion of women in society is discussed as it occurs in one of its extreme forms—rape. Researchers have contributed very recently to this discussion, and they argue that solutions to the problem of rape will require changes in the social, legal, and economic position of women.

Contemporary changes in sex roles—what women do and are expected to do or be in society—are hinted at in a recently published review of experimental studies in social psychology. Other indications come from the changes observed in the roles of both partners in marriage, with women moving, in some cases, from the status of junior partner to the status of equal partner.

CHAPTER 5:
SOCIAL PSYCHOLOGY—THREE UNITS OF STUDY

Social psychology is shown to cover an extremely wide variety of topics that can best be organized by answering the question, "What is the unit of study?" The answer is threefold: the unit of study could be the individual, the dyad (two persons), or the small group. For each of these, there is a choice of research methods: experiments, observation in everyday life, interviews, or questionnaires. Methods have been adapted from other areas of psychology but research designs have also been created especially for social situations, and we go into some detail about these.

Theory in social psychology usually comes from suggesting tentative explanations. Starting from an informal guess, we can suggest a *hypothesis* or probable explanation and then search for evidence (from experiments, observation, or questionnaires) either confirming or disconfirming it. It may be that certain specific explanations will hold from one situation to another and we are, thus, on the way to generalizing about social relations. In Chapter 4 we encounter a similar process, in which evidence of female social skills was found in several contexts. From this evidence it may be possible to construct generalizations about the relationship between social competence and female gender.

We discuss why research on social behavior cannot be objective to the same degree as research in the physical sciences. Some methods are discussed that are unique to social psychology, such as the sociometric tests (to measure friendship patterns) and attitude scales (to measure people's opinions and intentions). In our laboratory classes we can gain an understanding of the scientific method by careful arrangement of experiments, and we illustrate this by describing experiments with individuals, dyads, and groups.

CHAPTER 6: LANGUAGE AND SOCIAL BEHAVIOR

In Chapter 4 we see some of the implications of speech styles in social situations. Now we examine the issue of bilingualism and relationships between different language communities. Our examples are taken from the United States, Canada, and Europe, but all show a general tendency for people to follow rules concerning which language or dialect (we can refer to either as a "code") should be spoken *when*, *where*, *to whom*, and *about what*.

People often have a choice among languages, dialects, or accents, and they may switch from one to another depending on whether the situation is a formal or informal one or whether they are speaking to friends or strangers. These situations can be classified into "domains." By observing which language or code is generally spoken in each domain, it becomes possible to establish that there are rules for code-switching and rules to predict generally, but quite confidently, how the rules will operate.

Social psychology contributes theories that are useful in explaining why individuals switch codes. Language and personality are connected, and we consider how far a person's personality and behavior also change when code-switching happens.

One way in which speech expresses the quality of a relationship between two persons is by the form of address used. We use the examples of the French forms *tu* or *vous*. In English, although we no longer use the equivalent *thou* or *ye*, we also have available some subtle classification possibilities, through the use of titles, first names, and their diminutives.

A detailed study of the social aspects of diglossia and bilingualism is discussed, using as an example the Acadians in Atlantic Canada, a language community similar in many speech characteristics to the Chicanos of the Southwest. Situations like these are studied by observation of everyday behavior, but other social aspects of speech have been subjected to intensive laboratory study.

Results of long-term research are also available on French immersion teaching (that is, teaching all subjects through the medium of French) in Canadian schools. Here, English-speaking children are likely to show some changes in social attitudes in addition to knowledge of a second language.

Finally, the enterprise of systematic research confirms that speech is a key element in understanding the relations between individuals and between groups.

CHAPTERS 7 AND 8: COGNITIVE AND SOCIAL DEVELOPMENT—COMMUNICATION SKILLS

In 1962 a historian of science, Thomas Kuhn, introduced the concept of the scientific "paradigm." A paradigm includes the various methods, beliefs, and assumptions shared by a particular scientific community. When the conventional paradigm is no longer considered satisfactory, a paradigm "shift" occurs, and it is replaced by a new paradigm. Kuhn's discussion could not have been more timely for the science of psychology. During the early 1960s, more and more psychologists were moving away from the "old" psychological paradigm, behaviorism, with its rejection of all "mentalistic" concepts, such as "expectancy," "purpose," and even "self." New developments in the psychology of language, for example, made it clear that thought processes could no longer be ignored; human behavior is quite likely to be governed by such unseen, mentalistic phenomena as plans, rules, and self concepts. The new paradigm was dubbed *cognitive* psychology.

It was also about that time that a Swiss philosopher-psychologist named Jean Piaget was "discovered" by North American child psychologists—despite the fact that Piaget had been publishing his work (mostly in French) for nearly 40 years and was already familiar to a number of English-speaking psychologists. Because of this sudden interest in Piaget's theory of "cognitive development," child psychology was changed dramatically. Chapters 7 and 8 reflect the influence of cognitive psychology in general and Piaget's ideas in particular on the recent study of child development.

Chapter 7 traces the course of social perception from infancy to adulthood. The discussion on infancy reflects a burgeoning interest in what infants *can*, rather than cannot, do, in both the perceptual and the social realms. Generally, there seems to be considerable continuity between social perception and nonsocial perception, and, in fact, many psychologists of infancy are claiming that perceptual and social development progress together. The recent emphasis on the infant's social and perceptual *competencies* belies the old description of the infant's world as a "blooming, buzzing confusion."

Also discussed are the child's ability to recognize faces and to perceive emotions in others and his tendency (depending on age level) to evaluate others. We note that children demonstrate biases in their social perceptions, such as ethnic and sex-role stereotyping.

The discussion of moral judgments would probably not have been included in a chapter on social perception had it been written by someone nurtured on the "old," behaviorist paradigm, which would not have allowed mentalistic terms to intervene in the stimulus-response formula. However, it has been made compellingly clear that the same action may be responded to quite differently by a perceiver on different occasions, depending on how the perceiver interprets the behavior. The most important interpretative factor is the *attribution of intent*, which will greatly affect moral judgments and retaliation to inflicted harm. Later we consider the development of more "positive" forms of social perception, such as empathy and judgments of kindness.

A particular social percept may in fact be influenced very much by inferences, suppositions, and hunches; indeed, people seem so inclined to "go beyond the information given" that some psychologists prefer the term social *cognition* over social perception. Chapter 8 discusses the role (and development) of such social cognitions in one especially important mode of social interaction: the communication process. Skills that are assumed to be necessary for effective communication are discussed, as well as the factors in the child's life that are conducive to the development of communication competence. Cognitive development is one such factor, and indeed Piaget's influence is clearly evident throughout the discussion.

Next we give attention to the skill called perspective-taking ability, and its opposite, egocentrism. It was Piaget who first suggested how important it is for the child to learn to take another's perspective in order to communicate effectively. However, it seems that Piaget himself—who was among the first to marvel at the child's mental world—might have overestimated the young child's egocentrism and apparent lack of communicative intent. Research now indicates that even toddlers may have remarkable perspective-taking and communication ability.

Chapter 8, like the previous chapter, also discusses some of the ingenious methods child psychologists have recently devised in order to uncover just how much young children *know* and can *do*. Older methods of testing or experimenting with children tended to be mere simplifications of procedures typically used with adult subjects; the methods were especially inclined to overtax the child's verbal facility, for example. Now researchers are coming up with tasks and procedures more appropriate or "natural" for the child's age level. The results in many instances are no less than startling. Perhaps there is something of a miniature "paradigm shift" in the works for the study of child development.

CHAPTER 9: ETHOLOGY

Animals, like humans, have to coordinate activities among themselves. This coordination requires some means of communication or "animal language," in which a variety of the senses can be used. A dog uses hearing by barking or whining, smell by marking objects with urine, and sight by wagging its tail or baring its teeth.

The discipline concerned with animal communication is ethology, which examines the animal behavior primarily in its natural habitat. Two schools of animal behavior have emerged over the last 40 years: the comparative psychologists and the ethologists. The former were primarily concerned with learning and conducted their experiments for the most part in laboratories, using rats as test animals. Ethologists studied many species of animals in a natural environment and focused on unlearned behavior. The overlapping interests of the two groups led to controversy and rapid expansion of the study of animal behavior.

Anthropologists and sociologists recognized that the techniques of the ethologists might be useful for human studies, and they have subsequently adopted the ethological approach. One question that often arises is: How relevant can animal behavior be to the understanding of human behavior? The question is discussed at length; the argument for "continuity" between animal and human studies, not a new issue but still a lively one, is presented.

Ethology employs a number of methods. The first method is to make an extensive and accurate catalogue or "ethogram" of all behavior patterns the animal exhibits. Emphasis is placed on study in as natural a habitat as possible to minimize the effect of captivity on behavior.

A second method is to observe the development of a specific behavior pattern. When does it first appear in the animal's life? What are the factors that precipitate it for the first time? Does it come about through learning, or is it inherited? This can be determined by isolating animals from others to see what behavior they show when they have had no opportunity to imitate others. In this fashion innate or inborn patterns can be determined.

A third set of methods focuses on motivation. What are the factors that lead to the occurrence of a pattern at a specific time and place? (A female adopts a courtship posture *because* her mate is present and he performs courtship displays that stimulate her.) Certain "releasing stimuli" can activate behavior. (A male stickleback attacks crude models with red stomach regions. The "red below" releases the attack response.)

Signaling behaviors are called "expressive behavior." Many of these behaviors have become "ritualized" or enhanced to exaggerate the signaling function. A peacock not only has developed a very elaborate, enormous, multicolored tail but also exhibits it in a spectacular fashion. It is spread during the courtship display to its full extent and is vibrated. The color, the size, the spread, and the vibration all enhance its signal value. Different species of animals show different amounts of expressive display. As one would expect, a very social (high-contact) species has many more expressive patterns that are more elaborate than those of relatively solitary (low-contact) species. Presumably a high-contact species requires more means of coordinating activities than a low-contact species.

Another observation made by ethologists concerns a form of behavior called a "fixed action pattern." A fixed action pattern is stereotyped and is inherited. For example, all dogs show the same pattern before sleeping. They turn in circles "preparing the bedding," sometimes scratching the surface before lying down. The behavior is stereotyped and once started seems to continue automatically.

Ethology has provided a much better understanding of behavior observed in different species. These systems appear to be shaped by evolution, just as body forms are, and they appear to be just as stable.

We may attempt to apply some of the ethological concepts to human actions. Parental responses to children seem to have been produced by "releasing stimuli" akin to those that are observed in animal studies. These have been exaggerated in cartoons and in other media to create a "supernormal" response to such things as Disney characters, dolls, or some species of dogs.

Humans also exhibit a much more complex behavior shared by many species of animals, that is, territorialism. People defend many more things than any other species of animal, a fact that is probably an extension of the complexity of our present technology. We use libel laws to defend our names, and we defend our houses, cars, gardens, and many other possessions or territories in a variety of ways. This defense of things is very similar basically to that observed in many species of animals.

In summary, as Chapter 9 illustrates, it seems we have more bio-logically based behaviors than we previously suspected. For many years it was widely accepted that our highly developed learning ability accounted for most, if not all, of our behavior. Now a more balanced view is held. Learning is still a major factor in shaping our behavior, but our genetic background plays a large part as well.

CHAPTER 10: ENVIRONMENTAL PSYCHOLOGY

Considerable interest in the human environment has developed over the last few years. Overcrowding in cities, with their ghettos and impersonality, has been blamed for the rising rates of crime and vandalism. Can humankind really adapt to urban life? Over millions of years our ancestors evolved a hunting-gathering form of existence, where limited groups moved about in a nomadic fashion collecting food. Ten thousand years ago a dramatic change in life style came about with the advent of farming; a few humans could feed many. Populations increased in numbers as food limitations were removed through improved farming.

Many of our present-day behaviors suggest we may be reaching our limits in terms of our ability to survive the urban environments. "Back to nature" trends, such as moving to the country, camping, organic gardening, and communal living, are on the increase. City dwellers are questioning, and in many cases stopping, many forms of urban development such as high-rise buildings and highway develop-ment. The effects urban development has on humans are now of primary concern. Previously, urban administrations often gave more consideration to traffic flow problems and the potential tax revenue of new buildings than they did to the problem of the human living condi-tions in urban areas.

The problem of our genetic limitations cannot be resolved; we have no way of determining our limitations. However, it can be argued that we have not had sufficient time to respond in an evolutionary sense to the urban environment. Evolution normally requires many thousands of generations before a genetic response to environmental conditions comes about.

One factor that is often cited as the source of many human prob-lems is crowding. This, on examination, is somewhat difficult to prove. In Hong Kong, densities of 2,000 people per square acre are observed, whereas the maximum allowed in London, England, is 200 people per square acre. Cultural factors somehow intervene in one's perception of "crowded." Some evidence based on number of people per room suggests that high densities are correlated with homicide, juvenile crimes, and civil disorder. Mental and physical illnesses have also been found more frequently in crowded conditions. Other factors influence crime rates. Building design can affect the rates of crime in and around them. On a per capita basis, crime in two to three floor apartments has been shown to be half what it is in apartments sixteen or more floors in height.

High vandalism rates are found in many public-housing units. These could result from the frustration and anger often brought about by forced rehousing from central slum areas to new public housing. Many slum dwellers are happy. They have close friends nearby, are close to downtown facilities, and have very low rents. The new housing usually has higher rent levels, it is far from shopping and other facilities, and friends are dispersed. In spite of improved housing, the people are worse off than before.

Building design has also been cited as a major factor contributing to widespread vandalism. In high-rise family apartments mothers can no longer keep track of their children once they are out of the apartment. Free from parental or adult supervision, children can and do vandalize with relative impunity. Another factor contributing to vandalism is a response to "hard architecture." New buildings are made of concrete; picnic tables are concrete and are embedded deep in the ground. Playgrounds are covered with asphalt, and in some cities even the rivers are lined with cement. Subways are lined with glazed tiles, and the subway car seats are hard and uncomfortable. These impersonal surroundings are personalized with graffiti or are rejected through vandalism.

What can be done to combat some of these problems? In high-rise family apartments facilities for children's play should be available, along with some form of adult supervision. Otherwise, more traditional forms of housing should be encouraged, in order to allow parental control. Attempts should be made to soften concrete environments with flowers, trees, and lawns. Public housing should be built at the slum sites where friends and facilities remain accessible. Consideration of these approaches could alleviate many of the problems before they arise.

Some cities are considered to be more pleasant than others, and city "legibility" may be an important factor. If a city has distinctive features, such as specific centers of activity, clear-cut boundaries, such as rivers or lake shores, and recognizable districts and landmarks, it is considered to have more of a "personality" than a city without these features. People are more comfortable living in or even visiting a "legible" city, since they can maintain their orientation more easily than they can in a monotonous city, where one district or area seems much like another.

Residential satisfaction has been examined in various types of neighborhoods, with surprising results. In upper-middle-class communities people were most satisfied in the least dense neighborhoods, where neighbors took good care of lawns, houses, and flowerbeds. On the other hand, in an urban slum the two main factors associated with neighborhood satisfaction were the feeling that the community and area outside the home was an integral part of the home and a high level of kinship and neighbor contacts. Since most planning and development is carried out by middle-class individuals, caution must be exercised. Middle-class standards do not apply to all situations. If public housing is to be developed, consideration must be given to the inhabitants. Their wishes and lifestyle must be understood before planning takes place. This could eliminate many of the problems that develop after people are moved to these public-housing developments.

The interest in how buildings shape our behavior has led to many fascinating observations in recent years. We are now aware that buildings can indeed alter human behavior.

Chapter 2
BRAIN AND BEHAVIOR
Recent Topics in
Human Neuropsychology

Irmingard I. Lenzer

How can an understanding of the working of the brain contribute to an understanding of the human mind and the experience of the self? Some believe that coming to grips with the working of the brain is a simpler undertaking than coming to grips with that "inner core," the self, around which mental states revolve. Some believe, further, that it is impossible to understand the self by studying the brain, because this "inner core" does not lend itself to scientific investigation. It is the aim of this chapter to examine such views in the light of experimental data gathered from the normal and the damaged human brain.

Our understanding of the relationship of brain functioning to the human experience of the self would be one step ahead if we could agree on a definition of the *self*. English and English (1958) offered the following as possible definitions:

> All that a person is tempted to call by the name of *me* or *mine*.

> That aspect or part of the person or organism which carries out psychic, mental, or psychological acts.

The first definition stresses the all-inclusiveness of actions and experiences, while the second emphasizes the self as the origin or originator of experience and activities. However, no matter whether the self is viewed as the sum total of the "me experiences" or as the agent giving shape to these experiences, the self as a concept remains elusive.

Our experiences are seemingly coordinated, integrated, and organized, but when we search for the "central core," the "I," we are unable to find a distinct part that could properly be regarded as the self. Yet, the experience of the self at a given moment of introspection persists.

It is not, however, the purpose of this discussion to settle on a definition of self or to investigate the self from a philosophical point of view. Rather, let us assume the reality of the self, however conceived, and proceed to examine research on normal and brain-damaged humans to see what light is shed on the relationship between brain and the experience of self. The discussion focuses first on some psychological functions that contribute to what we think of as mind and subsequently on the self that lies behind or is at the core of these functions. These functions are not indivisible but rather they dissociate themselves on occasion, as in the example (discussed later) of the brain-bisected patient who with one hand wanted to harm his wife, while with the other hand he tried to protect her. The experimental findings and case reports show the difficulty of keeping psychological functions, and indeed the self, always wrapped up in a neat bundle. The confrontation of our "intuitive" notion of self with the paradoxical findings of the laboratory and the clinic (e.g., through the study of brain-damaged patients) may perhaps leave us still somewhat perplexed. The following discussion puts together neuroanatomical, physiological, and psychological data that give us the basis at least to ask the right questions about brain processes and the human self.

EVOLUTION OF THE BRAIN

Millions of years of evolution have made the human brain the most intricately packed matter known. At the same time, the brains of lower animals, while they are less complex, have the same recognizable ground plan as the human brain. As a rule, once a bodily structure has been developed at a rudimentary level, nature does not abandon this structure in a high species, but rather integrates the older structure within the more complicated design of the newer. This is clearly so in the case of the brain.

Neuroanatomists divide the brain into three large regions: the hindbrain, the midbrain, and the forebrain. The *forebrain* has undergone the greatest development in the human, particularly the part called the cerebral cortex. In lower vertebrates, such as fish, there is no cerebral cortex. In humans, on the other hand, approximately 9 billion brains cells out of an estimated total 12 billion are in the cerebral cortex. Thus, three-fourths of all the brain cells have come to lie in a part of the brain that made its appearance relatively late in the evolutionary history of the brain. It is this part of the brain that is so important for the crucial human processes, such as reasoning and problem solving.

The enormous increase in the human cerebral cortex has led to its mantle-like (cortex literally means bark) coverage of the rest of the brain. As the mass of the mammalian cortex increased from species to species, it was pushed upward and backward, because of the physical restrictions the skull placed on further forward expansion, until it came to envelop the rest of the brain. In the limited space of the skull, the cortex is like a large piece of cloth pushed into a small container. As the surface area of the cloth increases, so do the number of folds and the extent to which the walls of the folds touch each other. In neuroanatomical terms, the top elevation of a fold is called a gyrus or *convolution*; the part of the fold that is buried and that constitutes the groove is called a *sulcus* or *fissure*. The convolutions and fissures are used as geographical landmarks when we subdivide the cortex into different "lobes." Four such lobes are recognized: the frontal lobe (the cortex in front of the cerebral sulcus), the parietal lobe (lying behind the central sulcus), the temporal lobe (below the lateral fissure), and the occipital lobe (lying posterior to the parietal and temporal lobes). However, dividing the brain into large regions should not lead us to underestimate the heterogeneity that exists, even within small regions of the brain.

STRUCTURE AND FUNCTION

The study of the *structure* of the brain (and the nervous system as a whole) is called neuroanatomy. The study of the *functions* of the various brain structures is called neurophysiology or neuropsychology depending on whether the focus of study is on the physical and chemical or on the behavioral and mental. What does it mean to say that a given structure has a particular function? What does *function* mean? Do we have an adequate grasp of behavioral and mental processes when we say that a specific process is a function of a given structure or group of structures?

Luria (1969), the Russian neuropsychologist, has discussed the meaning of "function" in the context of the relation between brain organization and mental activity. He distinguished two different meanings of the word "function." In one sense, we say that a structure has a certain function when it is highly specialized to do a certain job. For example, the function of the cells of the pancreas is to produce insulin; the cells are engaged in a specific job, localized in a specific area of the body. The second meaning of the word function has a much broader scope, as, for example, in the term "intellectual functions." Clearly, when talking about intellectual functions, we are referring to a complex adaptive mechanism by which the organism relates to the environment. Luria argued that function, in this broad sense, refers to a system composed of many parts, the relations between which may vary according to the requirements of the situation.

The following example illustrates the adaptability of behavior in relation to an environmental change. A rat that is taught to run a maze to receive food in a goal box may, when faced with a maze filled with water, *swim* to the goal box. The important point here is that goals may be reached by various means involving a change from certain subroutes to others, and this gives the organism flexibility in the execution of a task. Such behavior cannot be located as a function of any one specific area of the brain.

In our efforts to discover the workings of the brain, we may be tempted to search for structures that have, locked within them, the secrets of intelligence and memory. However, this would be wrongheaded, Luria suggested. All attempts to "localize" higher mental functions prove to be fruitless. Nonspatial (abstract) concepts, such as intelligence and memory, cannot be imposed on the spatial layout of the brain. Instead, we should try to understand how a given brain area may be important for a particular function, relative to other brain areas. In order to find what brain areas are involved in particular complex mental processes, these same processes must not be studied as if they were "indivisible."

Let us follow up this approach. At a very basic and general level the functions of the cortex can be divided into three categories: sensory, motor, and associative. Cortical areas that have sensory functions are those that process information coming through the senses (e.g., the visual, auditory, or tactual sense). Cortical areas that have motor functions are those that send out signals to muscles, bringing about movement. Cortical areas that have associative functions are those areas that deal with the integration of information. Originally, the terms sensory, motor, and associative arose from experimental work with animals. In the sensory cortex, electrical signals are recorded when a sensory modality is stimulated (e.g., light stimulus to the eye). The motor cortex consists of areas that, when electrically stimulated, give rise to body movement. The associative cortex does not respond to sensory input directly, nor does it give rise to motor responses when stimulated; it is the cortex that is "silent" in this context. The associative cortex areas have increased most in humans in terms of sheer mass. We learn more and more about their various specific functions from patients with brain damage as they are studied by clinical neuropsychologists and neurologists.

From this starting point, dividing the cortex into sensory, motor, or associative areas, we look within each of these areas for more specific functions. For example, in the occipital lobes lie the primary visual sensory areas, and in the parietal lobes lie the primary sensory areas for touch. Within the motor cortex are the cells that control movement of individual muscles or groups of muscles. Within the associative cortex are areas crucial to intelligence, memory, and problem-solving ability. Evidence shows, for example, that damage to associative areas in the temporal lobes may bring about a permanent loss of long-term memory, starting at the time the damage to the brain occurs.

In recent years much attention has been focused on the concept of *lateralization* of cortical functions. Some functions seem to depend much more heavily on the left side of the brain than on the right, while for other functions the reverse is true. Lateralization applies particularly to the higher mental functions. Since the concept is so significant for the purposes of this discussion, let us examine it at some length.

TWO IN ONE

Investigations have shown that the brain is not a single structure with various regions, but rather a *paired* structure; i.e., two identical singles that are mirror images of each other. We speak, therefore, of *two* cerebral hemispheres, *two* brain halves covered with cortex. This duplication is not surprising when it is remembered that throughout evolution the primary function of the nervous system has been to communicate with and control the body, which is symmetrical (at least in motile animals) around a central body axis. Thus, generally speaking, each half of the brain has come to control one-half of the body. The left half of the brain has taken on the right side of the body and the right half of the brain the left side of the body. This relationship holds for most motor functions and for some, although not all, sensory functions. For example, the right visual field is represented in the left occipital area and the left visual field in the right occipital area. *Contralateral* hook-up is the term used to describe the relationship that exists between one brain-half and the *opposite* body-half. There also exists an *ipsilateral* control between one brain-half and the *same* body-half, but this type of control (when present) is weaker and less clearly understood than contralateral control. It is important, however, to keep ipsilateral control in mind, because when contralateral control is failing or no longer possible (e.g., as a result of brain damage) ipsilateral control may in certain instances prevail.

How do the right cortex and the left cortex remain mutually informed? After all, the two sides of the body are locked into one organism, and one hand knows what the other is doing. Clearly, this question involves a strong subjective component; our everyday experience is of the *unity* of behavior and awareness. How are two brain-halves doing so well what we feel to be the work of one? The answer (although by far not the entire answer) lies in the structural link-up between the two hemispheres.

COMMISSURAL CROSS-TALK

The left and right cerebral cortices are interconnected by nerve fibers; there are specific hook-ups between corresponding brain cells of the two cortical halves. The name given to a collection of these hook-ups is *commissure*. There are several commissures, varying in size, location, and importance. The largest, most researched, and most interesting with respect to human behavior is the commissure called the *corpus callosum*.

The evolutionary appearance of the corpus callosum is much more recent than that of the cortex itself. Rudimentary appearance of the corpus callosum is first noted in marsupials (e.g., kangaroos and oppossums). The corpus callosum reaches its greatest density (in terms of number of fibers) in the human brain. Dimond (1972), who has written extensively on this subject, pointed to the enormous potentialities of a cross-communication system like the corpus callosum for the effective and speedy integration of information between the two hemispheres. The evidence is that the efficiency of the corpus callosum, measured in terms of time taken to transmit information between hemispheres, is greatest in the human.

As the most recent addition to the human brain, the corpus callosum has thus made the brain into a more efficient information processor without significantly adding to the space problem resulting after millions of years of evolution. The efficient commissural integration of information between the two hemispheres is especially important for the higher mental functions, many of which are lateralized (that is, only one side of the brain is involved in the processing of information that then has to be made available to the other side).

CEREBRAL DOMINANCE

Sensory and motor processing occur in both hemispheres of the brain, although the material that is processed in one hemisphere is not the same as that processed in the other (which is another way of expressing the idea of contralateral control). Certain kinds of processing, including many of the complex kinds, are largely limited to one hemisphere, which brings us to the concept of cerebral dominance. Cerebral dominance does not refer to the dominance of the cerebrum over the rest of the brain, but rather to the dominance of one hemisphere over the other in the operation of certain mental functions. To find out what may account for cerebral dominance, a number of recent investigations into the structural differences between the two hemispheres have been undertaken (see, for example, Galaburda et al., 1978).

The concept of cerebral dominance has a long history, going back to the 1860s, when Broca, a French surgeon, published his findings about language representation in the brain. He showed that there exists in the frontal lobes an area that has language functions. This area lies close to the cortical areas governing the muscles of speech production, also in the frontal lobe. Broca further argued that it was the area in the *left* frontal lobe that had language functions, and not the corresponding area in the right frontal lobe. He based his argument on studies of patients with aphasia (a term used to describe certain language disorders resulting from brain damage). Over the years, the view has come to be accepted that this brain area (since called Broca's area) is essential for language. The general clinical characteristics of Broca's aphasia are slowness of speech and poor articulation. The deficit is evidently not the result of paralysis of speech muscles, the cortical control of which is also centered near Broca's area. For example, Geschwind (1972) reported that aphasic patients, who were unable to speak, could still sing a melody.

Broca's clinical accounts of aphasia were soon followed by reports of language disorders resulting from damage to a second area lying in the posterior part of the left cerebral hemisphere at the border of the lateral fissure near the "confluence" of the parietal-occipital-temporal regions. This is now called Wernicke's area, after the German psychiatrist who first described aphasia resulting from damage to this region. Wernicke's aphasia is characterized by rapid production of speech with little "content." It is not certain at present how these two language areas communicate with each other, nor is it clear how the integration of sensory and expressive aspects takes place to produce meaningful, fluent language. According to Geschwind, there is evidence that the fiber system called the *arcuate bundle* is the connecting link between Broca's and Wernicke's area.

Historically, then, the concept of cerebral dominance grew out of studies on aphasia that involved areas in the left hemisphere. This led to the view that the left half of the brain was the *dominant* hemisphere, while the right half was less important. However, in recent years, with growing understanding of right-hemispheric functions, the concept of unilateral dominance, i.e., dominance of the left hemisphere, has been abandoned. We now know that the right hemisphere is dominant for some functions, such as visual-spatial processing.

HANDEDNESS

It is hardly possible to discuss lateralization of functions without touching on the subject of handedness. Right-handedness in humans has been with us for a long time and has been traced back at least 5,000 years. Coren and Porac (1977) examined artwork from which hand preference could be deduced. They showed that the right hand was used in 93% of the cases; these results support a physiological theory of handedness rather than a theory that posits that handedness is the result of cultural and social pressures.

Nowadays about 90% of all people are right-handed, i.e., the right hand is the dominant (preferred) hand in the execution of most tasks, and 10% are left-handed. "Mixed" handers are also included within these two groups, making for a gray zone between pure right handers (dextrals) and pure left handers (sinistrals). When establishing handedness, the task required of a person is of considerable importance. For example, experienced typists who are right-handed attain equal or better speed with the left hand. Other tasks, such as playing the violin or the piano, rely heavily on the left hand even though the person may be right-handed. These examples are important to remember when adjectives like "preferred" or "dominant" are used.

Handedness probably does not exist in subhuman species. It is true that some animals, in the execution of some tasks, preferentially use one hand or forelimb. However, compared to the strong bias toward the right hand in humans, forelimb preference in subhuman species seems almost random, with 25% preferring right forelimb, 25% preferring left, and 50% showing mixed preferences. Unlike humans, animals shift easily from preferred to non-preferred forelimbs.

Handedness develops slowly in children and becomes fully established much later than language does. Research shows that most children do not show a clear hand preference before the age of three, and that handedness is only established firmly at about six years. One theory is that the slow emergence of hand preference is the result of the later neuronal development of the corpus callosum. This would suggest that the normal infant has, in effect, a "split-brain," in the sense that the corpus callosum has not sufficiently developed to allow cross-integration and cross-control of the two cerebral hemispheres; the child thus finds it difficult to shift activities from hand to hand, and in particular from the left to the right hand.

THE HANDEDNESS-SPEECH LINK

The link between handedness and cerebral dominance for speech is far from being fully understood. One of the major reasons for this is that, while handedness may be fairly easy to determine in a given person, cerebral dominance for speech is not. However, two technical advances may help.

The first is a technique, now referred to as the Wada test, by which cerebral speech dominance may be determined. The technique involves the injection of sodium amytal, a barbiturate, into the intracarotid artery of the subject. The subject is conscious and engaged in talking, but when the drug reaches the hemisphere controlling speech, he becomes aphasic. Thus, the hemisphere controlling speech can be identified by the time it takes after injection for aphasia to set in. It is obvious, however, that routine use of the test on normal individuals is not warranted, and so the findings from the Wada test apply mostly to patients undergoing brain surgery.

There is a second technique that has been used with normal individuals to establish the hemisphere dominant for speech. It is called the dichotic listening technique and involves the simultaneous presentation of pairs of different stimuli (words or numbers) to both ears via earphones. Those subjects who report more of the words or numbers heard with their right ear than those heard with their left ear are assumed to have left-hemispheric dominance for speech.

Research studies in which hemispheric speech dominance has been demonstrated by means of these tests indicate that almost all dextrals have left-hemispheric speech dominance. One implication of this is that a right-handed person who shows aphasia upon damage to the right hemisphere can be suspected of being originally *left*-handed.

This suggests that we consider further the relationship between handedness and speech in left-handers.

The Origins of Left-Handedness

Some cases of left-handedness are clearly of genetic origin. This holds for individuals who show not only dominance of the left hand but also dominance of the left eye and left foot. There are others who are genetically left-handed, but who have been pressured to use the right hand for writing. These individuals will use the left hand more frequently than pure right-handers do on tasks other than writing. A third group includes those whose left-handedness resulted from damage to the right hand or arm or from damage to the left cerebral hemisphere. If damage to the brain occurred before two years of age (e.g., brain damage at birth), the shift from the damaged to the healthy hemisphere may go unnoticed.

How is language lateralized in sinistrals? Studies on language deficits resulting from brain damage in sinistrals show that aphasia may occur as a result of damage to *either* hemisphere. Remarkably, sinistrals often recover from aphasia faster than dextral patients; this may be because language is not as strongly lateralized in some sinistrals as it is in dextrals. From tests for lateralization of speech it has been learned that more than 50% of normal and brain-damaged sinistrals have left-hemispheric language dominance, while less than 50% have language representation in the right hemisphere or in both. These data account for the fact that aphasia may occur in sinistrals as a result of damage to either hemisphere.

Let us examine more closely one theory of the beginnings of the link between handedness and speech in the young child: before the age of two, when the child's corpus callosum has not fully developed, the child uses the right hand more often (because of genetic predisposition or social pressures) than the left hand, making the left hemisphere more active in a sense than the right hemisphere. The additive effects of the increased use of the right hand give the left hemisphere the advantage of a greater number of memory traces and practice in performance of the task compared to the right hemisphere. The increased use of the left hemisphere makes it a more competent hemisphere that absorbs more information from the environment and generally takes the lead. Another aspect of this theory nicely explains the primitive language functions that have been observed in the right hemisphere: in the young child, before the right hand becomes the preferred hand, use of the left hand engages the right hemisphere in memory storage and instructions to and from the world;

some form of a language system, although primitive, is set up in the right hemisphere. This theory explains why damage to the left hemisphere in the young child (under two years, before the functional hook-up of the corpus callosum has taken place) is less disruptive to language acquisition than it would be later on in the development, because the right hemisphere may take on the tasks that would have been done by the left hemisphere. This theory, which emphasizes hand preference in determining hemispheric abilities, is very probably deficient in that it overlooks the structural differences between the hemispheres already seen in the fetus.

SPLIT-BRAINS IN ANIMALS

Recently, as a result of the development of a surgical technique, lateralization of functions has been studied more intensely than ever. In the 1950s investigators began to look systematically at the role the corpus callosum plays in behavior. The question was all the more intriguing because in previous research commissurotomy (cutting of the commissures) in animals did not seem to produce changes in behavior. However, a new turn was taken when findings were reported from research with cats whose corpus callosum and that part of the visual tract that connects one eye with the opposite visual cortex were sectioned. After such an operation each eye was connected to one hemisphere only; that is, visual stimulation of the cat's eye was transmitted to the cerebral hemisphere on the same side as the eye and not to the other hemisphere. Cutting the corpus callosum halted the transfer of information between the two hemispheres.

A cat with an operation of this type was able to do something a normal cat could not do: learn two contradictory tasks without conflict. The experimental set-up for such learning involved the use of an eye patch over one of the cat's eyes. In one study the task presented to the uncovered *left* eye was to choose between a circle and a square. A reward followed the correct choice. The cat learned to discriminate between the rewarded and the nonrewarded symbol; that is, the left hemisphere learned the task. Then with the left eye covered the cat learned to choose between the symbols, but this time the reward was given for choosing the symbol that was previously not rewarded. Cutting the corpus callosum (and other commissures) produced a brain split into two independently functioning units, with one unit not knowing what the other knew. By precisely controlling the destination of the visual input in the brain (a situation not encountered by the cat outside the experimental set-up) through the placement of an eyepatch on one of the eyes, the experimenter was able to teach "contradictory" responses (Sperry, 1964).

HUMAN SPLIT-BRAINS

In the 1960s operations involving commissural transection were performed on human patients with epilepsy. Their purpose was to prevent the spread of abnormal firing of brain cells (bringing about the epileptic attack) from one hemisphere to the other. Gazzaniga (1967), who studied patients with commissural transections, reported the case histories of the first patients receiving this operation. As expected, bisection of the brain did not give rise to gross behavioral deficits. However, carefully designed testing procedures soon revealed a host of deficits peculiar to the bisected-brain patient.

Before going into discussion of these deficits, a word is in order concerning the term "bisection" of the brain. Bisection of the brain does not usually entail *complete* transection of the two hemispheres; there are still alternate routes of crossed transfer possible in the bisected brain. However, investigators are able to create conditions so that specified kinds of information cannot be transferred from one hemisphere to the other.

Much of the testing of bisected brain patients involved the use of visual material. This stands to reason given the precise neuroanatomical hook-up between the eyes and the brain. Imagine that you fix your eyes on a point in front of you; the scene thus perceived is called the *visual field*. This can be divided into a left visual field (to the left of the fixation point) and a right visual field (to the right of the fixation point). Representation of the left visual field is in the right occipital lobe of the cortex, and representation of the right visual field is in the left occipital lobe of the cortex. The location of the left and right visual fields depends, therefore, on the fixation point. As the point of fixation changes, so do the visual fields. The duration of fixation on one given point is usually very short, a fraction of a second. One way to circumvent the problem of changing points of fixation and changing visual fields (and therefore changing cortical representation) in an experimental situation is to ask the person to fixate on a point, and then to flash a visual stimulus for a short period of time (around 1/20th of a second), too brief a time for eye movements. The instrument used for the presentation of visual stimuli for durations of a "split second" is called a *tachistoscope*. Gazzaniga described some early experiments with visual material. In one experiment the picture of a spoon was presented tachistoscopically to the left hemisphere (i.e., the picture was projected to the brain-bisected patient's right visual field). The patient was able to report verbally what he saw. Then the same picture was projected to the left visual field. This time, however, the patient was unable to give a verbal or written report of what he had seen. The results suggested that disconnection of the commissures prevented 1) the transfer of visual information from one hemisphere to the other and 2) the transfer of visual information from the right hemisphere to the language area in the left hemisphere. Thus the functional asymmetry regarding language that has been previously shown in left-hemispheric brain-damaged patients could be demonstrated in a brain-bisected patient through manipulation of visual input.

The question of awareness inevitably arises. Gazzaniga discussed a patient who was asked to select with his left hand (controlled by the right hemisphere) from a number of items hidden from view the item that had previously been presented to the right hemisphere (a spoon). (The assumption here is that the visual information is contained in the same hemisphere that guides that hand.) Would the patient be able to select the correct item? The answer is yes; but the patient was still unable to describe the object that was "seen" in the right hemisphere and felt and selected with the left hand. Thus, asking the patient to indicate nonverbally what the right hemisphere had seen brought about the correct response, at least behaviorally. But was the patient *aware* of the spoon?

Let us consider another report that bears on the enigma of awareness in the split-brain patient. In this experiment by Gazzaniga (1970) visual material of neutral or provocative content was tachistoscopically presented to the left or right visual field of a split-brain patient. The experiment was designed to show whether or not emotional responses could be elicited. The procedure involved the showing of an unexpected picture of a nude woman, among a series of neutral pictures, to either the right or the left hemisphere. When the picture was shown to the right hemisphere, the female patient grinned and chuckled but nevertheless reported that she had seen nothing. When asked by the examiner the reason for her laugh, she did not know but speculated that the machine may have been funny. When the picture was shown to her left hemisphere she also laughed, but now she knew the cause of her laughter; that is, she reported the pin-up. Translating these results into psychoanalytic language, we could say that the person's behavior in the first instance was governed by unconscious processes (the perceiving of the pin-up in the right hemisphere) and by conscious as well as unconscious processes in the second instance. [As a matter of fact, the double-mind theory (Feher, 1973) places the unconscious in the right hemisphere.] The presence of language areas in the left hemisphere seems to have added a dimension of consciousness.

Through study with brain-bisected patients, lateralization of certain complex functions in the *right* hemisphere has been demonstrated. This research of necessity involves nonverbal methods of testing, that is, ways of communication not involving language. Gazzaniga (1967) described the behavior of a brain-bisected patient given the task of copying drawings of three-dimensional objects, for example, a house or a cube. When asked to copy the drawing of the house, he was able to do so only with his left hand (under the control of the right hemisphere) even though he was right-handed. The drawings he did make with his right hand were poor reproductions, leaving out three-dimensional lines and other important spatial features. Why is it then that the patient was able to complete the task with his left hand but not with his right hand? The answer appears to be that spatial analysis requires right-hemispheric control, manifesting itself in the differential performance of the drawing task. The patient was able to evaluate his own performance, criticizing the poor quality of the right-handed reproduction, but was unable to translate his judgment into the practical application; the left hemisphere failed to give proper guidance to the right hand for proper performance of this spatial task.

Clinical data that have contributed to our growing understanding of right-hemispheric functions have used what is called the *split-stimulus* technique (Levy, 1974). When a bilaterally symmetric stimulus is projected exactly on the midline of the visual fields (i.e., the left half of the stimulus lies to the left of the point of fixation and the right half of the stimulus to the right of the point of fixation) something unexpected happens: the brain-bisected patient sees the total picture. It is unexpected, because the left hemisphere receives only the right visual field (containing half of the stimulus), and the right hemisphere receives only the left visual field (containing the other half of the visual stimulus). Each hemisphere must thus *complete* the missing half of the stimulus in the absence of interhemispheric transfer. As long as the stimulus is made up of two identical halves, this perceptual feat will not be apparent. What happens when one-half of the stimulus is exchanged for a different stimulus? One experiment (as described by Levy, 1974), using faces as the visual material, did just that. Photographs of two faces were cut in half at the face's midline, and a new face was created by joining the left half of one face to the right half of the other face, thus creating a "chimeric" face. The patient, after having seen the chimeric face by the split-stimulus technique, is asked to select from photographs of faces, the face he has seen previously. The patients select the face seen in the right hemisphere. Unlike the patients in the previous experiment who can judge poor right-handed drawing, the patients in this experiment are not aware (at least not by verbal indications) of the chimeric nature of the face shown by the split-stimulus technique.

From experiments like these involving the use of brain-bisected patients, hemispheric differences in processing various types of stimulus material have been uncovered. The study of the bisection syndrome has opened a whole new way of studying the human brain, with new testing techniques for the study of brain-damaged patients or normal subjects, and indeed a new approach to the understanding of mental processes, consciousness, and the self.

"WHO AM I?"

Neuropsychological work with animals and humans shows how sensory stimulation is transmitted along the various pathways within the nervous system until it arrives in the cerebral cortex. Recording electrical activity of single neurons within the various sensory systems of animals shows how the sensory input is processed, or "shaped," according to the rules of the system. The riddle that remains unanswered is how the final transformation is accomplished; how the sensory input is transformed into an *experience* of an object. Similar questions apply to behavior. Electrical stimulation of the motor cortex elicits movement in animals and humans. However, humans (and also animals, though perhaps to a lesser extent) follow a course of action in everyday life, according to internal and external commands, that exceeds in complexity any behavior so far achieved by experimental stimulation. In other words, there is a *will*, which sometimes seems to stand behind behavior, even resisting the commands of the environment and of the body.

As mentioned at the beginning of this chapter, doubts have been raised that the self can be understood through scientific investigation; the riddle of the experiencing subject seems not to yield to mechanical probing. It is tempting to assume some kind of "homunculus," or "little man inside the head," engaged in the task of combining the primary sensory data of lines, form, surface texture, color, sound, and so on into the experience of the percept (or similarly controlling behavior).

Are these doubts justified in the light of present knowledge? Let us look a little more closely at some of the characteristics of the self as "perceiver," characteristics that manifest themselves in humans with brain damage or brain dysfunction. From the large neuropsychological and neurological literature that is available on this subject we shall address ourselves to only one kind of dysfunction in order to show that transformation of sensory data into percepts does not always take place, or takes place in a fractioned way. The clinical example is *astereognosis*, which refers to the inability to recognize objects by touch alone. Critchley (1966), a famous neurologist, argued in his discussion of astereognosis that recognition of an object involves two distinct operations: first, the *unisensorial* recognition of the properties of the object (such as size, shape, smell, texture) and second, the *plurisensorial* recognition of the identity of the object. He further argued that these two types of recognition are not necessarily sequential. He cites individuals who fail to recognize an object, even though they can correctly describe the basic qualities (such as size and weight) of the object. Other individuals may recognize an object but be unable to describe one or all of the unisensorial properties of the object. Again, the perceptual experience may depend on which part of the body is involved in the process of identification: percepts may emerge from the left hand but not from the right hand. A similar argument has been advanced by Hebb (1968). He believes that perceiving and being aware of having perceived are not feats accomplished single-handedly by a "perceiver" but rather are possible because of the involvement of a hierarchy of levels of perceptions. Underlying this perceptual hierarchy, in Hebb's view, are assemblies of cortical neurons of increasing complexity. For example, when a child sees a chair, he will not only see the parts (primary level of perception) of the chair but also the entire chair as a single object (secondary level of perception) or as an object to sit on (a tertiary level of perception). It is the different orders of cell assemblies that are accountable for our various levels of perception. Faults in perception may occur at any of these levels.

The clinical picture of astereognosis shows that some part of the "perceiver" has become faulty. The test materials are commonly used objects, which, to the normal individual, pose no difficulty; the percept emerges instantaneously. For an individual with astereognosis the percept may not emerge at all, or it may be a fractional percept. Where is the "inner man" in all this?

Fractionation of the self in its role as the "perceiver" is apparent in many other clinical observations. As we described earlier, some brain-bisected patients are unable to comment on an object held in the left hand (although they are able to do so when it is held in the right hand). However, these patients are able to *match* the object in the left hand when allowed to search for it (among a number of items) with the left hand. Other patients with disorders of the body image occurring as a result of brain damage may neglect one side of the body to the point of not placing a shoe on the neglected foot, not combing the hair on one half of the head, or leaving one sleeve of the jacket empty. They will not rectify these omissions even though they can see them in a mirror. Then there is the example of the split-brain patient who behaved at times as if two selves were competing for expression. He would pull his pants down with one hand and up with the other, or, more drastically, he would shake his wife with one hand, while with the other he would come to the rescue. We have already recounted the case of the woman patient shown a pin-up in a series of otherwise neutral pictures. When the pin-up was projected to the right hemisphere, her reaction was to laugh but confusedly, not knowing why. When the picture was projected to the left hemisphere, she also laughed, but this time she knew why and was not confused. The visual input gave rise to a different *experience*, depending on which half of the brain did the processing.

These cases and others that could be recounted, argue against the notion of a *unitary* self existing above and beyond brain processes. Our intuitive sense of a unitary self may prove to be a myth we construct from the materials of memory and dreams, through the magic of everyday language. What we picture to ourselves in language as a whole, we can then *feel* and *intuit* as a whole. The fractionation of the self that is evident in the clinic dispels the myth, or forces one to the absurd notion of two or more "inner men," each with its own domain of experience.

"WHERE AM I?"

The question "Where am I?" can be taken even further. We have been assuming that every person has a sense of self, even if it is fractionated. However, recent research suggests that severely retarded humans lack a sense of self altogether.

The experimental definition of self in this research is whether or not the subject responds to his mirror image in a manner that indicates self-recognition. The assumption is that a minimal condition for a sense of self is recognition in a mirror (or photograph) of the "me." Animal research shows (Gallup, 1970) that self-recognition is present in great apes but not in monkeys and lower primates. Profoundly mentally retarded humans are also unable to recognize themselves in a mirror or photograph (Harris, 1977).

It therefore appears that to recognize oneself (and, by inference, to have a sense of self) requires brain structures, neural connections, and processes that are absent in lower primates and in severely retarded humans.

CONCLUSION

Some may have doubts about the inroads of science into the most elusive human essence, the self. Others may feel confident that ultimately research will achieve its objective. Meanwhile, we have attempted to draw a rough outline of the research in neuropsychology through which the ultimate question may be pursued: "How does the brain manage to crystallize for us a sense of unitary self in the presence of billions of active neurons?"

REFERENCES

Coren, S., and C. Porac. 1977. Fifty centuries of right-handedness: The historical record. Science 198:631–632.

Critchley, M. 1966. The Parietal Lobes. Hafner Press, New York.

Dimond, S. 1972. The Double Brain. Churchill Livingstone, New York.

English, H. B., and A. C. English 1958. A Comprehensive Dictionary of Psychological and Psychoanalytical Terms. Longmans, Green and Co., New York.

Feher, L. 1973. Double-mind theory. Am. J. Psychoanal. 33:210–213.

Galaburda, A. M., M. LeMay, T. L. Kemper, and N. Geschwind. 1978. Right-left asymmetries in the brain. Science 199:852–856.

Gallup, G. G., Jr. 1970. Chimpanzees: Self-recognition. Science 167:86–87.

Gazzaniga, M. S. 1967. The split brain in man. Sci. Am. 217:24–29.

Gazzaniga, M. S. 1970. The Bisected Brain. Appleton-Century-Crofts, New York.

Geschwind, N. 1972. Language and the brain. Sci. Am. 226:76–83.

Harris, L. P. 1977. Self-recognition among institutionalized profoundly retarded males: A replication. Bull. Psychon. Soc. 9:43–44.

Hebb, D. O. 1968. Concerning imagery. Psychol. Rev. 75:466–477.

Levy, J. 1974. Psychobiological implications of bilateral asymmetry. In: S. J. Dimond and J. G. Beaumont (eds.), Hemisphere Function in the Human Brain, pp. 121–183. John Wiley & Sons, New York.

Luria, A. R. 1969. Human brain and psychological processes. In: K. H. Pribram (ed.), Brain and Behaviour: Mood, States and Mind, Vol. 1, pp. 37–53. Penguin Books, New York.

Sperry, R. W. 1964. The great cerebral commissure. Sci. Am. 210:42–52.

Chapter 3
SEX DIFFERENCES AND SIMILARITIES

Irmingard I. Lenzer

When we say "male" and "female" we are assuming that humans come in two versions, and that each version has its own range of culturally and biologically determined behaviors and experiences. However, language often dichotomizes where a clear-cut dichotomy does not exist in reality. The purpose of this discussion is to examine the limits of the male-female dichotomy in terms of physical and physiological factors as well as psychological factors. The discussion is divided into two parts. The first is a look at the development of male-female differences before birth, in the hope of seeing past, as far as possible, the powerful cultural influences that come after birth. This does not mean, however, that environmental influences are nonexistent before birth; not only does the intra-uterine environment importantly affect the developing fetus, but also the intra-uterine environment is, in turn, influenced by the external environment of the mother. In the second part, intrapersonal and cultural factors are examined.

SEX DIFFERENCES: IN THE BEGINNING . . .

Determination of Sex

A human sets out on the journey of life as a zygote, which is the union of the male and female germ cells, the egg and the sperm. The program for the formation of the entire organism rests in the 23 pairs of chromosomes of the zygote. One member of each pair of chromosomes is donated by the mother and one member of each is donated by the father. The pair of chromosomes that determine the sex of the person are called sex chromosomes, XX for females and XY for males. The task of the chromosomes or the associated genes is to initiate and direct biochemical processes that in turn govern morphological (structural) development.

The first indication of male-female dimorphism, the first difference in outward appearance in the human organism, appears at about six weeks of intra-uterine life. The male (genetically defined) embryo shows differentiation of the *primitive* sex glands or gonads (which, up to then, is the same for males and females) into testes. For the female (genetic) embryo, development of the primitive gonad into an ovary begins somewhat later. It is the presence of the Y chromosome that guides the embryonic development into a male. The absence of the Y chromosome means female development. The influence of the Y chromosome in male development has been shown in humans with anomalous sex chromosomes. In cases where the sex chromosomes fail to separate normally, patterns such as XXY, XYY, or XXX result; the first two patterns result in males, the third in females.

Following the differentiation of the primitive gonads into either ovaries or testes, the genital ducts develop into the internal accessory structures (uterus and fallopian tubes in the female, and epididymis, vas deferens, and seminal vesicles in the male). The ground plan for *both* male and female accessory structures is present in the eight-week-old fetus. However, during the third month, the "unused" set regresses while the sex-appropriate ground plan becomes dominant. Also, around the eighth fetal week the rudiments of the external genitals appear. The clitoris and the penis take their origin from the *same* primitive structure, the genital tubercle. At around twelve weeks of fetal life, external genital differences are apparent. However, changes in phallic size may be observed throughout fetal development (Wilkins, 1965).

To summarize, gonads as well as external genitalia are present, at one point in life, in the same rudimentary form in both females and males. Later, through genetic and hormonal initiative, differentiation begins. However, in order for the genetic instructions to be followed, an environment supportive of these instructions is necessary. In the normally developing organism, genetic instructions and intra-uterine environment go hand in glove. However, the "normal" path is sometimes missed, and these instances prove enlightening. Animal experiments have been especially useful in showing the important events that take place in the process of sex differentiation.

HORMONAL TIMETABLE

What, then, are the important events in the course of sex differentiation? In the male fetus, after the primitive gonads have developed according to genetic instructions into testes, the testes, in turn, secrete a hormone, testosterone, which influences development of the male structures (internal accessory structures and external genitalia). In addition to testosterone, the developing testes secrete what is called the mullerian-inhibiting substance. This substance *suppresses* the formation of the female accessory structures, for example, the uterus, which derive from the primitive mullerian ducts (remember that both male *and* female ground plans for these accessory structures are present earlier in the fetus). Thus, the male gonads ensure that the different parts of the reproductive system get on, and follow, the male path at the fork of sexual differentiation. If this path is not taken, because of accidental or experimental interferences with the production or availability of the male hormone, the sex structures follow the path of female development. It should be emphasized that these events follow a precise timetable of fetal development; there is a *critical period* during which certain events must take place if normal development is to occur. The critical period for the occurrence of a given event varies between species. It was in the rabbit that the interaction between gonads and the development of the remaining sex structures (accessory and external) was first demonstrated. If the developing male-rabbit embryo is castrated (removing the testes and thereby removing the testosterone) before 21 days of embryonic life—that is, within the critical period—it will from then on develop as a female. If a rabbit is castrated on the 24th day of embryonic life or later—after the critical period—it will still develop as a male.

In the female the presence of gonads and associated hormones (estrogen and progesterone) is not necessary for the development of internal and external structures. Not only are they not necessary, but there is normally no embryonic secretion of ovarian hormones. In fact, ovarian hormones are produced in measurable amounts only later, around the age of ten or after. That the secretion of ovarian hormones in the fetus is not essential for female-body morphology (body-build) is shown in Turner's syndrome. In this condition, the fetus has ovaries that are best described as "ovarian streaks," without eggs and without the ability to produce hormones (for further description of this syndrome see Wilkins, 1965, and Money, 1968), yet the fetus develops female internal accessory structures and external genitals.

It seems then that the basic model nature makes is female; only upon further "instructions" (by testosterone and the Mullerian-inhibiting substance) does nature deviate from its basic course and produce the male.

What was true for the male is also true for the female: if the male hormone, testosterone, is introduced experimentally into the embryonic environment during the "critical period," this shifts development in the male direction and results in the virilization of female sex structures. It was demonstrated that injection of testosterone into the pregnant guinea pig (thereby changing the hormonal environment of the embryo at a critical period) produced virilization of the female offspring; the female guinea pigs had external genitalia that were indistinguishable in appearance from those of newborn males. There is a human analog to this. In the 1950s, when pregnant mothers were given, either intramuscularly or orally, the hormone progestin (which has testosterone-like properties) to prevent threatened abortion, they often gave birth to female babies whose external genitals were masculinized, giving rise to a condition called progestin-induced hermaphroditism (see, for example, Wilkins, 1965).

Thus, we can conclude that, in nature, the embryonic environment acts in concordance with the genetic sex instructions to produce the male-female dichotomy or dimorphism. If, for one reason or another, there is nonconcordance between the genes and the embryonic environment, developments result that blur the male-female dimorphism and open the way to a shift in concepts from *dichotomy* to *continuum*.

Early Sexual Bias

Given the evidence on the development of sex structures and their associated functions in the male or female, what can be said about the biasing of the brain prenatally toward behavioral, perhaps also mental, maleness or femaleness? This is mainly a question of the effects of the sex hormones on the developing brain. It is believed that sex hormones in the developing embryo, in addition to controlling the growth of genitalia, also "throw a neuronal switch" *within the brain* toward male or female sexual behavior as manifested later in life. Are some of these behavioral differences the outcome of an early (prenatal) polarization of the brain resulting from the action of sex hormones? The pitfalls to this inquiry are manifold, the primary one being that while sex behavior in lower animals is largely controlled by sex hormones, in humans it depends upon cultural factors that are present throughout life. How, then, do we apply animal research, extensive as it is, to the human situation without misusing the former and distorting the latter? Before we consider this question, let us first have a look at the animal research as such.

The laboratory rat is a likely subject here, because its behavior is easily and precisely observable and manipulable, and its sexual behavior in particular is very much under hormonal control. Seymour

Levine (1966) reported changes in sexual behavior in male and female rats following hormonal interference during the critical period of development (which in the rat occurs during the first few days *after* birth). Specifically, he found that the presence or absence of testosterone at this time affects sexual behavior at maturity. When female rats received a single injection of testosterone during the critical period, they displayed, when reinjected with testosterone in adulthood, male sexual ritualistic behaviors. When males were castrated during the critical period, thus eliminating the gonadal testosterone, they showed in adulthood, when injected with estrogen and progesterone (the female ovarian hormones), the sexual behavior normally found in female rats. That these changes in adult behavior were *not* the *direct result of hormonal action* was indicated by the following findings: when normal females were injected with testosterone or normal males were injected with progesterone-estrogen, no "abnormal" behaviors were observed. From this it was concluded that the *early* hormonal manipulations had permanently changed or biased the brain, and this was the basis for the abnormal adult behavior.

Early hormonal interference has been found to affect nonsexual behavior as well as sexual behavior. In the rat, exploratory behavior in an "open field" apparatus is different in the two sexes; females tend to be more active and to defecate less often than males. When females were given testosterone during the critical period, the male pattern of behavior emerged. Similar results have been reported for pup-killing behavior. In the rat pup-killing is restricted to the male. It has been shown that neonatal castration of the male rats reduces this behavior. It is not the elimination of testosterone itself that is the important factor (since castration in adulthood does not reduce pup-killing), but rather it is the effect of lack of testosterone on the developing brain. The sex difference with regard to this particular form of aggression thus seems to be the result of the presence or absence of testosterone *during the critical period* and the consequent biasing of the brain.

Other research shows how early hormonal manipulation may alter sex-appropriate behavior. Pregnant rats restrained over illuminated plexiglass tubes experience stress. The adult behavior of the male offspring of these stressed mothers is affected in two ways. The sexual behavior in some instances is sex-appropriate but reduced in frequency. In other instances, it is changed to the female pattern (although the female pattern is not elicited as often as in normal females). Such changes, it has been argued, are caused by a decrease in the availability of testosterone to the developing fetus with a resultant "feminizing" of the brain. This is explained in the following way: when an animal (in this case the mother rat) is stressed, the adrenal cortex secretes increased amounts of androgen. Androgen is often called a male hormone in the sense that it is a close relative to testosterone, the most biologically potent of the androgens. Since the type of androgen secreted by the adrenal cortex is weaker than that secreted by the testes (testosterone), the relative amounts of the maternal adrenal androgen to fetal testosterone is much higher, and androgen washes out the "stronger" testosterone.

What information do we have on the human to add to the picture we get from the animal research on early hormonal manipulation? Cases of endocrine abnormality have been noted and studied, and these provide data for evaluation and grounds for conjecture. The two principal types of endocrine abnormality are the *testicular feminizing syndrome* and *progestin-induced hermaphroditism*. The testicular feminizing syndrome emerges as follows. The XY embryo begins to develop male gonads and internal structures. The male hormone, however, proves to be ineffective in moving the fetus along the path to maleness, with the result that at birth the baby appears to be a female and is often subsequently raised as one. When chromosomal, gonadal, and external genital sex do not coincide, external development usually determines the gender of the child. In addition, at puberty estrogen, which is the "female" hormone but is also secreted by the mature testes, has a large effect, feminizing the body. Because the gonads are male, and because the fetal testes secreted the mullerian-inhibiting substance, the internal female structures were not developed, and reproductive and associated functions are absent.

Money and his research associates have found that individuals undergoing such development show typical female traits: they enjoy homecrafts, they are greatly interested in babies and child care, even though they cannot bear children, they play with dolls in childhood, and they prove to be "good mothers" (these women have adopted children). In general, they *live* as females. Is this finding attributable to an early biasing of their brains toward femaleness because of an insufficiency of testosterone, or to a process of socialization following the initial assumption of gender identity?

The second type of endocrine abnormality, progestin-induced hermaphroditism, is a human analog of the experimentally induced masculinization of female animals prenatally. As discussed above, cases of progestin-induced hermaphroditism were created when progestin, a testosterone-like hormone, was administered to pregnant mothers to prevent spontaneous abortion. Some of the female (XX) offspring of these mothers showed varying degrees of masculinization of the external genitalia. Follow-up reports on those individuals whose sex assignment at birth was female indicate that tomboyism, rough-and-tumble play, career orientation, and other "male" traits were more pronounced in them than in their normal female counterparts. Again, the question is whether these behaviors and traits are due to an early biasing of the brain or to a process of socialization given the effect of the early hormonal intervention on gender—in this instance not to change the gender but to make it ambiguous.

SEX DIFFERENCES: BIRTH AND AFTER . . .

"It's a boy!" "It's a girl!"—these are pronouncements with long-lasting consequences. With sex assignment made, the male or female is channeled into roles society has established for each sex. What started out as a biological category—male and female—becomes now a socially defined category—masculinity or femininity. How far does culture build on sex differences already "present" at birth? Does it manufacture differences that would not otherwise exist? What is the relation between biology and culture? How much does each contribute and in what way?

Four Theories

What we have been skirting in the discussion so far is a *biological* theory of sex differences, which seeks to explain sex differences in terms of biological processes, whether directly or indirectly genetic, mediated, for example, by hormonal processes. Three other theories can be briefly sketched here: the social-learning theory, the cognitive-developmental theory, and the psychoanalytical theory.

The social-learning theory holds that the acquisition of sex-typed behavior is the result of a history of rewards and punishments. Sex differences stem from differences in reinforcement history. As the child grows up "boy-behaviors" and "girl-behaviors" are rewarded differentially for boys and girls. A more sophisticated version of the theory distinguishes two types of reinforcement, one coming from the environment and the other coming from "inside" the child. The theory allows for the importance of imitation behavior in the child; a large part of the child's repertoire of sex-role behaviors is acquired by observing "models" (from family life, movies, stories, etc.).

The cognitive-developmental theory pictures the growing child as controlling in a significant way its own history of rewards and punishments. At an early age, around 18–24 months, the child takes on a gender identity, realizing that he is a boy or that she is a girl. On this basis, the child is able to organize reality and give meaning and value to environmental input. "Boy things" then become more reinforcing for the child who identifies himself as a boy, and "girl things" become more reinforcing for the child who identifies herself as a girl. In this theory the child becomes an active organizer of the many experiences that he encounters. The child's sexual identity (i.e., the child's personal experience of being a boy or a girl) is developed and finally stabilized at a relatively early age (around four years), while sex-role attitudes and behaviors are acquired slowly over the years. This theory is cognitive in that it holds that the child's thought processes are crucial in shaping later sex-role attitudes. It is developmental in its concern for age-related changes in sex-role development. The theory is closely related to Piaget's theory of cognitive development. It is argued, for example, that the child must have developed a good grasp of category constancies in the physical world (e.g., a dog that has been trained to walk on its hindlegs does not become a person) before he will accept the constancy of his own sexual identity. It is not the social rewards but rather the child's internal cognitive organization that ultimately shapes his sex-role behaviors. The possibilities for ambiguity and blurring of sex-role behaviors are obvious once the complexities of this organizational process are understood.

The psychoanalytic theory places major explanatory weight on certain unconscious processes accompanying the critical phases of early childhood. The very young child is "bisexual," not in the sense that the male and the female are completely alike sexually (it is posited, for example, that the male has more libido, or sexual energy, than the female), but in the sense that both the male and the female relate sexually to both parents and in a similar time sequence. However, around the age of four or five the two sexes clearly diverge. The male child enters the Oedipal phase: his love is directed to his mother, and his father becomes an outsider. Fear of the father develops, giving rise to the "castration complex." The conflict is resolved and the fear is overcome when the boy suppresses the desires and ideas associated with the Oedipal phase and identifies with the father. Certain patterns of sexual behavior emerge; the masculine character takes root. In the girl the castration complex precedes the Oedipal phase, because she already has a sense of lacking what the boy has: a penis. The Oedipal phase in the girl develops when she begins to feel antipathy for the mother and directs her sexual energy toward her father. Through a process of the unconscious, she equates penis and baby. By having her father's (later her husband's) baby, she hopes to get the desired penis. The "feminine character" grows in this context. Unconscious processes are central here, as they are not in the other theories. A key conjecture is that it is much more difficult for the girl to overcome the conflicts of the Oedipal phase than it is for the boy.

To summarize, the four theories discussed explain the acquisition of sex-typed behaviors from different theoretical positions, placing weight on different, although not mutually exclusive, determiners of sex-typed behaviors. Biological theory reminds us of the influence that the "male" hormone exerts on morphological and behavioral features of the organism; hand in hand with this goes the assumption that at least some aspects of sexual stereotyping are based on innate biological differences. Cognitive developmental theory places the fulcrum of the lever that swings in the male or female direction within the cognitive sphere of the child. The social learning theory looks to the environment for the setting up of reinforcement contingencies for sex-appropriate behavior. Psychoanalytic theory places emphasis on the morphological genital differences as they are perceived by the growing child within the context of the family and the culture. What separates psychoanalytic theory from the other three theories and renders it problematical in the eyes of many is that it is based on clinical and observational material, much of it anecdotal in nature.

Behavioral Watershed

The list of behaviors that can be classified by sex is long, and the task of explaining the roots of these differences is difficult. As an example, let us look briefly at one area of behavior where sex differences are believed to exist and where more research has been done than on any other: aggression. The term aggression covers a wide range of behaviors, including physical aggression, verbal aggression, prosocial aggression (when one person or group lays down a rule and threatens punishment if another person or group breaks the rule), and antisocial aggression. Social learning theorists maintain that boys display more physical aggression than girls, because boys are encouraged, or at least allowed, to engage in such behavior. Girls, on the other hand, are encouraged or permitted to be verbally and prosocially aggressive. The sex differences in aggressivity are principally the result of differences in "sanctions," "expectations," and "rewards" set up by the culture and delivered by peers, parents, or others.

However, is there not a biological basis for physical aggression in boys? The *average* boy is heavier at birth, and this difference holds throughout life. Do these simple biological factors not account for the difference in physical aggression? The reality is not simple. Physical aggression in the adult includes not only "brute" force, at which the male may indeed be constitutionally superior, but also "weapon-mediated" force, and the female skilled in karate or in the use of the pistol may suffer no biological handicap in this case. Superior physical strength may be unrelated to the factors that give *rise* to physical aggression.

What are these factors? Animal studies have shown the hormone testosterone to play an important role in the *elicitation* of aggressive behaviors. Fighting between male mice, which is elicited by placing a pair together after a period of isolation, can be turned off by castration and turned on again by subsequent replacement therapy with exogeneous testosterone. Normal adult female mice do not fight, even following isolation, and cannot be made to fight by administration of testosterone. However, female rats that receive testosterone injections at birth do fight when treated with testosterone at maturity. Therefore, it is not testosterone level *per se* that triggers aggressive behavior but rather testosterone level in conjunction with a particular neural make-up determined by early hormonal conditions.

Similar findings have been reported for primates. The female offspring of rhesus monkey mothers treated during pregnancy with testosterone proprionate are more aggressive than their normal counterparts, showing male-like behaviors, such as threatening and rough-and-tumble play, as observed during the first five months of life.

In the human the effects of early (prenatal) testosterone have been studied in progestin-induced hermaphrodites. It should be recalled from the previous discussion that we are dealing here with female offspring of mothers receiving progestin (which has testosterone-like effects) during pregnancy. The question of interest is whether these females, who were thus fetally masculinized, show higher aggression than normal female controls. The answer seems to be no, neither in terms of "picking fights" nor in terms of securing a place in the dominance hierarchy of their group. Perhaps this is because these girls realize that transgression of the culturally defined right to dominance for males leads to eviction from the recreational group to which they belonged (Money and Ehrhardt, 1972). Thus, aggression, a sex-related, dimorphic behavior in rodents, has lost its bipolar qualities in the human and has become interwoven with other variables. While a greater *potential* for aggression (or striving for dominance hierarchy) cannot be disproved for the male or the progestin-treated female, it does not manifest itself unless it can pass through the cultural screen of appropriate and expected sex-role behavior.

Role of Culture

The cultural overlay on behavioral sex differences is complex, and anthropology, sociology, and social psychology are gradually isolating its various facets. For the present discussion let us focus on three concepts that are and have been of great interest because they appear to be the core concepts to understanding cultural determinants of behavioral sex differences. The three concepts are role, position, and sex-role.

The term "role" refers broadly to patterns of behavior that are associated with certain positions. Thus "the term *position* is used by social scientists to describe the niche, or slot, occupied by the individual within a society, and the term *role* applies to the stabilized patterns of behavior associated with a position" (McDavid and Harari, 1974, p. 145). This definition suggests that it is the position that sets the requirements for role behavior. Yet, from daily observations we know that the type of behavior we expect from a person in a given position depends not only on the *position* within the social set-up but to a large degree on the *sex* of the person. This point was brought out dramatically in an experiment by Horner (1969). She asked male and female students to expand the following statement into a story: "After first-term finals, John (Anne)" (male students were given the statement with the name John, females with the name Anne) "finds himself (herself) at the top of his medical-school class." Expansion of a statement of this nature, as required in the experiment, gave the students the opportunity to project (and thereby reveal to the experimenter) their own personal feelings, expected life-goals, and expected future behaviors of the fictitious character of the story. Horner then analyzed the stories for achievement motivation. Specifically, Horner wanted to find out whether differences existed in the way male students came to grips with John's success and how female students treated Anne's success. Male students portrayed John as a dedicated young man, hard-working, and well-deserved of his success. On the other hand, female students described Anne as a person unhappy with herself as well as disliked by others.

This experiment illustrates that appropriate and expected behavior in a given position varies with the sex of the role-playing person. John, like Anne, showed appropriate role behavior; both were hard-working, high-achieving medical students. Yet, sex-role prescriptions placed negative injunctions on Anne's behavior, or as one student put it, "Anne is pretty darn proud of herself, but everyone hates and envies her" (Horner, 1969, p. 38).

The experiment by Horner illustrates still another point, namely, that certain forms of sex-role behavior may make it difficult to remain in a social position or to aspire to certain social positions. So-called female behaviors, such as passivity and dependence (psychoanalytic theory regards them as part of the feminine character), may place barriers between the woman and the attainment of a goal (for instance, becoming a medical doctor). Horner calls it the "motive to avoid success." Eventually, the social position requiring behaviors in conflict with the appropriate sex-role behavior will be abandoned for a cozier social niche where the requirements for independence and decision making are at a minimum.

Over the years, Horner's findings have been reinterpreted and replicated, and new material is accumulating on the topic of fear of success. Condry and Dyer (1976) suggested that what Horner may have been observing in her study is not so much a personality trait of fear of success but rather the realistic assessment of negative consequences of sex-role deviancy ["If a girl's achievement threatens her boyfriend, she will be left alone" (p. 74)].

One of the many replications of Horner's study was done by Hoffman (1974). The experiment was conducted at the same university as Horner's experiment. Hoffman, too, found a high percentage (65%) of women reporting fear-of-success themes. Unlike Horner's study, however, where only 8% of the males reported fear-of-success stories, Hoffman's reported 77%. Hoffman analyzed the content of fear for the female and male stories and found that women were more concerned with affiliative loss ["Anne will stay in school and become a good doctor but she will never have many close friends" (p. 356)], but men questioned the value of achievement ["It's great for his parents, but he doesn't give a shit" (p. 356)]. Hoffman suggested that the male students' change in response from 1965 to 1971 (when Horner and Hoffman collected their data, respectively) may be a reflection of the increasing tendency of white college men to question academic and career success. On the other hand, the feelings for the males in the Hoffman study may simply also reflect the changing male sex role. Pleck (1976) suggested that, as the modern male sex role emerges, traditional male role expectations may become less dominant. Maybe what we are seeing here is that these young men are no longer consistently socialized for the male role.

For now, what can be said in reply to the claim that cultural stereotypes of sex-role behavior are just reinforcing biological undercurrents that nature has set in motion ages ago? In answer, investigators have looked at different societies, especially at primitive societies; one assumption might be that similarity of sex-roles in different cultural communities reflects deeper biological determinants. However, no easy answers come our way from this direction. As Ruth Benedict (1934) wrote, "The diversity of cultures can be endlessly documented" (p. 41). She reminds us how human behavior is organized, shaped, and reshaped into many different patterns, recognizable in some cultures, and barely recognizable in others.

As an example, the diversity of patterns of behavior is well documented for aggression. Aggression is a behavior that positively sex types males in our culture and negatively sex types females. As discussed above, there is considerable evidence that aggression, at least at the animal level, has strong biological roots. Different cultures, however, deal with aggression differently. The two cultures that are most often singled out in demonstrating cultural caprice are the Arapesh and the Mundugumor, two primitive societies in New Guinea. The Arapesh heavily disapprove of aggressive behavior in both males and females; "both men and women were expected to be succoring and cherishing and equally concerned with the growth of children" (Mead, 1975, p. 214). On the other hand, in the Mundugumor, aggression was the expected form of behavior from both males and females: "Most difficult of all for me to bear was the Mundugumor attitude toward children. Women wanted sons and men wanted daughters, and babies of the wrong sex were tossed into the river, still alive, wrapped in a bark sheath" (Mead, p. 225).

An instance of cultural influence on stylization of behavior does not, however, rule out the possibility that aggression, if and when it falls along sex lines, is a manifestation of biological determinants that differ for the sexes. What can be suggested at this point is that cultures may "override" natural tendencies and not allow their expression. In the past, evidence for biologically rooted differences was a weapon in the hands of those who would place females back in the home ("Woman's place is in the home"), in square one! Tiger, in his book *Men in Groups* (1971), carries on this tradition when he writes: "Should cross-cultural studies suggest that males and females differ concretely in not only reproductive but other kinds of major behaviour, there would be immediate consequences for those theories about social activity which are principally concerned with explaining the structure and process of social systems in social terms" (p. 16). However, anthropology does not provide us with evidence for concrete behavioral differences immutably locked into cultures, not even in the case of behaviors that are biologically rooted, such as aggression. In the case of other social behaviors, such as altruism, the evidence is even more tenuous.

Furthermore, it is crude optimism to wait for the isolation of a behavioral variable that once and for all marks the dividing line between males and females. Behavioral variability within a group of males or females is large, and overlap, rather than separation, of male and female behavior is the rule. Thus, behavioral requirements for the male sex-role may come easily to some males but be difficult for others. The same applies to females; cultural requirements favor some and disfavor others. Benedict stressed this point over forty years ago when she wrote:

> Obviously, adequate personal adjustment does not depend upon follow-
> ing certain motivations and eschewing others. The correlation is in a dif-
> ferent direction. Just as those are favored whose congenial responses are
> closest to that behaviour which characterizes their society, so those are
> disoriented whose congenial responses fall in that arc of behaviour which
> is not capitalized by their culture. These abnormals are those who are
> not supported by the institutions of their civilization. They are the excep-
> tions who have not easily taken traditional forms of their culture
> (p. 238).

In a recent book, *Female of the Species* (1975), Martin and Voorhies have extended the scope of analysis of sex-roles by compar- ing cultures of different ecological adaptations, ranging from foraging and hunting cultures to industrial cultures. The authors maintain that sex-roles were, and are, a universal feature of human culture, even though not statistically fixed across cultures. They are of the opinion that sex-roles will be of lesser significance in the future than they have been in the past, if only to allow greater individual development, unrestrained by sex-role boundaries. Once the social expectations for masculine and feminine behavioral sterotypes are removed, males and females may select from a wide variety of behaviors to suit their own inclinations. To use Diamond's (1978) expression, the "smorgasbord of choice" of sex-role behaviors from which to select is large.

However, opening of the sex-role boundaries will produce a wave that touches on the shores of many areas, not only the psychological area. The economist J. K. Galbraith in his book *Economics and the Public Purpose* (1973) traces the duties and "virtues" of woman from the preindustrial to the modern society. He shows that women's roles and activities have been closely intertwined with the economic necessities of the day. In the present consumer society says Galbraith, the woman at home plays a vital role, as the manager and administrator of the consumption of goods. "Women's work" is still an indispensable (although hidden) asset to the economic system (Galbraith estimates it to be about one-fourth of the total Gross National Product in the U.S.).

The shape of the sex-role boundaries is determined by a number of factors. Hoffman (1977) points to three converging factors that bring about changes in family roles, socialization, and sex differences: smaller family size, longer life expectancy, and higher employment rates for women throughout the life cycle. These are not just trends, but pervasive factors that will stay with us. Little wonder that Hoffman, too, concludes that differences between the sexes will disappear.

The view that sex-role differences will disappear is not shared by others. Some hold the view that past, present, and future cultures have tended, and will tend, to maximize, or even invent, sex-role differences. Rosenberg and Sutton-Smith in their book, *Sex and Identity* (1972), suggest for example that sexual stereotypes may make a society both more colorful and more productive. Whether, in fact, sex-role polarization is conducive to greater productivity of a society is problematical, and we might want to question the importance of such criteria.

REFERENCES

Benedict, R. 1951, c1934. Patterns of Culture. The New American Library, New York.

Condry, J. and S. Dyer. 1976. Fear of success: Attribution of cause to the victim. J. Soc. Iss. 32:63–83.

Diamond, M. 1978. Sexual identity and sex roles. The Humanist 38:16–19.

Galbraith, J. K. 1973. Economics and the Public Purpose. Houghton Mifflin Co., Boston.

Hoffman, L. W. 1974. Fear of success in males and females: 1965 and 1971. J. Consult. Clin. Psychol. 42:353–358.

Hoffman, L. W. 1977. Changes in family roles, socialization, and sex differences. Am. Psychol. 32:644–657.

Horner, M. S. 1969. Fail: bright women. Psychol. Today 3: pp. 36, 38, & 62.

Levine, S. 1966. Sex differences in the brain. Sci. Am. 214:84–90.

McDavid, J. W., and H. Harari. 1974. Psychology and Social Behavior. Harper & Row, New York.

Martin, M. K., and B. Voorhies. 1975. Female of the Species. Columbia University Press, New York.

Mead, M. 1975. Blackberry Winter. Pocket Books, New York.

Money, J. 1968. Sex Errors of the Body. The Johns Hopkins University Press, Baltimore.

Money, J., and A. A. Ehrhardt. 1972. Man & Woman, Boy & Girl. The Johns Hopkins University Press, Baltimore.

Pleck, J. H. 1976. The male sex role: Definitions, problems, and sources of change. J. Soc. Iss. 32:155–164.

Rosenberg, B. G., and B. Sutton-Smith. 1972. Sex and Identity. Holt, Rinehart & Winston, New York.

Tiger, L. 1971. Men in Groups. Panther Books Ltd., London.

Wilkins, L. 1965. The Diagnosis and Treatment of Endocrine Disorders in Childhood and Adolescence, 3rd ed. Charles C Thomas, Springfield, Ill.

Chapter 4
SEX DIFFERENCES IN SOCIAL BEHAVIOR

J. K. Chadwick-Jones

It is inevitable in a discussion of the biological influences on behavior of the sexes that cultural influences also be mentioned. The large issues of sex differences and of sex discrimination in society have been the subject of books like Juanita Williams' *Psychology of Women* (1977). This chapter examines some of the behavioral differences between the sexes as these have recently been observed, in quite subtle and perhaps unsuspected ways, in empirical studies.

We discuss evidence, first, from recent empirical enquiry into speech style, and second from studies of nonverbal communication. Under the category of speech style, we discuss the evidence of sex differences in grammatical speech, "correct" pronunciations, and intonation patterns. The aspect of nonverbal behavior discussed is "looking" behavior, specifically duration of eye contact between persons. In each of these research areas we seek to show "how" the sex differences occur. To discover "why" these differences occur, we turn to controversial questions about patriarchal society and feminist opinions. Lastly, we mention some indications of changing sex-roles in contemporary society.

SEX DIFFERENCES IN SPEECH

One rather revealing sex difference occurs in language and, more precisely, in the use of speech forms. We must discuss first, however, certain general characteristics of speech, because only then can we appreciate the influences of gender. As we mention in Chapter 6, the varieties of dialect or speech codes within a language community are classified as either *standard* or *nonstandard*. Standard English is the form that has the most prestige, is the language of government, and is used formally. It is the variety of English taught in schools, used on the radio and on television, and considered generally to be the "correct" form. This standard form is known as "Received Pronunciation" (RP). Other varieties of English are, by the same criteria, considered to be nonstandard dialects and differ from the standard variety in such characteristics as accent, pronunciation, and grammar.

Peter Trudgill (1974) discusses several dialect surveys that illustrate how "correct" speech is used more in some socioeconomic groups or classes than in others. One study in Detroit, by Shuy et al. (1967), of the use of the double negative ("I can't eat nothing" instead of "I can't eat anything") showed a clear relationship between social class and the use of this grammatical construction.

The study was carried out in the following way. Individuals were assigned to class groupings on the basis of their occupation, income, and education. Next, samples of their speech were tape-recorded, and the frequency of double negatives was counted. While the results do not reveal sharp dividing lines between class groupings, it can easily be seen that there *are* differences in the relative frequencies of particular grammatical features.

Table 1 presents the frequency of the nonstandard double negative as a percentage of the negatives used. In Norwich, England, in a similar survey, percentages were computed of pronunciations of individual vowels and consonants. Three pronunciation features were isolated:

1. *N'* as opposed to standard *ng* in "walking" or "running"
2. Glottal stop as opposed to *t* in "butter" or "water" (The glottal stop is roughly the omission of the *t* sound: "bu'er," "wa'er")
3. Dropped *h* as opposed to h in "hammer" or "hat"

The results shown in Table 2 establish that the use of these three features is an indicator of social-class position.

Trudgill, in his excellent discussion of these results, pointed to a continuum, with social class differences appearing clearly in the use of

Table 1.   Double negatives in Detroit

Class	Percentage
Upper-Middle	2
Lower-Middle	11
Upper-Working	38
Lower-Working	70

From Trudgill, 1974, p. 47.

Table 2.   Non-RP forms for three consonants in Norwich, England

Class	Percentage of		
	n'	glottal stop	dropped h
Middle-Middle	31	41	6
Lower-Middle	42	62	14
Upper-Working	87	89	40
Middle-Working	95	92	59
Lower-Working	100	94	61

From Trudgill, 1974, p. 48.

these pronunciations. The studies quantify, in an effective way, what people know through everyday experience about social class and speech.

Having demonstrated these class differences, we find that *if we hold class membership constant*, differences will emerge between men and women within a given class grouping. First, we take some examples, again from Trudgill's book, and then we can discuss their possible significance.

The Detroit figures on frequencies of double negatives provide us with clear evidence of sex differences within the social-class categories. The lower-middle and lower-working-class groupings reveal especially large differences. Men are much more likely to use constructions like "I can't eat nothing," as Table 3 demonstrates.

It appears that women tend to avoid incorrect grammar. Why? Is it because correct speech, like "nicer" or more "refined" behavior, is expected more of women than of men? Is it because of certain expectations of women's behavior? Or are women more skilled at following the standard speech conventions? It could be that, compared to men, women are more sensitive to the requirements of different social situations and will therefore tend to switch to more correct speech forms when the occasion (such as a tape recording) demands. Are women more sensitive because of their more dependent position in society? Murstein (1972) discussed the question of dependence of women in the context of courtship and marriage: "They tend to improve their stand-

Table 3.   Percentages of double negatives

	Upper-middle	Lower-middle	Upper-working	Lower-working
Men	6.3	32.4	40.0	90.1
Women	0.0	1.4	35.6	58.9

From Trudgill, 1974, p. 91.

ard of living and status more by marriage than do men" (p. 621). He argues that it is more important for women that they marry at a relatively young age. They are "in the market" over a shorter period than men, and because women are less powerful in the courtship situation, they may well be more alert and sensitive to their partner's needs. Murstein asked 98 young couples questions about their partner's personality and "ideal self" and, in fact, females did tend to be more accurate in their judgments about their male partners than the males were about their female partners. However, we have not yet finished with the linguistic evidence.

In Detroit where, as in other American cities, the *postvocalic r* is a prestige feature of pronunciation, women tend to use it far more frequently than men. Postvocalic *r*, which means *r* after a vowel, refers to the emphatic *r* pronunciation in such words as *car* and *cart*. In New York City, for example, an accent with this *r* is considered more "correct" than one without it. People in higher social positions tend to use it more frequently than those in lower socioeconomic levels. Table 4 shows the percentages of postvocalic *r* in speech samples recorded from the black population in Detroit.

Again, in this situation women lead the way in the use of correct speech forms. The same trend has been found in studies in a variety of countries. In England, women are less likely than men to say "walkin'" instead of "walking," or to use the glottal stop in words like "butter" ("bu'er"). Similar tendencies are found in South African English.

Trudgill gives us one further insight: he argues that, in a given society, the greater the sex-role differences the larger the linguistic differences. "It seems that the larger and more inflexible the difference between social roles of men and women in a particular community the larger and more rigid the linguistic tendencies tend to be" (Trudgill, 1974, p. 95).

To support this statement there is evidence from studies of primitive communities with food-gathering or nomadic economies, such as the American Indians, where sex roles are very sharply differentiated and male and female speech varieties are distinct in a much more

Table 4.   Postvocalic *r* in the black population of Detroit

	Upper-middle	Lower-middle	Upper-working	Lower-working
Men	66.7	52.5	20.0	25.0
Women	90.0	70.0	44.2	31.7

From Trudgill, 1974, p. 92.

contrasting way than in our society. In these societies the linguistic forms used by women appear to be older historically, and changes have taken place in the speech forms used by men that apparently have not been adopted in women's speech. According to this evidence, women's speech seems to be more conservative. There are also some indications, according to Trudgill, that women's speech forms were not only different in these communities but were considered to be better—a tendency similar to our contemporary research evidence that women's speech is more correct.

However, there is contrary evidence mentioned by Trudgill: in new speech forms having high prestige, women tend to be the innovators, as studies in the United States and Norway confirm. Thus, women are conservative only when the older speech forms are considered to be better. When the newer ones are thought to be more correct, it is women who seem to take the lead in the change.

There is one other influential factor which, up to now, we have not mentioned: the association of certain speech forms with the masculine image. For instance, in studies of Carib Indians, some words could be used only by adult men on warlike expeditions. In effect, these were taboo words, that is, words that are held to be improper and "forbidden." The notion of taboo certainly is not unfamiliar in our own society. For instance, swearing seems to be more acceptable in men. If women do swear, they may be doing so consciously to break the taboo or prohibition. Breaking the rules in this way can be used as a step away from the existing restrictions on women. Of course, the use of swear words by men also varies greatly between individuals and groups. So it is as well not to oversimplify and reduce the interpretation of swearing into the male-female context only. Nevertheless, groups in which swearing is frequent, whether they are servicemen, unskilled laborers, or schoolboys, may possibly value, maintain, or aspire to certain notions of masculinity.

This brings us to the question of working-class speech and incorrect grammar, and the significance these also have for masculinity or "toughness." It seems that working-class speech has a definite significance for "manliness." This is the reversal of the idea that correct speech denotes prestige. The prestige associated with incorrect speech has been called *covert prestige* by Labov (1972). It is a kind of rejection of the middle-class and "nice" conventions of speech.

One last study gives us an additional view of a difference in social attitudes between the sexes. In the study of the dialects in Norwich, England, a "self-evaluation" test was carried out to see whether people's reports on their own speech were accurate. This was done by comparing their tape-recorded speech with the pronunciation they claimed they used. Some claimed they spoke more correctly than they actually did, these were the "over-reporters." Others said they spoke less correctly than was actually the case, they were the "under-reporters." Comparing men and women respondents, it was found 1) that men tended to be more accurate than women, 2) that men were definitely more likely to be under-reporters, and 3) that women had more tendency to over-report than men. Table 5 demonstrates these differences as revealed in the Norwich data showing the results of the "self-evaluation" test for the vowel sounds in words like *ear* and *here* (working-class pronunciation in Norwich would resemble *air* and *hair*).

The table shows that the majority of women perceived themselves as using the correct forms even when they did not; they over-reported. However, half of the men were under-reporters, claiming to use more incorrect forms than they actually did.

Although it seems that women try to follow middle-class conventions for pronunciation, the data from men respondents indicates that their working-class style was of greater personal value. Presumably, for reasons of maintaining masculinity, that was *their* appropriate speech form.

Before Trudgill (1974), Labov (1966, 1972), and others were inclined toward the view that women are more sensitive to the stigma of incorrect speech, but it could be that women are (or have learned to be) more competent in their speech styles and can switch from one speech "code" to another more effectively than men. Other psychological facts must be taken into account. For instance, there are the well-established differences between males and females in verbal abilities. "Girls talk earlier and, especially after age 11, girls do superior work in spelling and in English courses at school. Adult women tend to be superior to men on the verbal sections of intelligence tests"

Table 5. Over- and under-reporting of the pronunciation of *ear* in Norwich, England

	Total	Percentage of informants	
		Men	Women
Over-reporting	43	22	68
Under-reporting	33	50	14
Accurate	23	28	18
	99	100	100

From Trudgill, 1974, p. 98.

(McKeachie, Doyle, and Moffett, 1976, p. 318). Again, Schlesinger and Groves (1976), summarizing the available information on sex differences in abilities, stated that: "Girls are usually ahead of boys in developing language skills. They say their first words sooner, articulate more clearly at an earlier age, and use longer, often more complex, sentences . . . girls show consistent superiority throughout school years . . . (in) grammar, spelling, and word fluency" (p. 293). Lastly, Wrightsman and Sanford (1975) mentioned evidence that girls do better at tasks involving language and social skills, and that "a number of studies have found that girls are superior to boys on verbal skills . . . (which) may be only a matter of verbal fluency" (p. 161).

It is not unlikely that these same tendencies are reflected also in our linguistic studies, although, of course, there is no direct connection between female speech styles and tests of female verbal abilities. The entirely speculative condition of our "explanations" at the moment (as we have no direct evidence that a dependent position in society produces correct speech!) does suggest caution.

It should be understood that what we have been discussing are descriptive studies of language usage, which do not provide us, in themselves, with satisfactory explanations. We can only guess at what may be producing the differences. Since we have no direct support for any particular explanation, we can only suggest probable relationships that will have to be studied more closely in the future. We would have to investigate a variety of contexts in which women might speak more correctly. Is this tendency more pronounced in some situations than in others? Compared to men at different social levels, do women switch more from one speech form to another, in the home, on the telephone, or in talking to another person of a higher or lower socioeconomic level? Are basic values involved concerning what is appropriate for women, as contrasted to men, in speech situations?

Nonverbal Communication

We have been discussing some sex differences in speech of which many people are probably unaware. There are other indicators, just as subtle, in nonverbal communication. "Eye contact" is one form of behavior that has been observed systematically in experiments and that also shows variation between the sexes. "Eye contact" refers to *mutual gaze*, when two people look at each other in the region of the eyes.

There is evidence that women, in conversation with other women and with men, tend to have more eye contact than men. Social psychologists, the foremost of whom are Michael Argyle in England

and Ralph Exline in the United States, have specialized in measuring eye contact under different conditions (see Argyle 1969, 1975) and have provided us with a good deal of carefully recorded information.

The typical pattern of gaze in an everyday conversation between two people consists of intermittent glances lasting between 1 and 10 seconds. The proportion of the conversation during which each person looks at the other varies between 25 and 75% of the total conversation time. Actually, the duration of eye contact or mutual gaze is much less than the total time spent looking at the other. One person may be looking at the other, but the other may be looking away. The person who is talking, after a preliminary glance at the listener, tends not to look again until the ending of the utterance. The speaker looks less, to avoid distraction; the listener tends to look at the speaker considerably more. Thus, conversation can be thought of as a coordinated task in which people look at others to seek information or to give information.

Argyle (1975) has noted that "sex differences have appeared in many studies of gaze." For example, studies show that pairs of women, as compared to pairs of men and mixed-sex pairs, have the highest levels of mutual gaze. In general, it seems that women look more and pay more attention to visual cues.

This kind of evidence might suggest a conclusion similar to one we have drawn from the speech samples: that women are more sensitive to social "signals." Also it could be that sensitivity involves a position of greater dependency or of less power. Women may need more feedback about the reactions of others.

Bearing in mind that these are no more than plausible hypotheses, we might suppose that women attend more to visual cues, either because they are more alert socially or because they learn to be more so in a society where their position is less secure, more vulnerable, than that of men.

There is other evidence, however, that suggests we should avoid this kind of general statement. One study of black Americans suggested that avoidance of eye contact is a way to show respect toward people in authority and emphasized that black people may "have been taught since childhood that it is disrespectful to look other people straight in the eyes" (Tubbs and Moss, 1978). Because of such cultural influences, we need to be careful, at this stage, in drawing conclusions about sex differences in eye contact, even though, in experiments, the differences may be confirmed. The effects of a given social relationship, such as relative status, age, social class, and degree of attraction or acquaintance, on eye contact still await further study.

SPEECH INTONATION

Grammar and the pronunciation of words are not the only linguistic differences between men and women. Intonation, the "tunes" in which we speak, must be mentioned as a highly significant part of being "feminine" and "masculine." Sally McConnell-Ginet (1978) argues from a feminist point of view that there is a need to understand how talking works to create and maintain "sex stereotyping and male dominance," especially because "differences in female and male speech melodies are apparently heard by the male-dominated ear of our culture as signalling women's relative instability (and, from the male viewpoint, incompetence) . . ." (p. 542).

The intonation of speech involves its pitch, rhythm, and variations in loudness. The fact that women speak at a higher pitch than men is partly the effect of their smaller vocal cords, but there are other factors that suggest this is not the whole story. First, there is actually an overlap in the pitch ranges used by individual men and women. Second, there are important cultural rules that operate to make different segments of the pitch range more suitable, for women or for men, in different societies. American men, for instance, tend to use a lower speaking pitch than some Europeans. Pitch rhythms vary in different languages; in some there are more "glissando" effects, changes of pitch, or "glides," than in English. Men students learning Russian have been known to show reluctance to speak with the rapid glides that they associate with American feminine speech; the extreme of masculine speech in our culture tends toward the monotone. As McConnell-Ginet emphasizes, there is other evidence of this kind that suggests that sex-stereotyped intonations are not universal. The use of higher "registers" or levels of pitch by women may not only reflect a biological difference but may well be the result of our training of the young to "sound" feminine or masculine.

Typically, women use a relatively wide pitch range, rising and falling with greater shifts in loudness. The result is that a cluster of characteristics is identified that gives a women's speech a more "dynamic" intonation. It seems that men rarely use the higher levels of pitch that women use and that men have fewer levels of intonation.

However, a further complication is that the dynamic aspect of women's speech may also be associated with emotional expressiveness. The greater a speaker's range of pitch, the greater is the degree of emotionality perceived by listeners. McConnell-Ginet writes: "It is possible that part of women's being emotional in our culture derives from our sounding emotional" (p. 552). In other words, an equivalent degree of "dynamic" speech is only encountered in men under conditions of heightened emotion. For McConnell-Ginet, the problem is not that women are stereotyped as emotionally expressive but that in our culture certain other things go along with being an emotional person, including being unstable and unpredictable.

The characteristics of the female voice could thus be used, as in male impersonation or derisory imitation, to emphasize women's inferiority. Higher pitch and intonation variability could be taken to mean that women have less self-control than men, although there is no rational connection between expressive speech and instability or inferiority. Such ideas can operate to the disadvantage of women in general, and feminists would argue that numerous (if not all) men have an interest in maintaining women in an inferior position and in exploiting them. Women's roles in society are usually subordinate ones, and it is not at all inconceivable that some men wish to maintain this state of affairs.

An obvious question to ask at this point is whether or not expressive speech is *learned behavior* similar to the sex-typing of emotional expression. If, for instance, it is permissible for women, but not for men, to express sadness by weeping, is expressive speech also permissible only in women? Or are there innate tendencies producing greater expressiveness in women? One possibility is that expressiveness is part of a social skill, like women's greater use of gaze in conversation, developed to achieve ends otherwise not attainable given their subordinate roles.

Finally, situational demands are also important. As McConnell-Ginet commented, child care requires emotional expressiveness; repairing telephone lines does not. This is similar to Judy Gahagan's (1975) comment when she discussed the tendency for women to conform more to group pressures: "Women have, in the past, been socialized (if not genetically endowed with the capacity) to attend to, or orient themselves to the social world, where men seem more concerned with objective tasks . . ." (p. 95). There is a widespread uniformity in the facts that are known about women's roles in society, that is, about what women actually do, think they should do, and are expected to do. Zelditch (1955) showed that women's role in most societies has been that of comforting, caring, and sustaining others in the family, especially children. Is it the female parent who has the greatest share in maintaining the family and who carries out more of the socioemotional tasks of consoling, reconciling, and loving? Zelditch discussed the evidence from fifty-six societies, modern and primitive, and in families consisting of a male, a female, and their children. He drew the following broad conclusion: it is the male who is the task specialist oriented to the external environment to obtain food and materials for the family; the female is the maintenance specialist in the internal relations of the family, providing affection and reducing anxieties. Zelditch concluded that, with some exceptions, such as the Arapesh and Mundugomor (see Chapter 3), the father's role was usually instrumental (task-oriented), and the mother's role was usually expressive (maintenance-oriented).

Are women, by their nature, more fitted for the socioemotional tasks? Or have they learned to be more socially sensitive and skillful in their traditional maintenance role in the family? When men have been involved in the external, material support roles, women have been in charge of the interpersonal relationships and, especially, of the feelings and personal development of children.

One thing to take note of is the immense change in the achievement and status of women in our society during the last few decades. Who can say what will happen in the next fifty years? Most important of all is the quite recent emergence of women into a much greater diversity of occupational activities. As Alice Heim (1970), in her discussion of "The Mediocrity of Women," argues, there are questions concerning the nature of male and female capacities that "may become clarified within the next half-century" (p. 136). Heim discusses the tendency of males to achieve more than females, whether on intelligence tests, on academic examinations, or in other career fields. Furthermore, men are found in greater relative proportions at both extremes—the high and the low. "There are more male geniuses . . . criminals . . . mental defectives, suicides, and stutterers, more colour blind males, than females. The list is a long one, with relatively few exceptions" (p. 136).

Concerning whether these tendencies are the result of cognitive differences or social artifacts, Heim comments that, "it is hard to tell as long as society continues to treat women as intellectually different from men" (p. 140).

She concludes that the key to *why* men are found both at "the top rungs of the achievement ladder" *and* "on the bottom rungs of this and other ladders" will not be found "until women have had strictly equal vocational, social, and educational opportunities *for many generations*" (p. 140).

It may be significant, however, that "many women believe that women are generally less competent than men and that this belief becomes a self-fulfilling prophecy" (Wrightsman and Sanford, 1975) with women subsequently achieving less, and wanting to achieve less, than men. Similar beliefs have already been mentioned in the context of the "fear of success" in Chapter 3, and social pressures may even play a part in the fact, noted by Alice Heim, that boys (by their early teens) tend "to catch up with girls even in verbally biased problems" (p. 139). Females' performance on verbal tests show less superiority relative to the males' after adolescence. This tendency is also consistent with the fact that, on the upper levels of academic achievement, women's progress similarly fades. Although the proportion of women graduates is now relatively high, the proportion of those who go on to advanced degrees is much less. Could it be that women, irrespective of their potential abilities, are *expected* not to achieve any more? According to evidence discussed by Middlebrook (1974) and many others, the answer is definitely yes.

FEMINIST VIEWPOINTS

In our discussion of speech intonation, we have touched on some of the feminist arguments that converge on the conclusion that sex differences are distorted by stereotypes of female roles, that is, by certain fixed ideas about what women can or should do and be.

We would probably be mistaken, however, if we were to conclude that a battle between the sexes is needed to put things right, or that it is all a question of male dominance in contemporary society. We should try to avoid a polemical statement of women's rights against "male dominance" lest it lead us into mere superficiality. Some of the very deep questions involved are discussed by Juliet Mitchell in her book *Psychoanalysis and Feminism* (1974). She states that anthropological evidence overwhelmingly supports the view that the most general form of society is patriarchal, with men always at the head of families, groups, or organizations. Furthermore, anthropologists, describing the structure of societies, have drawn attention to fundamental rules governing relationships between families and groups. These rules typically regulate the exchange of women in marriage: something of value is given so that something of equal value can be received in turn—"the exchange is all" (p. 372). Of course, "exchange" is here the kind of "transaction" involved when a woman belonging to one family or group of families marries a man of another family, on the understanding that, perhaps even a generation later, a woman from the latter family will marry a man of the former. Mitchell comments that such rules are "coexistent with society itself" (p. 373). In industrial societies the rules are less visible and, among the lower socioeconomic levels, may not exist at all, but in the upper levels some form of these "exchanges" continues.

She quotes from the work of the anthropologist Claude Lévi-Strauss in order to underline the importance of the exchange process: "The objects of value in the kinship system that are to be exchanged are women, and those who conduct the exchange are men . . . Lévi-Strauss suggests that there is no theoretical reason why women should not exchange men, but empirically this has never taken place in *any* human society. Such a fact again warns us against the Utopian matriarchal reconstructions . . ." (p. 372).

If, as the anthropologists' evidence shows, society has always tended to be patriarchal, the notion of women's freedom must be revolutionary, in a very general, cultural sense of the term. However, in a narrower sense, feminist movements that aim to change existing conditions of society are, by definition, revolutionary movements. So it should not be surprising that the social and sexual emancipation of women is a political question that merges, in some countries such as France, with radical politics. A further complication in France is the merging of current feminist thinking with an interest in Freudian theory, for example, in the group "Psychoanalyse et Politique" within the "Mouvement de la Liberation de la Femme." This adds an interesting twist to the view of Freud as a protagonist of masculine values and male dominance. The group "Psychoanalyse et Politique" opposes the American feminist rejection of Freudian theory.

Juliet Mitchell herself also shares this view. She argues that, while we should not accept Freud's patriarchal ideas, we should seek an alternative within Freudian theory. The position can be summarized as follows: we should aim to continue with the general framework of Freudian ideas concerning the unconscious mind but work toward a different "filling" inside the overall framework. Mitchell contends that Freudian theory might be salvaged from its patriarchal bias, thus preserving what is of value in the psychoanalytic approach to the unconscious for understanding the development of sexuality and sex differences.

However, Mitchell makes effective criticisms of feminists who are in danger of "replacing biological dualism with social dualism." That is, instead of attacking the assumption that women's restricted roles derive from innate biological differences, they now see the enemy in "male domination." Things are not so simple, Mitchell argues: the oppression of women derives instead from the patriarchal structure of the "father-dominated" society. She defends Freud for reporting on the status quo of patriarchy, thereby revealing how "the human animal with a bisexual psychological disposition becomes the sexed social creature—the man or the woman" (p. 402). In Chapter 3 bisexual development in the child through the Oedipal phase is described, and this is what Mitchell refers to in the quotation.

Mitchell argues that Freudian theories "give us the beginnings of an explanation of the inferiorized and alternative (second sex) psychology of women under patriarchy" (p. 402). Although there is a complete absence of empirical citations in her book, it provides a source of ideas, some of them very profound and searching, and we now intend to show why it is useful to discuss them.

First, there is the remarkable insight that her discussion gives into fresh arguments, different from those we usually find in our textbooks. For example, she emphasizes the contrasting opinions about Freud's work among feminists in various countries, and writes:

> From my own experience in America I cannot say I have heard a word said even in favour of an interest in Freud's writings; with varying degrees of subtlety, he is portrayed as one of the greatest misogynists (women-haters) of all time. In England there is general prejudice against psychoanalysis . . . Among Scandinavians I have found surprise at the thought of feminists utilizing his work . . . In France there is the large and important women's liberation group calling itself Psychoanalyse et Politique . . . (p. 297).

Mitchell quotes from an English version of the manifesto of "Psychoanalyse et Politique," which announces that Freudian theory is of value because "In the ideological and sexual fight, the only discourse that exists today on sexuality and the unconscious . . . is the discourse of psychoanalysis . . ." (p. xxi). Thus, a "descending scale of opposition" to Freudian theory is revealed, depending largely on the ways and with what emphasis Freud's work has been interpreted and used by psychoanalysts in these countries.

Mitchell denies that Freud's theory gave "a mandate on how to be a true woman" or dictated how women *should* be. Actually what he did was make "his observations on how a girl is supposed to become a woman, what repressions . . . what inhibitions, what prohibitions, what possibilities she may hope for" (p. 338). By expanding the concept of the unconscious mind, Freud was able to show how the cultural demands for different sex-roles are imposed; of course, the demands that Freud described were those of a father-dominated society, and a strictly dominated one at that.

To return to Mitchell's argument that patriarchy can be identified with all human history: any solution to the question of woman's inferior position now seems much further away than if it were only a matter of current male exploitation. Can we find solutions in other directions? Is there really an alternative in an "ecological revolution"—what Mitchell calls a "brave new world of extra-uterine babies," with technology conquering both the "biological handicap" of physical weakness and the "painful ability to give birth." Or should we think of going for political solutions to equalize legal and economic power? Mitchell sees a solution as coming, inevitably, out of pressures already present in Western society to undermine the family as a socializing agent and thus to undermine patriarchal values. In psychoanalytic terms, the cultural demands that are introduced into the child's unconscious mind at the Oedipal stage of development (see Chapter 3) might themselves be changed if the patriarchal family is no longer their agent. There are, according to Mitchell, a variety of changes in society that make this "undermining" plausible. For instance, large-scale social welfare structures in the spread of child-care facilities and the increase of dual-career marriages. These, she thinks, are the right conditions for "a transformation of all previous ideology," although whether this will occur in the face of the prevalence of patriarchy in all kinds of historical accounts is a question that produces serious flaws in the argument. Nevertheless, under present conditions the patriarchal system may be growing more and more irrational.

In conclusion, we are indebted to Juliet Mitchell because her ideas "turn the tables" on the preconceptions of more conventional thinking. If we are to discuss some of the bigger social psychological problems from as many sides and directions as possible, her ideas serve us well. Especially, they pose one central question: do we *need* patriarchy?

RAPE AND SOCIETY

Some of the feminist advocacy against male domination focuses on attitudes toward rape in our society, identifying rape as an extreme form of the general male coercion of females. Two researchers, Lorenne Clark and Debra Lewis (1977), have made a study of the incidence of rape in Canada. Understanding the social context of rape involves some very far-reaching questions, and the solution to current problems connected with rape will necessitate, according to Clark and Lewis, undermining the legal, economic, and social institutions that preserve the unequal status of men and women. This means that women must have the larger objectives of attaining "control over aspects of their persons and their lives by acquiring rights of ownership to the various goods and benefits which were formerly reserved exclusively to the ownership of men" (p. 178). Attaining these objectives will bring about the result that "women will emerge from their status as objects, rather than subjects of property rights . . . as new approaches must be based on the assumption that rape is a violation of every woman's right to sexual autonomy, and wrong because it is an unjustified interference with her physical person, no different in kind from any other form of physical interference" (p. 179). Clark and Lewis present arguments for changes in the legal position so that rape can be treated as any other form of assault on the person rather than in a special sexual context, with possibly "excusable" features. They refer to common attitudes and legal practices that are detrimental to women's rights, and they emphasize that "it is totally arbitrary to conceptualize female sexual organs as being governed by a different legal framework than that which governs other bodily parts . . . Since sexual organs are just parts of the body, an attack on the sexual organs is as threatening to life and health as an unprovoked attack on any of the other bodily parts" (p. 167).

There seem to be at least two levels for the discussion of rape. The first is the individual level. Here we can discuss the personal strategies that women can use to evade rapists. For instance, in pamphlets issued by the police, such as "Woman Alone," a variety of precautions are listed, although the depressing effect of these warnings is to demonstrate how restricted is the amount of freedom and independence that women have in our society as compared to men. Then there are strategies of resistance. How can women resist an attacker? In some cases, the rapists' victims escaped because they "out-talked" the man—telling him someone was watching, giving the victim an opportunity to get to the door. One of the Boston Strangler's victims escaped by keeping up a continual loud screaming and biting his finger down to the bone.

Second, in contrast to this level of individual strategies, there is the theoretical attempt to analyze the general social context of rape and particularly the attempt to understand social attitudes toward or about women, the degree to which rape is the result of these attitudes, and how they may be changed. For example, the expectation that women should be submissive, and women's own inclination to be so, can be understood as a social product involving legal, economic, or traditional structures in society. Susan Brownmiller (1975), who has written a historical and contempory, if lurid, discussion of rape, comments on these influences when she recalls that in her first karate class, the attitudes of submissiveness were so strong in herself that she found she could not even attempt the physical attack.

> At the start of our lessons our Japanese instructor freely invited all the women in the class, one by one, to punch him in the chest. It was not a foolhardy invitation, for we discovered that the inhibition against hitting was so strong in each of us that on the first try none of us could make the physical contact. Indeed, the inhibition against striking out proved to be a greater hindrance to our becoming fighting women than our pathetic underdeveloped muscles (improvement in both departments was amazingly swift) . . . (p. 453).

The conclusions of Clark and Lewis suggest the need for basic legal changes as a beginning in the task of combating the problem of rape, and certainly, as Brownmiller argues, there can be no "private solutions."

SEX ROLES AND SUBMISSIVENESS

Although in the previous section we mainly discuss current ideas about sex differences, I also mention that our aim in social psychology, as a discipline, is primarily to carry out and seek explanations from empirical studies. In the following chapter we consider the nature of this empirical task more fully.

There are a variety of research studies already available on the topic of sex differences. Many of them have suggested that certain effects follow from the dependent position of women in society. Alice Eagly (1978) has summarized the experimental evidence concerning women's reaction to social pressures, their susceptibility to influence, which may be the result of sex roles, defined as "normative pressures characterizing our culture and prescribing that females shall yield to social influence and that men shall remain relatively independent" (p. 87). This norm of submissiveness is assumed to be learned as a product of childhood "training" that stresses passive behavior and yielding. Eagly has reviewed all experimental studies reporting statistical tests of sex differences and divided them into three main categories: 1) studies of persuasion, 2) group-pressure studies of conformity, and 3) conformity studies not involving surveillance. Let us now examine her results, taking each category in turn.

1. In *persuasion research* an influencing agent (the experimenter) presents opinions or arguments, and the subject's subsequent degree of agreement is assessed. The most common result in the 62 studies of this category showed no sex difference, and only 10

studies (16%) showed significantly more female persuasibility. One study (2%) reported more male persuasibility.

2. *Group-pressure* studies involve members of a small group (confederates of the experimenter) exerting influence by their majority opinion on subjects who believe their responses are under surveillance by the other group members. Out of a total of 61 studies, the most frequent result (62%) showed no sex difference. Twenty-one (34%) found females to be significantly more conforming, and 2 (3%) found males to be so.

3. In conformity studies *without group pressure* or surveillance, influence is typically exerted by reading out opinion statements, but the subjects' responses are not exposed "publicly." Of 22 studies of this kind 19 (86%) reported no difference, 2 (9%) reported significantly greater conformity among females, and 1 (5%) reported greater male conformity.

In summary, Eagly concludes that the most frequent finding in the totality of these three categories is for no difference between the sexes. Only in the group conformity experiments is there a substantial minority of studies showing greater female yielding. Eagly is, however, able to point to a pronounced difference in the distribution of findings by comparing studies published before 1970 with those published in the 1970s. The studies showing female influenceability in each of the categories tend to be those carried out *before* 1970. Thus, 16 of 37 group pressure studies before 1970 (43%) showed greater yielding by females, contrasted with 5 of 24 (5%) for the 1970s.

This kind of evidence corroborates the indications of social change that we mentioned earlier in relation to sex differences in achievement. Still, the greater incidence of female conformity in group-pressure situations remains without a satisfactory explanation, unless it might be the speculative possibility that women are more concerned with ensuring social harmony within the group and for this reason go along with the majority. However, Eagly also brought our attention very clearly to the change and transition in women's attitudes. We can examine further the probability of recent and current modifications in sex roles by examining contemporary patterns of marriage.

CHANGING MARRIAGE

Several times in this chapter the extent to which sex roles are changing is mentioned. Scanzoni (1972) analyzes the changing female role in marriage by focusing on the ratios of married women's obligations and rights at different time periods. For instance, with the beginning of feminist activities in the nineteenth century, there was a movement away from the women's status as *property*. More recently, together with the greater pressures from feminist movements and general social changes, married women's rights have increased, he suggests, along a continuum from *complementary* status, to *junior partner*, and finally to *equal partner*.

The change of women's role from the status of property to complement brought with it greater amounts of affection and consideration from husbands. As complement, Scanzoni notes, the married women becomes "a friend to her husband." Later, as more and more women took jobs in industry and commerce, women came to have a share in the instrumental roles of marriage, bringing in material input and also assuming a greater part in marital decisions. At this stage, Scanzoni writes: "We can label (wives) as being somewhat beyond complement and as a kind of *junior partner* chiefly because there is evidence from several sources that the working wife has more family authority than her non-working counterpart" (p. 39).

The greatest degree of reciprocal sharing in rights as well as duties is found, obviously, in dual-career marriages, where both partners are engaged in occupational careers, sometimes within the same occupation or professions, such as teachers, managers, physicians, academics, administrators, journalists, and so on. The decision-making within the family and the rights-duties ratios are now those of equal partners.

The proportion of working-couple marriages throughout the socioeconomic levels of society must be high and increasing (Rapaport and Rapaport, 1978). However, all three marriage types—complement, junior partner, and equal partner—are found in our society. A good example, and a relatively early one, of a useful research approach to discovering more about the internal patterns of marriage is Blood and Wolfe's (1960) questionnaire concerning everyday decisions. This questionnaire has eight items asking *who makes the final decision* about, for example, what car to get, whether or not to buy life insurance, what job the husband should take, and where to go on vacation. The replies are combined in a single index of "family decision-making." The index has been applied frequently in various countries with the following results: husbands have more power, and the higher the job status of the husband, the more decisions he controls.

Scanzoni refers to further questionnaire evidence suggesting that the husbands with higher social status had more legitimate power because they bring more resources to the marriage, whereas lower status husbands may simply seize nonlegitimate power. A further qualification has to be made by the tendency of husbands of higher social status to share power with their wives.

Whether the kind of questionnaire approach we have just mentioned captures the essence or subtlety of marriage relationships is doubtful. We would also have to consider such other marital factors as mutual consideration, self-sacrifice, altruism, and the tendency, not to be discounted, of partners to idealize each other. Nevertheless, the discussion of power within marriage does call for fact-finding by questionnaires and interviews with husbands and wives. Scanzoni also touches on a distinction that is helpful in understanding feminist movements. He distinguishes between individual opposition and collective opposition to power. If an isolated individual (for example, a wife) perceives a power situation (her marriage) as unjust, her disapproval is not of general significance. As in Brownmiller's comment, which we mentioned above, there can be no "private solutions." However, if numbers of individuals have similar perceptions, then social movements may result, with the possibility of changing an entire social structure. Clearly, this process is underway for the structure of marriages.

CONCLUSIONS

Studies of social behavior reveal some marked sex differences in such areas as speech forms (grammar, accent, intonation) and nonverbal communication (eye contact). The descriptive evidence of these is consistent in suggesting either that women are more competent in social skills or that they have to be more alert and sensitive in social situations because of their dependent, less powerful position in society. However, while the evidence is clear, the interpretation of what it may mean or how it is to be explained is still an undecided question. Are women innately different in social situations or are they trained to be so, in a society where men have the power? It could be that both possibilities account for the differences that have been observed. It could also be that in a society that frequently treats women as inferior, we may be a very long way from any more precise answers.

The process of change in existing sex roles can be better understood by examining current feminist ideas and how they represent the priorities for change. Arguments have been put forward that the prime target for change is the structure of patriarchy itself, even though there is historical support for patriarchy as the prototype of almost all societies.

In the meantime changes in female social behavior are happening, some of which have been noted in recent experimental studies of conforming behavior. Other changes are obviously taking place in the resource or power structure of marriages. There are many issues yet to be studied, many hypotheses to be tested by research. We are now ready to discuss, in the next chapter, the more general topic of the methods and approaches that are available to us for our use in carrying out research in social psychology.

REFERENCES

Argyle, M. 1969. Social Interaction. Methuen, London.

Argyle, M. 1975. Bodily Communication. Methuen, London.

Blood, R. O., and D. M. Wolfe. 1960. Husbands and Wives. The Free Press, New York.

Brownmiller, S. 1975. Against Our Will: Men, Women, and Rape. Bantam Books, New York.

Clark, L., and D. Lewis. 1977. Rape: The Price of Coercive Sexuality. The Women's Press, Toronto.

Eagly, A. H. 1978. Sex Differences in Influenceability. Psychol. Bull. 85:86–116.

Gahagan, J. 1975. Interpersonal and Group Behavior. Methuen, London.

Heim, A. 1970. Intelligence and Personality: Their Assessment and Relationship. Penguin Books, New York.

Labov, W. 1966. The Social Stratification of English in New York City. Center for Applied Linguistics, Washington, D.C.

Labov, W. 1972. The Study of Language in its Social Context. In: P. P. Giglioli (ed.), Language and Social Context, pp. 283–307. Penguin Books, New York.

McConnell-Ginet, S. 1978. Intonation in a Man's World. Signs: J. Wom. Cult. Soc. 3:541–559.

McKeachie, W. J., C. L. Doyle, M. M. Moffett. 1976. Psychology, 3rd Ed. Addison-Wesley, Reading, Massachusetts.

Middlebrook, P. N. 1974. Social Psychology and Modern Life. Alfred A. Knopf, New York.

Mitchell, J. 1974. Psychoanalysis and Feminism. Penguin Books, New York.

Murstein, B. I. 1972. Person perception and courtship progress among premarital couples. J. Marr. Fam. November, 621–626.

Rapoport, R., and R. N. Rapoport. 1978. Working Couples. Routledge & Kegan Paul, Boston.

Scanzoni, J. 1972. Sexual Bargaining: Power Politics in the American Marriage. Prentice-Hall, Englewood Cliffs, New Jersey.

Schlesinger, K., and P. M. Groves. 1976. Psychology: A Dynamic Science. William C. Brown, Dubuque, Iowa.

Shuy, R., W. Wolfman, and W. K. Riley. 1967. A Study of the Social Dialects in Detroit, Final Report, Project 6-1347, Office of Education, Washington, D.C.

Trudgill, P. 1974. Sociolinguistics: An Introduction. Penguin Books, New York.

Tubbs, S. L., and S. Moss. 1978. Interpersonal Communication. Random House, New York.

Williams, J. H. 1977. Psychology of Women. Norton, New York.

Wrightsman, L. S., and F. H. Sanford. 1975. Psychology: A Scientific Study of Human Behavior. Fourth Edition, Brooks Cole, Monterey, California.

Zelditch, M. 1955. Role Differentiation in the Nuclear Family: A Comparative Study. In: T. Parsons and R. F. Bales (eds.), Family, Socialization and Interaction Process, pp. 307-351. The Free Press, New York.

Chapter 5
SOCIAL PSYCHOLOGY

J. K. Chadwick-Jones

In most introductory texts the section on social psychology appears at the end. It is usually preceded by chapters on the physiology and neurology of human and animal behavior and by chapters on perception, learning, personality, and motivation. Only after studying all this is the reader supposedly prepared to study the person in relationships with others, in groups, and in social situations of different kinds. Leaving social psychology to the end is a result of the logical unfolding of our discipline from individual to social factors. However, some cautions are in order.

Krech and his colleagues in their introductory text (1976) made an interesting comment on this tendency to leave social psychology to the end when they remarked that "in real life, psychological processes do not go forward one chapter at a time." They suggested that we, the readers, may not have realized that they have been dealing with social psychology all through their book, "just as Le Bourgeois Gentilhomme in Moliere's play was unaware that he had been speaking prose all through his life . . . "

In the approach to psychology as the scientific study of mind and behavior, it is necessary to examine certain "core" functions of the individual organism. These functions are the subject matter of experiments that test how the individual reacts to certain stimuli: light, visual displays, sounds, tastes, touch, lifting weights, and so on. This is the field of perception. Other experiments focus on how well specific tasks are performed under controlled conditions of prior experience. This is the field of learning. Experiments are aimed at measuring motivation when performance is recorded, for example, after fasting or when incentives, such as food and money, are offered. These areas of perception, learning, and motivation largely exclude the social context because careful laboratory controls are used that minimize the extraneous influences of everyday social behavior. However, if we consider development in children, for example, we can see immediately how socially saturated all psychological processes are.

Children build a "self-image" partly because they are trained to do so by others, especially adults. By seeing a "reflection" in the admiration, approval, or disapproval of adults, the notion of self develops as a mirror image of the reactions and behaviors of other people. Thus, for a full sense of "I," social interaction is required, since the "I" develops through awareness and acceptance of the evaluations made by others. Examples of what happens when social influences are absent can be found in the phenomena of wild or feral children who have spent their childhood away from human contact. There is no evidence of normal development; these children seem to have both cognitive and social incapacity.

Studies of such diverse areas as mental health, intelligence, language, and work behavior have shown that social factors are among the foremost and most decisive factors affecting these areas. In language studies this has been recognized only recently. For instance, Wrightman (1972) included language as a major area in social psychology at a moment when most textbooks left it out.

It is not claimed herein (although it is tempting) that *all* psychology is social psychology, but we should remember that much of human thinking and behavior is socially and culturally influenced, at least in the particular forms that human characteristics—morality, intelligence, language, personality—are found to take.

We, therefore, have to modify the impression that we may have had from our introductory texts that social psychology can be neatly parcelled into a small section about "contemporary problems" or about some favorite laboratory topics, such as obedience, conformity, or deviance. Instead, we should recognize that social psychology is a very broad field of study. It is a field that we will already have started to discover in observing how a child becomes a social being, how a child learns language, how adults refer to social standards of what is "normal," or how personality absorbs the acceptable social roles for male and female.

When we examine the topics involved in social psychology, we find that the subject matter concerns both how persons act toward others and how they perceive the relationship between themselves and others. We must try to study social behavior as it occurs, and try to understand also how people think in social situations. This will be difficult because we cannot describe the process directly; we can only suggest the possible ways in which such thoughts operate.

For instance, let us attempt to express how we think about other persons. We have to consider our feelings about them, what we think are likely to be their responses, and what they assume or think about us. Moreover, we may have to guess what others think that we think about them or even what others believe we think that they think about us. In this way we touch on the subtle ways in which we think about other persons even in everyday situations. Unfortunately our language is not very well adapted to describing such subtleties. A better approach could be to express the relationships in diagrams, so that their interactive quality appears more clearly. One device used recently by George Levinger (and discussed in Schneider, 1976) is to represent different stages of interpersonal relationships by means of intersecting circles—minor, major, and complete intersections expressing development from surface contact to increasing degrees of mutual attachment.

THE UNIT OF STUDY

It may seem relatively easy to study only the acts that we can observe, record, and measure, but even here we will have a further problem, which can be expressed in the question, "What is to be our unit of study?" The unit of study could be the individual—how the individual perceives or acts in various social situations—but equally well, or perhaps better, it could be two or three persons. What, simultaneously, are their thoughts and their mutual actions toward and reactions to each other? There is yet a third possibility: we can observe whole groups of people whose actions and reactions we can record. So we see there are three units of study to choose from: 1) the individual, 2) the two-person relationship (the dyad), and 3) the group (usually a primary group of up to 8–12 persons).

These three alternatives represent the actual choices of social psychologists. Some study the individual's social world, his perceptions, motives, and ideas. Others focus their study on two persons and examine the interaction between the two (sometimes three) individuals as the prototype of all social relations. A third "school" of social psychologists studies groups of persons and attempts to analyze the many relationships that form simultaneously and interact.

By emphasizing that there is a choice of "units," we can avoid the impression that social psychologists simply rush out to study "social behavior" in general. Also, as well as recognizing the fact that this is not the way it is done, we have adopted a framework that will help us to understand what social psychology is about.

In recent years dyads have been receiving much attention, probably more attention than individuals or groups, partly because they constitute a convenient unit for laboratory study and partly because of the many forms and elaborations devised for two-persons games, such as the Prisoner's Dilemma (a game in which the players choose between sharing or exploiting, each choice carrying its advantages and risks).

The popularity among social psychologists of these units of study—individuals, dyads or groups—is a matter of current fashion. Up to about ten years ago it was the group unit that was most often used, with the individual as runner-up and the dyad relatively less studied. Since then, there has been a great increase in two-person experiments.

Let us consider some typical examples of these three units.

1. If the unit chosen is the individual, then the approach we use will be something like the following example:

    Objective: To observe an individual's reactions to a variety of social stimuli.

    Actual task: The individual selects among a check list of descriptive adjectives after he is presented with pictures of people of different racial appearance.

    Results: We are able to discuss tendencies to ethnic stereotyping, that is labeling all individuals of one ethnic group with the same personal qualities (usually negative). We thus try to answer the question, "What are the characteristics of stereotypes?" (Lindgren, 1973).

2. If the unit is the dyad—two persons in interaction—then we can take as our example a laboratory session where student volunteers are observed in conversation and the amount of their eye contact is recorded.

    Objective: To observe the effects of varying distances between people in conversation.

    Actual task: Pairs of subjects are observed in conversation in three conditions of proximity: 2 feet, 6 feet, and 10 feet.

    Results: When two people are placed closer together, eye contact is greatly reduced (Argyle, 1969).

3. If the unit is the face-to-face group, which we refer to as a *primary group*, then a typical example would be a situation where

we can measure the effects of group size in producing conformity to the majority's judgments.

Objective: To observe and record how conformity with others' judgments is affected by the number of others present.

Actual task: One student volunteer and a varying number of confederates of the experimenter have to carry out a task requiring judging the length of lines.

Results: When the group consists of only one confederate and one genuine subject, the subject forms an independent judgment and does not conform. When a second confederate is introduced, conformity occurs on 14% of the judgments. When a third confederate is added, conformity rises to over 30% and stays at this level with subsequent additions of confederates (Wheldall, 1975).

So we see that social psychologists give their attention either to individuals in their relationships with others or to the two-person relationship, or to group members in direct contact. Also we have noted that this is a matter largely of current fashion in universities. Very recently the group unit seems to have been out of fashion, and the dyad has attracted more interest, but the focus on the individual has always been prominent, because at this level social psychology is closest to general and "mainstream" individual psychology. The social psychologist who studies effects of the social environment on individuals achieves a greater precision and control in experimental design than can be achieved either with dyads or with primary groups. Because the individual approach is closest to the experimental model, it probably enjoys greater academic prestige.

Social psychologists are somewhat divided over which of these three approaches *should* take priority in university courses, in teaching, in textbooks, and in research or support from endowment funds. We accept, here, that a diversity of approaches is a good idea and that the deficiencies of one may be compensated for by the others. How this diversity actually exists and operates is illustrated below.

Individuals

Many psychologists who collect their research data in the laboratory adapt techniques from the classic experiments in 1) perception, 2) learning, and 3) motivation, in order to study 1) social perception, 2) social learning, and 3) social motivation.

With learning and motivation, the individual "laws" or principles can be applied very plausibly to social situations. For example, explaining the actions of a child by referring to rewards in the form of food or candy seems very similar to explaining the child's behavior in terms of social rewards, that is, when rewards are in the form of approval or praise by adults. Much of the time, the individual's motives are inseparably biological and social. Social behavior often expresses a biological drive, and social motives develop from biological ones.

Some social motives are discussed in introductory texts, as a matter of individual biological needs expressed in socially distinct ways in different cultures. However, motives such as competition, affiliation, and power-seeking are studied exclusively within their own context of social behavior, because they represent important problem areas in our own culture.

The continuity of principles referring to both physical and social perception is emphasized in many texts. For instance, the tendency to stability in person perception is similar to the consistencies of physical perceptions. We can notice the same tendency to order and to systematize and thus to achieve some control and predictability in the environment, whether it is the environment of physical objects and events or the environment of social activities. In social situations this tendency to order what we perceive is found in the way we form impressions about other people; we tend to generalize from our initial impressions, from even one or two characteristics, presumably because we try to predict how other persons will behave in future situations.

Dyads

The two-person game is a very popular laboratory design. For example, the experimenter may want to observe the effects of different instructions on the outcome of the game. Subjects may be told either to compete for the greatest possible gain or to cooperate and share as much as possible. Experimenters may manipulate certain conditions, such as the amounts of monetary rewards to each partner in the game, and introduce the possibility of threats to expropriate more than a fair share, with counterthreats to take some alternative option detrimental to the other partner. The experimenter always hopes to achieve understanding of conflict as it occurs outside the laboratory in actual social situations. The two-person game may involve an exchange of written messages, and a series of choices between pairs of alternatives. Its exponents argue that there are factors at work in the two-person situation that are the essence of social conflicts, whether they occur between individuals or between groups, such as employees and unions. To resolve a conflict of interests the partners in the game may be given opportunity to negotiate or to bargain over a mutually acceptable solution. Although there is no firm bridge between the laboratory, on the one hand, and actual bargaining situations, on the other, there have been attempts by brilliant researchers, such as Harold Kelley (1966), to establish principles of bargaining that must certainly be taken seriously. They do appear to apply to everyday situations.

Kelley showed how typical bargaining starts at a much higher demand level than the eventual agreement levels, and he suggested the following "guides to negotiation": 1) avoid early commitments; 2) try to get the other party to make concessions; 3) make concessions yourself; and 4) seek out information on what would be considered a reasonable outcome. This last point is especially important. It concerns information about each person's limits—how far can one party's offer go up and how far can the other party's demands come down? We can think of these "guides" operating in all sorts of situations where bargaining is undertaken, and so we see that information exchange is a very important part of bargaining.

There are other interesting aspects of the social psychology of negotiation that are currently being studied, especially the use of threats and power. For instance, "power" is defined as one partner's control over the allocations of points between two partners in a laboratory game; "counterpower" is defined as the weaker partner's option to seek an alternative outside the "partnership." Thus, each partner may threaten to use "power" or "counterpower" in the process of negotiating an agreement. Finally, a successful negotiation can be seen as a process of collusion where both the bargaining parties manage to emerge with a feeling that they have obtained not only a good deal but the best possible deal under the circumstances—in other words, they have "a bargain"!

The Group

This is the level of greatest complexity for research in social psychology. The group, even a small, temporary meeting of several persons, involves multiple relationships, and it is very hard to keep track of them all. Not only may there be conversations, communications, and different degrees of liking and disliking between each mutual pair (for a group of 8 persons there would be 28 such pairs) but there may otherwise be coalitions, "mutual-admiration societies," consisting of several members.

The work of the observer is difficult; the main problem is how to collect reliable information without interfering with the group. How far is the group going to accept the social psychologist as an observer? Can the group members be sure about the use to be made of the information? Will the information be "objective"? Will it be treated "objectively," or will it be used for interests other than those of the group, perhaps of some controlling or manipulating body?

How can the observer obtain precise, objective data? Fortunately, there are standard procedures that researchers have worked out for such situations, but still it is not easy. How about the people being observed, don't they object? This question raises the possibility of "observer effects," in other words, those under observation will modify their usual behavior and will not behave as they would normally. Because of this problem, most observational studies, especially those outside the laboratory, have been done with groups of children, who are used to being watched by adults and are therefore not on the defensive. Children's behavior is, in any case, a much better subject for observation since it is more open, spontaneous, and expressive than adults'.

In the laboratory, adults' social behavior can be effectively studied in discussion groups, with the use of one-way observation screens, and in these discussions the group members often appear to forget they are being observed. It is a different matter observing groups in natural situations. Whether these people are at leisure or at work, the group may react negatively, not necessarily by rejecting the observer but by subtle modifications in behavior.

Some of our classic studies of small groups have been carried out with preschool, nursery school, and high school children. Children's behavior is, in its own right, an extremely rich subject for study. Perhaps the most famous "field experiment" on intergroup relations, hostility, and prejudice was done by observing and interviewing two groups of schoolboys for several weeks at a summer camp.

To observe and question groups of professional people, politicians, or people in their everyday occupations or in leisure groups, however, is a very tough proposition. Even when such a study is successfully carried out, the results cannot be analyzed in the neat format of experimental designs. There may be an even bigger difficulty over the matter of publishing them: how can this be done without embarrassing and discomforting those who supplied the information? This time, it is not a relationship with so many experimental subjects paid to attend for an hour but with people who have helped to produce the results, perhaps over a long period of time.

So, we can see that for each approach—individual, dyad, or group—there are suitable methods, designs, and theories. Some of the methods and designs are adapted from experiments on individuals, for example, in perception or learning; other methods have been created especially for social situations, and this is usually the case for experiments with groups and dyads.

THEORIES IN SOCIAL PSYCHOLOGY

There is no tidy, neat, matching of theories to each of these three areas. On the contrary, social psychology is at an early stage of theory building. There are no generally accepted, elaborated theories, although many theories have been, or currently are, in fashion. They usually suggest tentative explanations. We see that certain "causes" might be at work so we make a guess, form a hypothesis, and then search for evidence to confirm it.

We are only able to suggest, cautiously, that certain specific explanations may hold from one situation to another, and we try to proceed from facts about social events toward generalizing statements, but we are still no further than constructing sketches of what an explanatory framework—a theory—might be in the future.

As students this should not discourage us. That we have few hard-and-fast explanations does not mean that we are not scientists. It does mean that our science is at an early stage of development and that there are special difficulties, some of which may mean that our branch of science will always be different.

These special difficulties arise because in observing social behavior, we cannot, as in the physical sciences, pursue our data by setting up measuring instruments and then studying their quantitative results. In our case, we have humans as observers (researchers) or as reporters (subjects, actors) instead of measuring instruments, and so our "results" may well mean more or less than we think, and the interpretations of them will vary. All this makes the enterprise of systematic research a problematical issue in social psychology. Observation of natural situations is less powerful as a technique than the laboratory experiment, but even in the latter we may only have achieved the appearance of precision because of factors usually operative (for example, personal or cultural history) that we have not taken into account.

These sources of errors add to the difficulty of filling in on the theory sketch, and many social psychologists have abandoned the optimism that was an earlier characteristic of the discipline. They no longer expect to find a "break-through" experiment but take the view that we shall make progress relatively slowly, cumulatively, and by critical discussion within the discipline. In the earlier optimistic period, the notion of theory building implied a search for explanations of specific events, which could then be connected to each other, as a family of similar explanations—propositions, corollaries, and derivations—and that beyond them it would be possible to locate a small number of general premises from which eventually a whole set of specific explanations (hypotheses) might be deduced. This would be a theoretical structure along the classic lines of the physical sciences. However, this kind of ordered structure is not to be found in social psychology nor in psychology. Only sketches of how such a theory might work are found (Chadwick-Jones, 1976). In contrast, what we do have are *empirical generalizations*, that is, explanations that have had some support in our experiments or systematic observations and from which we try to generalize and to predict that they will hold for any similar situations. Here again, we cannot be very precise, because it is extremely hard to identify the variety of factors that may combine to support or disconfirm our generalization in a future situation. Nevertheless, there are general propositions that can be identified: for example, that learning occurs under certain conditions more effectively than under others, that social interaction during childhood influences adult behavior, that social structures always involve rules of sexual behavior, that the flow of social interaction is influenced by the relative prestige of participants, or that rules of equity determine how social interaction occurs, and so on.

As evidence that such general propositions hold, we can note that more than ten years ago one textbook claimed to be a "digest of the important and better supported generalizations that have emerged from recent decades of behavioral study" (Berelson and Steiner, 1967).

SOCIOMETRIC TESTS AND ATTITUDE MEASURES

We have discussed problems of measurement and have seen that there are special conditions in defining social psychology as a science. At the same time, we cannot underestimate the degree of achievement. In social psychology we find, over and over again, that the shared characteristic of all empirical work is the attempt to collect and analyze facts by rigorous objective standards.

Actually, there has been a considerable advance, especially with some methods that are creatively unique to social psychology, such as sociometric tests, attitude scales, and laboratory designs with a high degree of technical expertise.

Sociometric tests measure the number of choices of persons in a group by other persons in the same group by asking questions like, "who would you like to be your friend?" Then we sum the choices and study the results of this "popularity poll" for each group member. We can also present these results in a diagram, by means of arrows that show who was chosen least frequently, who was a "social star," who was an "isolate," and who formed "mutual admiration societies."

To measure attitudes we can give persons a list of opinion statements about some interesting topic—maybe about student behavior, Women's Lib, or even some political issue—and ask them to agree or disagree with each statement. More precisely, the participants check off their own position on a five-point scale: *strongly agree, agree, neither agree nor disagree, disagree,* or *strongly disagree.* We can then score this pro-con scale from high to low (agree equals five, disagree equals one). Eventually, with a large number of such statements, we can compare the scores of each individual on the attitude scale and also compute the average scores of groups or persons for the topic in question.

As students of social psychology learning our discipline we gain our understanding of scientific method by means of laboratory experiments. This is the easiest way to grasp the essentials of stringency and rigor in research, to appreciate the problems involved in achieving an objective statement of evidence. What we accept as facts are produced by investigators using careful, controlled observation. We must trust that different investigators will have used similar controls to achieve results that are, as far as possible, objective. These essentials apply to all our scientific efforts in social psychology. "Success" in our attempts to show that a given hypothesis explains our observation is to be judged by whether or not the hypothesis "works" as a guide to the objective assembling of evidence; whether it produces positive or negative results when it is tested is another matter: it may be supported or it may be disconfirmed.

FASHIONS IN SOCIAL PSYCHOLOGY

Psychologists, in their preferences and choices among different kinds of subject matter, are inevitably biased toward prevailing fashions. Over the long term, an interchanging variety of topics will be fashionable. Not only do we have social psychologists actively training students in their own favorite kind of experiment or theoretical approach but they, as social psychologists, come under subtle pressures from society to consider some fields of study more important then others and therefore more worthy of attention. For instance, it may be violence that is thought to be the biggest social problem, or it may be racism, obedience to authority, greater productivity of workers, or the rates of suicide, and so on. Depending on such influences of context, psychologists may be happy to concentrate on studying social skills, how to win friends, behavior within organizations, relationships in work groups, child development, or language as a function of social class. For example, if we pick up a textbook from France or England, we will find a rather different distribution of "problems" from those currently identified in North America (see Triandis, 1977).

Social psychologists may have their interests determined by their occupations; whether they work in industry, government, welfare, or education, their day-to-day practical tasks will influence where and how they collect their information—it is now a matter of useful applications to practical problems. In these situations, the opportunity may occur to implement techniques that have been developed through research, such as group therapy, leadership training, and training in social skills. It is also probable that psychological expertise may be of use in situations of social change and of innovation. Usually psychologists and other social scientists observe and comment on the effects of innovations; it is not so probable that they will intervene actively in planning ahead for changes, simply because they have little leverage in the power structure of organizations. Their intervention will not be direct, then, but may be limited to critical commentary. On the other hand, there is always a danger that psychological expertise may be used by powerful interests to their exclusive advantage.

What is certain is that psychologists cannot pretend to stand outside their society just for the purposes of research. They cannot be detached, as physical scientists might be, from their subject matter. Some psychologists have pointed out that the use of the laboratory experiment in social psychology has constituted an illusory attempt to achieve such detachment because the external social world cannot be excluded and laboratory "subjects" and experimenters are themselves engaged in social relationships with each other. However, the problem is still more complicated. It is a dilemma: either to stay with clinically "pure" laboratory experiments or to attempt the study of actual social problems.

If he makes the first choice, a researcher will probably face criticisms of triviality or irrelevance and may be forced into the inconsistent position of generalizing, somehow, from his laboratory results to actual situations. If it is the second choice, the researcher has to accept a less-than-perfect approach to the design of studies, with many more difficulties in achieving a standard systematic design. Even if this is done reasonably well, there is then the further snare in a society of conflicting interests (parties in power and opposition parties): who will utilize (or profit from) the results when they are published?

In general, research outside the laboratory tends to focus on current social problems in a given society. To some extent we would therefore expect to find an American social psychology, a Canadian social psychology, a European social psychology, each "brand" identified by the social problems that are considered worth attention in each cultural environment. In fact, this is not completely the case because problems concerning race, conformity, industrial innovation, and violence are very general ones common to a variety of societies. There are also differences of emphasis and even local problems that are not shared by other societies. However, we should not think of our field of psychology as only a matter of relevant problems. Who decides if (and which) behavior (by whom) constitutes a problem? The "problem of leisure" was much discussed a few years ago but now has been dropped, presumably because increments in leisure for the great majority of persons, despite technological advances, have been relatively small. Given the transitory nature of some "problems" and the possibility that "problems" may only be pseudoproblems, it is as well to emphasize that our field of study should not be defined as a collection of social problems.

Our aims touch on more profound questions—even on the nature of humanity. In taking our psychology courses, we are setting out to learn about social behavior to see how psychologists put into systematic form many of the facts and bits of knowledge that we already know something about through our experiences as social beings. How do psychologists build on common-sense knowledge: do they go beyond it or do they show common sense can be wrong? Essentially, then, we want to learn more about social behavior and to understand more of what we are already, to a large extent, familiar with. What we are now entitled to expect is that we will be shown the extent and the limits of a scientific approach. Can we say that there are laws for social behavior, as there are laws for molecules or gases?

Greater understanding will be our main objective, and particularly greater understanding of our own society. Social psychology will not be a rapid means to the solution of problems; it will be a means toward deeper appreciation and insight, and, not least, toward insight into ourselves.

CONCLUSIONS

We have discussed some contemporary questions about what social psychology is or should be: how research is done, where, and for whom. There are probably more controversial questions in social psychology than in other traditional areas of psychology, such as perception, learning, motivation, or neuropsychology. In social psychology we also have available a large variety of methods and techniques, from experiments to observation of social behavior in everyday situations. We must insist that the experimental method be the basis of our training and be our teaching emphasis. It remains the most effective means for learning scientific methods. In addition, there are great and classic landmarks in experimental social psychology, such as the Asch and Sherif experiments on conformity, Sherif's field experiments in intergroup hostility, and French's experiments in group decision making, each of which helped to advance social psychology into the forefront of our discipline of psychology.

REFERENCES

Argyle, M. 1969. Social Interaction, Methuen, London.
Berelson, B., and G. A. Steiner. 1967. Human Behavior (Shorter Edition). Harcourt, Brace & World, New York.
Chadwick-Jones, J. K. 1976. Social Exchange Theory: Its Influence and Structure in Social Psychology. Academic Press, New York.
Kelley, H. H. 1966. A classroom study of the dilemmas in interpersonal negotiations. In: K. Archibald (ed.), Strategic Interaction and Conflict. University of California, Institute of Inter-personal Studies, Berkeley.
Krech, D., R. S. Crutchfield. and N. Livson. 1974. Elements of Psychology. Alfred A. Knopf, New York.
Lindgren, H. C. 1973. An Introduction to Social Psychology. John Wiley & Sons, New York.
Schneider, D. J. 1976. Social Psychology. Addison-Wiley, Reading, Mass.
Triandis, H. C. 1977. Interpersonal Behavior. Brooks/Cole, Monterey, California.
Wheldall, K. 1975. Social Behavior. Methuen, London.
Wrightsman, L. S. 1972. Social Psychology in the Seventies. Brooks/Cole, Monterey, California.

Chapter 6
LANGUAGE AND SOCIAL BEHAVIOR

J. K. Chadwick-Jones

Our aim in this chapter is to explore and to consider the available evidence and, in particular, to gain greater insights by examining language as an aspect of social behavior. For instance, differences between social groups often lead to hostility, and we seek to understand more of how language and speech styles contribute to these differences.

Especially, we discuss some of the topics that social psychologists have begun to study only during the past decade. Our perspectives are not confined to any one language; we are able to refer to a variety of language communities in proximity to each other and sometimes in a relationship of potential conflict. Some of our examples are provided by English and French in Canada, others by English and Spanish in the United States. Let us begin by defining *bilingualism* and *diglossia*. In the course of our discussion we will refer also to *standard* speech that we have already defined in Chapter 4.

BILINGUALISM AND DIGLOSSIA

Fishman (1967) defined bilingualism as a characteristic of individuals with the capacity to understand in some degree, or to speak, two languages. William Mackey (1968) has made a useful comment in pointing out that "bilingualism is not a phenomenon of language; it is a characteristic of its use. If language is the property of the group, bilingualism is the property of the individual. An individual's use of two languages supposes the existence of two different language communities; it does not suppose the existence of a bilingual community" (p. 554).

Mackey emphasizes that bilingualism requires the existence of two separate language communities, suggesting that individuals from each of the monolingual communities may, to a varying degree, have need of the other language. Thus, "the *bilingual community* can only be regarded as a dependent collection of individuals who have reasons for being bilingual, since a closed community in which everyone is fluent in two languages could get along just as well with one language. As long as there are different monolingual communities, however, there is likelihood of contact between them; this contact results in bilingualism" (p. 555).

Mackey describes bilingualism as an individual's capacity to negotiate, to some extent, social relations in two languages, and he states also the social fact that bilingualism presupposes the existence of two self-contained monolingual communities. In referring to bilingualism we are probably oversimplifying, because many individuals have the capacity to speak *several* languages, or dialects (which we refer to as "codes") as they move from contacts in one social group to another.

Individuals can be said to be *multilingual* in the Southwest of the United States, where there are two major languages and a variety of English, Spanish, and Chicano dialects. There are many other situations where varieties of languages or dialects reflect a social structure in which individuals may exercise choice and possess the capacity or inclination to use several languages.

In situations like these, bilingual individuals move from one speech community to another. However, there is one kind of situation, usually referred to as *diglossia*, where the entire speech community changes from one language or dialect to another, using, for example, one code for everyday occasions and another for more important, formal ones (e.g., High German is a formal code, and Swiss German (Schweitzerdeutsch) is the "low" variety; Hebrew is the "high" or formal code, and Yiddish is the "low" dialect). The term *diglossia* is used for the kind of social situation where two varieties of a given language (high/formal, low/informal) coexist.

The definition can also be extended and used where two different languages coexist in the same society (Peñalosa, 1975), such as Spanish and English in the Southwest and French and English in the Atlantic Provinces of Canada. Again, as in the initial definition, the main emphasis of the term diglossia rests on the social organization of a language community and on the way *everyone* in the community follows the speech rules. Later we will illustrate diglossia in the use of the Acadian dialect of Atlantic Canada.

Diglossia has been discussed by Kloss (1966), who suggests we use "in-diglossia" for a relationship between closely related forms of speech and "out-diglossia" to refer to a similar relationship between languages not closely related. So, in Canada there is in-diglossia between the Acadian dialect and standard French, depending on the degree of formality of situations; at the same time, out-diglossia may also occur between the Acadian dialect and English, each one in its appropriate domains of family, work group, and city or rural centers.

Thus, in some situations two distinct languages may constitute the diglossia where one of them is used as standard speech and the other as nonstandard speech. In immigrant populations in North America, such as in Spanish, Italian, Polish, or German speech communities, English is the standard language and the minority language is used for less formal, more intimate relationships.

Complex diglossia is found in many situations; Fishman (1972) discusses a number of illustrative cases in Europe, Africa, the Arabic countries, and in the United States among immigrant communities. We now illustrate both diglossia and bilingualism with some further examples.

At the risk of oversimplifying we shall attempt to make clearer the definitions of diglossia and bilingualism. The difference between a situation of diglossia, on the one hand, and bilingualism, on the other, is illustrated in Figures 1 and 2. In Figure 1 an entire speech community (A) follows rules for speaking one or another of the two codes, depending on whether the speech style required is the "high," formal variety or the "low," informal variety. In Figure 2 a bilingual speech "pool" (D) derives from two monolingual speech communities (B and C), each contributing in varying proportions. The proportion contributed to the bilingual pool (D) by either B or C will depend on the relative dominance of the communities. For instance, where English is dominant, as in the Southwestern United States, most of the Spanish speakers will be bilingual but few English speakers will be. In France Breton speakers have to be bilingual, but few, if any, Frenchmen other than Bretons will also speak Breton. In Spain all Catalans (in the Northeast region) are bilingual, but few Castilian Spaniards of the Central region need to speak Catalan. In Canada the French speakers contribute more to the bilingual pool than English Canadians. Thus, it frequently happens that only one of the two communities contributes almost all of the bilinguals, as in Figure 3. Here members of a minority community (F) are required to speak the language of the dominant majority community (E) whose members have little interest in the minority language. Figure 3 represents a community (E) that is totally monolingual. In practice we might find a dominant majority (E) with, say, 5% or 10% of its number who are bilingual.

In the example of Figure 3, bilingualism exists where members of a minority language community speak their mother tongue *and* the language of the majority, as is the case for the Bretons in France or the Catalan minority in Spain. This is a situation frequently found in many countries of the world. More rarely, bilingualism also occurs when members of the majority or dominant language community also speak the minority language.

It was noted that we would have to oversimplify somewhat to discuss these differences. In actuality, it may sometimes be impossible to keep the definitions of bilingualism and diglossia separate. In those situations where all or almost all of one speech community is bilingual, the two languages in their actual usage (formal and informal) resemble a situation of diglossia within that community. It will be a matter of rules for the use of each language according to such factors as social circumstances (formal or intimate), location (home, school,

SPEECH COMMUNITY A

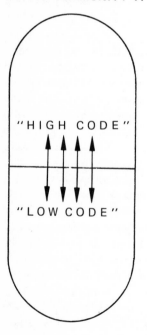

Figure 1.   Diglossia in speech community A.

SPEECH COMMUNITY B   SPEECH COMMUNITY C

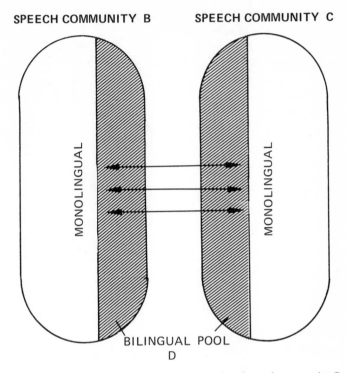

Figure 2.   Bilingualism in speech community B and speech community C.

or work), or topic (borrowing money or discussing politics). Such a situation exists, as we have mentioned, where one language community is dominant, and most minority members have no alternative but to become bilingual.

CODE-SWITCHING

When an individual changes from one language or dialect to another, this is referred to as code-switching. There seem to be generally accepted rules governing the appropriate use of each language according to the situation. However, these rules may also be resisted by groups where conflict arises between the minority and the dominant language communities. There may be a "backlash" reaction from Puerto Ricans, for example, who choose to speak Spanish as much, or as publicly, as possible; even when spoken to in English they may reply in Spanish. There is a similar situation in Quebec, with some

SPEECH COMMUNITY E   **SPEECH COMMUNITY F**

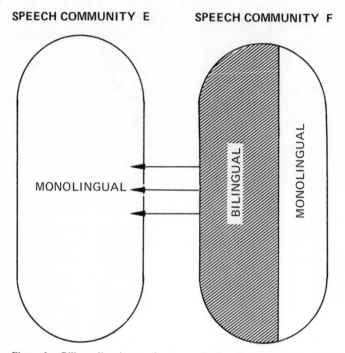

Figure 3.   Bilingualism in speech community E and speech community F.

French speakers choosing not to speak English although they could, of course, do so if they wished.

There is a further complication: not only does the dominant language usually carry more prestige than the other, but when members of the minority switch to the standard language, their version of the standard reveals an accent that itself implies lower status. In other words, the accent or intonation with which the minority member speaks the standard variety still marks that person as having a low, less prestigious position in society. The tendency would be to perceive such people as "outsiders," perhaps as outsiders wanting to come in.

CODES, STATUS, AND CLASS

We have now touched on a characteristic of speech style that, this time, does not relate to context or degree of formality of the situation but that signals to others that the speaker has a position of higher or lower social status. Certain language varieties may be generally accepted as the most prestigious on all occasions. These varieties are largely a matter of accent or pronunciation (see Chapter 4). In Britain the high prestige form is referred to as Received Pronunciation (RP). Needless to say, the opportunities for humor in the exaggerated use or misuse of this pronunciation are legion (e.g., in jokes about talking "lah-de-dah" or "posh"). However, in general, these differences of accent are of importance in conveying information about a person's social position, and they are empirically a part of the social-class structure.

Perhaps the most well-known example of codes connected with social class differences was Bernstein's (1961, 1971) postulate of two language codes: one was the simple, *restricted* code used in the family, home, and among intimate friends; the other a more complicated variety used in situations beyond the immediate group and called an *elaborated* code. Bernstein pointed to evidence that some British children of lower income parents acquired only a restricted code, whereas middle-class children became more proficient in an elaborated one as well. He argued that there are large differences between the range and kinds of social opportunities available to the lower class in contrast to the middle class. For instance, people in a lower-class bracket, such as unskilled workers, take on comparatively few, well-defined social roles, while middle-class parents and children travel more, have a wider range of social and occupational experiences, and generally have more social contacts. Thus, Bernstein drew the conclusion that members of lower socioeconomic groups have a restricted language code because of the limited opportunities of their position in the social structure. His evidence for this conclusion was taken from research data confirming that middle-class children, for example, used sentences of greater complexity. This evidence seemed to confirm what can be thought of as a traditional view of social-class differences. It was a plausible conclusion in the light of what is known about the considerable emphasis on language stimulation in the middle-class, compared to the lower-class, home. Typically, experiments have shown that middle-class mothers talk to their children more and use longer and more complex sentences than lower-class mothers (Hess and Shipman, 1965). However, Bernstein's view has now broadened not only toward the argument that the "restricted" code is not a manifestation of low cognitive development (see Chapter 8) but toward the assessment that it is an equally legitimate alternative (Saha, 1978).

Reaction to the traditional position came especially as a result of research by Labov (1972), who has presented the case that lower-class speech is rich and varied, although, of course, different from middle-class codes. Labov, by using methods of interviewing children *in informal conversations rather than by a formal approach through classroom testing*, has been able to suggest that lower-class speech also has its complex rules. Thus, Labov has attacked the "deficit" theory that is based on the idea that lower-class children only experience a deprived, restricted speech environment. Labov gives examples, among black children in New York, of their using grammatical constructions demonstrating a complex logic. The grammar is different from the "correct" version but is just as much a product of consistent rules. For instance, whereas standard English speech has an abbreviated form of "is" and "are" ("that's what they're. . . .") the nonstandard form will delete rather than contract, but just as consistently ("that what they . . ."). Thus, Cole and Bruner (1971) argue against language or style *deficiencies* as well as *differences*. Instead, they say that what may seem deficient or, at least, different (in thinking and problem solving) often is not even different. It is merely that the researcher did not ask suitable questions and did not make observational studies in the appropriate way.

FORMS OF ADDRESS

In expressing a particular relationship of closeness or distance and equality or inequality of status between individuals, certain speech forms are available. In many languages there are habitual and continual choices of *personal pronouns* to be made in referring to others; for example, *tu* or *vous*, (French), *du* or *sie* (German), *tu* or *usted* (Spanish), *ti* or *chwi* (Welsh), and *thou* or *ye* as they existed in older English speech. These pronouns are used to express social relationships of equality or inequality, of intimacy or formality. Much depends on which of the pronouns is used, but the special trick in their use is whether they are reciprocated or unreciprocated. Thus, reciprocated *tu* (T ⟷ T) means familiarity, but unreciprocated *tu* means superiority (T⟷V). When Person A uses *tu* to Person B, who uses *vous* in reply, it means that A is superior in authority or age. Reciprocated *vous* expresses a rather formal relationship between equals (V ⟷ V) but unreciprocated *vous* means deference and lower status (V⟷T).

Persons of superior status will use *tu* and will be addressed as *vous* by persons in lower positions. When adult strangers meet, they will more formally and respectfully use *vous* to address each other. Sometimes individuals or groups may decide to call everybody *tu* as a way of expressing what they see as a more egalitarian, free mode of behavior. There is also a variety of other possibilities, which are reported by Lambert and Tucker (1976) from their studies of French and Spanish speakers. They observed that, in Quebec, schoolteachers switched from *tu* to *vous* (thus increasing distance) as a method of control or punishment: "as a means of discipline, with certain difficult students, or when annoyed, or when being sarcastic. Many mentioned that *vous* creates a social distance between students and teachers that they found uncomfortable, but its discriminate use . . . can be of great value to the teacher" (p. 54).

The fact that, in English, these forms of address (*tu* and *vous*) no longer exist may mean that we have a more egalitarian outlook, in general, but at the same time we can express degrees of intimacy, distance, respect, or status by using the titles of Mr. and Mrs., Sir and Ma'am, or last name only as in "Hello, Smith" instead of "Hello, Jack" or "Hello, Mr. Smith."

Stephen Potter, in his humorous masterpiece, *Lifemanship*, caught the essence of the social implications of these forms of address when he listed the choices to be made up and down a hierarchy of social status, showing a variety of formal/informal and superior/inferior differences ranging from title and last name to the diminutive of the first name.

Potter illustrated what he called "Farr's Law of Mean Familiarity," as follows, with the hypothetical case of "Mr. Michael Yates" who might be addressed by the Managing Director of his company in the following ways, depending on his social position:

Co-Director	Mike
Assistant Director	Michael
Section Manager	Mr. Yates
Section Assistant	Yates
Secretary	Mr. Yates
Apprentice	Michael
Night-Watchman	Mike

However, this list does not take into account the critical component of reciprocity. Brown's (1965) classic analysis of unreciprocated, asymmetrical forms of address demonstrates how the one-sided use of the first name (FN) or title and last name (TLN) can express inequalities of power or status. For instance, inequality is expressed in the asymmetrical TLN ↔ FN; equal status friends use the reciprocated FN ↔ FN and equal status acquaintances or strangers will use TLN ↔ TLN. Status and age often occur together because older people are often in higher social positions, but obviously there may be quite frequent exceptions. In the event of older persons having a low social position, such as cleaners or janitors, FN may well be used toward them by younger people who have a higher occupational rank, and even though they have the "natural" status of older persons, the cleaners and janitors themselves will defer to achieved or "earned" status and reply with TLN.

Brown asks why egalitarians should attack unreciprocated *tu* or *vous* but tolerate nonreciprocation in other forms of address. He suggests that it could be a matter of the compulsion implied in the usage of *tu* or *vous*. One has to use one or the other; the pronouns cannot be avoided. In contrast, the forms of address FN or TLN can be bypassed with *you*, especially in situations of uncertainty that may occur by changes in relative personal status in an ascending or descending direction. In personal contacts over a period of time, acquaintanceship may change to familiarity, and between unequals if there is hesitancy over the transition in address, *you* will provide a comfortable evasion.

Lastly, if people feel even a little rebellious, their feeling can be gratified without any obvious (and possibly dangerous) defiance by avoiding the respectful forms and saying *you*. In Britain a more obvious and aggressive effect may be achieved and the other person (no doubt older or of higher social position) can be "taken down" simply by the addition of the word "mate" to the end of the sentence, i.e., "O.K., mate?"

LANGUAGE AND PERSONALITY

It has been noted that, as bilingual persons switch from one language to another, there are subtle changes in behavior or attitudes. When bilinguals have been asked to undertake personality tests in each of two languages, they tend to give different kinds of responses in one language than they do in the other (Ervin-Tripp, 1968; Taylor, 1976). In a test of Japanese-English bilinguals who were asked to finish uncompleted sentences, the bilinguals finished them differently in each language as in these examples:

> When my wishes conflict with my family's . . .
> it is a time of great unhappiness (Japanese)
> I do what I want (English)

> Real friends should . . .
> help each other (Japanese)
> be very frank (English)

What is the extent of such changes? Does a neurotic in one language cease to be one in another language? This seems highly unlikely.

Perhaps what has been observed are the influences of *cultural roles for behavior that are carried with the language*. It is most probable that, along with code-switching, certain changes occur in attitudes and behavior, but we really do not yet understand the extent and nature of such changes.

As Robinson (1972) notes, personality is a consistent entity and will not change with the switching of language, dialect, or style, but some aspects of behavior probably do change.

Now, given a change of language, what will influence the individual in deciding to change from one to the other? It is very important to understand that much more might be involved than the individual's own preference. What are the other factors? There are widespread social norms or rules that exist for language behavior governing which language or code is to be used in certain situations. Observers have found that bilinguals may switch from one language to another according to the place (where), the people (to whom), the occasion (when), and the topic (about what). These places, people, occasions, and topics are referred to as the "domains" of language, and "domains analysis" can reveal the social situations that are appropriate for different languages or dialects. Thus, we can chart the rules that operate for *diglossia* and discover when, with whom, and where people will switch from the "low" to the "high" code.

DOMAINS OF LANGUAGE

Investigators have described a number of domains from observations of the speech style or language used in particular situations. The variety of existing domains represents the actual spheres of activities open to individuals in a given society. According to Fishman (1971), the more complex a society grows in the range of social roles that it offers to individuals, the more diversified language repertoires become. In many societies only those people who live entirely within the home, such as preschoolers or retired elderly people, are likely not to have to change codes. As we shall see, the choice of which code to use is a function partly of the formality or seriousness of social situations and partly of the nature and closeness of interpersonal relationships.

The topic of conversation may influence a switch from one code (language, dialect, and style) to another. For certain topics the speakers may have received "training" in one language rather than another. They may be able to converse about world affairs, literature, or politics only in this "trained" language. This fact in itself will reflect that one language or style is considered more important than others. For more important topics, clearly a more important style of speech must be used!

The domains of language span from intimate relations among families and close friends to the more formal relations of teacher to pupil, employer to employee, buyer to seller, and so on. The continuum from informal to formal also relates to the different locations of family, church, work, and neighborhood.

So, if we were to ask people *about what*, *when*, *to whom*, and *where* one language is used rather than another, we might soon be able to chart the social structure of language use. One brief example from an empirical study will give us a typical view of such a structure. Greenfield (1968) used the technique of "self-report" (that is, people were asked about the persons, places, topics, and times of language use) to provide data on different occasions requiring Spanish-English code-switching. He concluded that there were five domains, involving: family, friendship, religion, education, and employment.

Greenfield's evidence supported the hypothesis that among bilinguals, Spanish was primarily associated with the family and secondarily associated with friendship (both family and friendship are intimacy domains). English tended to be used in situations involving religion, work, and education (status or formal domains).

Note that the description of domains is achieved by studying interpersonal conversations, that is, by research using methods familiar to social psychologists, such as direct observation, recording of face-to-face interaction, interviews, and questionnaires. The usefulness of domains analysis is particularly clear in studying the phenomenon of language maintenance or change between different age groups.

We might find that, comparing younger and older individuals, differentiation by domains is more marked with one age group code-switching across a greater number of domains than the other. In this way we could discover how children are socialized and trained in the family or school. Or we might discover that the younger generation is increasingly using a "new" language in preference to the one traditionally used by older people, as in the situation of "language-decline" or "language-death" reported by researchers in the Northwest of France. Here, Breton is becoming more and more confined to intimate and informal domains—to the home, or even only to conversations with grandparents. One researcher commented that some Bretons use Breton spontaneously only when they speak to animals!

THEORIES OF SPEECH BEHAVIOR

The analysis of *domains* is useful in allowing us to classify the occasions of language use in an orderly way. It therefore assists in our general understanding of the social meaning of language. If we want to explain code-switching by individuals or to predict, with some assurance, when individuals will change their language or speech style, then we have to find more subtle explanations. In other words, the general classification by domains is not able to account for all the variety of individual choices between one speech style or language and another.

Although the pattern of domains does provide an outline of general tendencies or norms, the notion of a behavioral norm assumes a standard or general pattern from which there will be many degrees and instances of deviance.

There are good reasons why such a general classification will fall short of what we expect in an explanation of the social functions of speech. First, the range of speech domains is descriptive of the structure of diglossia as it holds for an entire speech community, and the overall classification will not account for individual deviances from the rule in any given domain. In this respect, the domain rule operates rather like any other social norm where many or most people conform to it, but there will, at the same time, be a whole range of different degrees and occasions of departures from the norm.

Second, the classification by domains cannot predict individual speech strategies in a given interpersonal relationship. We must turn elsewhere for explanations of why bilinguals switch languages under some conditions but not others, or why people modify their accents in some conversations but not in others. After all, in social psychology this is precisely what we attempt to do; we aim to state the probability that under given conditions certain kinds of social behavior are likely to occur. Classifying by speech domains gives us an indication of the pattern of collective behavior, but it does not explain why individuals may change speech style in some interpersonal relationships but not in others. It is our task, as social psychologists, to find explanations at the level of individuals, dyads, and primary groups. Describing the overall structure of speech domains does not take us quite close enough to these units of study.

Giles and Powesland (1975) suggest a theoretical approach to explain code-switching that takes into account the *domain* rules we have just discussed and extends the explanation to a finer degree of measurement of interpersonal factors by introducing the concepts of *accommodative* and *divergent strategies.* Accommodative behavior occurs when at least one of the speakers in a two-person conversation adopts the style or code of the person to whom he is talking. Such convergence represents an attempt to conform or to identify with the other person. Alternatively, if one person adopts a speech style divergent from that of the other speaker, he is now identifying with some social group or language community different from the speaker's. Thus, a minority group retaining its own language in the face of pressure to speak the language of the majority might express divergent behavior. For example, as we mentioned earlier, a Chicano or Puerto Rican, spoken to in English, may reply in Spanish, and a French speaker in Quebec may refuse to speak English. Taylor and Simard (1975) explore the extent to which the pressure to be bilingual is felt to be a threat to an individual's identity resulting in the rejection of bilingualism by many French speakers in Quebec.

Thus, by accommodative behavior toward higher-status persons and subsequent association with them, a person could clearly raise his own status in the eyes of others and also seem more acceptable in the immediate relationship with the higher status individual. Exactly how language-switching occurs as part of interpersonal exchanges is likely to be a very fruitful area of research. There is, as yet, much to be discovered about the complexities of exchange and the symbolic meaning of different speech forms. For instance, what is actually exchanged when persons express accommodative or divergent speech behavior? They *gain* the approval either of the listener or of some other language group with which they identify, but they incur the *costs* of having to conform to the other's speech style showing deference to the other person. The listener may be extremely attractive to the speaker, but it may happen that the listener has no power to reward and that the gains of speech behavior consist precisely in the rejection of this person.

Giles and Powesland take their explanatory concepts from existing theories in social psychology to explain *why* speakers choose to be accommodative or divergent in their speech style or language. They seek underlying explanations in the hypotheses of social exchange theory, interpreting speech behavior as a means to improve and maintain status, or to gain approval from others. We should be quite eclectic and open to suggestion at our present stage of investigating language behavior on the question of which theory to use.

DIGLOSSIA AND BILINGUALISM: THE ACADIANS

As is mentioned earlier (Figures 1, 2, and 3) the term diglossia refers to a stable relationship between a primary dialect, used in ordinary conversations, and a "superimposed," more general form called *standard* speech that possesses a body of literature and a codified complex grammar (see Chapter 4). This "higher" speech form is also the written language. Unlike the primary dialect, it is not the language of the home but is learned in formal education. A characteristic of diglossia, according to Ferguson (1959), is that no part of a speech community regularly uses the "higher" form as a medium of everyday conversation. Therefore, we see in Figure 1 that an entire language community (A) switches from a lower to a higher code.

In many situations, diglossia between two forms of the same language is found side-by-side with switching into another language. Examples are provided in the Mexican-Spanish speech community of the United States and in the French-speaking Acadian minorities of the Atlantic Provinces of Canada, which we will discuss in detail here, because their situation illustrates quite a general phenomenon. The French dialect (Acadian) has been differentiated from the standard version of metropolitan France since it was brought into Canada by immigrants from the region of Poitou in France in the seventeenth century. This dialect has been maintained over a long period despite the fact that until recently the language taught in the schools was English.

An individual Canadian whose mother tongue is Acadian may have to "navigate" language behaviors in three forms—Acadian, English, and standard French—according to the nature of the occasion, the person spoken to, or the topic of conversation. Thus, speech 1) in the home, 2) with close friends, 3) with neighbours, 4) with strangers in the shopping center, 5) at work, 6) with the physician or priest, 7) with classmates at school, 8) over the radio, 9) on a television program, or 10) in a sermon at church are all instances of the range of speech occasions. The languages used may be Acadian (1, 2, 3, 6, 8), English (3, 4, 5, 6, 7, 8, 9) and standard French (6, 8, 9, 10). There may be some overlap between Acadian and English on occasions 3, 4, and 5 and between English and standard French on occasions 6, 8, and 9.

The use of Acadian on occasions 1, 2, and 3 means that the dialect dominates in frequency and duration. It is the language of everyday use, except that this usage may have to be suspended during work if the workplace is located away from the immediate neighborhood. It will also be noted that, across this range, there is an ascending order of formality. If we exclude radio and television, the speech occasions extend from the most frequent and informal, home and neighborhood use, to the more formal situations of work, school, and church. This could also be thought of as an ascending order of social prestige, from the chat by the back door to the formal lecture.

The Acadian dialect has been very durable over several hundred years. This characteristic of stability has been noted in other situations of diglossia. What is the future for Acadian speech? "Higher" forms of French may in the future absorb the primary dialect if Acadian speech communities merge with other French language groups, carriers of the higher forms. Or, less probably, the primary dialect may itself develop written and formal usages. There is now considerable awareness that the dialect, as a carrier of Acadian values and experience, should not be allowed to decline.

STEREOTYPES AND LANGUAGE

Earlier, the perception of *differences* between groups and the part this plays among other factors in generating hostility is mentioned. The *perceived differences* between language groups has been the subject of a number of studies by W. E. Lambert and his colleagues at McGill University in Montreal. This work, starting in the early 1960s, has influenced recent studies in many countries that have used or adapted the original research design.

An interesting feature of the studies was their conclusion that the stereotypes attributed by English speakers to the French-speaking community seem also to be accepted by the latter. In other words, the French speakers tended to repeat and echo the low opinions held by English speakers about them. Several sources have hinted at these stereotypes or clusters of personal negative traits, suggesting that French speakers in Quebec think of themselves as "beggars" and harbor feelings of inferiority, aggressiveness, and envy toward English speakers. Lambert's (1967) contribution was to provide evidence of the stereotypes attached to the language communities: how each labels the other, and how they label themselves. The experimental method used was the "matched-guise" technique, whereby recorded voices of French- and English-speaking Canadians were presented to students who were asked to rate the speakers on their personal qualities. Actually, each speaker successively assumed the "guise" of a Quebecois and an English speaker. There were ten bilingual speakers and each read a passage in both languages. The students listening were led to believe that it was a different person each time. The usefulness of the "guise" technique rests in the supposition that there are no actual differences between speakers, since each French passage is matched by an English passage read by the same person. After each reading the students marked, on checklists of fourteen adjectives, what they thought the personality traits of the speaker might be.

There were two notable results. First, the English-speaking students checked off the English speakers as more intelligent, dependable, ambitious, and so on. Second, the Quebecois students did the same thing, but more so. In fact, whereas the English-speaking students had related the English speakers higher on seven qualities, the Quebecois did so on ten qualities from the list of fourteen. They rated English speakers more favorably on such qualities as intelligence, self-confidence, dependability, ambition, and sociability. Thus, they expressed, toward their own group, a kind of self-disparagement and dislike. Lambert's demonstration of a fundamental problem in Quebecois-Anglophone relations has since been corroborated in a series of more recent studies by d'Anglejean, Tucker, and Taylor. The problem lies partly in the attitudes of the English-speaking community, in the disparagement they express toward the other group. This is a potentially dangerous tendency, if one language community offers only rejection or can only suggest self-hatred to the other as these results indicate. There is also the future possibility of a reaction to the negative attitudes of the superior group and counter-rejection on the part of the "inferior" group.

Lambert's interpretation of his results was that the French-speaking students showed "self-hate" because they had absorbed the English-speakers' negative stereotypes. There has been some critical discussion of the results by other psychologists, such as Robinson (1972), who points out that the particular personality traits included in the checklists might not be of significance in all intergroup situations or that others, not included, might be. Tajfel (1962) noted that the Francophones accentuated the superiority of the English speakers on "traits related to socio-economic success. The English section of the community does tend in Montreal to be socio-economically superior to the French one . . . It can be assumed that this situation is of direct and serious concern to the French subjects . . ." (p. 41).

Lambert's "matched-guise" experiments might have a limitation because in any everyday situation a person's voice would only be one feature in our evaluation. We would normally pay attention to appearance, to occupation, or to particular actions. It might also have happened, as Robinson (1972) suggests, that the speakers altered their intonation and their manner of speaking when they changed their languages, but whether they did so is not known.

Earlier in the chapter we defined bilingualism and considered some of the situations in which bilingual individuals might switch from one language to another. Now, let us examine a study by Lambert and Tucker (1972) in which they assess the influence of bilingual proficiency on social attitudes.

Lambert and Tucker subjected bilingualism to a profound analysis by investigating the social implications of French "immersion" courses in schools where French is used as the medium of teaching for all subjects all through the elementary grades. In this situation the researchers reported that the English-speaking children learned French effectively but something else also happened: The children's attitudes (tested initially before, and again after "immersion" training) changed favorably toward a more complex identity in which they were able to think of themselves as both English and French Canadians. These children were sufficiently competent in French to be able to form friendships with French-speaking children of their age. Lambert points out that they had "picked up a second identity effectively . . . they had become at ease in both cultural settings."

This research by Lambert and his colleagues (and there are a large number of studies besides the few mentioned here) brings to light one very optimistic, although speculative, possibility of second-language learning: that there might develop a situation where many individuals, of both language communities, have two mother-tongues. For instance, if French as well as English is learned early in childhood, then bilingual children, as Lambert says, "may well start life with the enormous advantage of having a more open, receptive mind about. . . . other people" (Lambert, 1967).

However, while there are certain positive indicators in these carefully implemented experimental studies, the external situation of stereotyping and of conflict between language communities continues. As Lambert (1973) has argued, being bilingual for English Canadians is *additive* and in no way threatens the use of English. On the other hand, bilingualism for French Canadians tends to be *subtractive*, meaning that when French Canadians learn English, it may end with the displacement of French because of the tremendous dominance of English-speech influence in North America.

CONCLUSIONS

We have now discussed bilingualism, diglossia, and code-switching. We also examined the relationship between language and intergroup stereotypes and some of the more far-reaching possible effects of immersion learning. These studies have illustrated a variety of methods, from field surveys, questionnaires, interviews, and systematic observation of behavior as it occurs in everyday life, to experiments in the laboratory and in the classroom. We note that there are several theories to assist our understanding of the social meaning of language behavior. The broadest explanations embrace the normative patterns or general rules of language use in a variety of societies, so we explore situations of diglossia. Other theories help us to explain interindividual behavior in switching languages or codes where language becomes part of an individual's strategies toward other persons. Here we apply exchange ideas to the study of speech behavior.

Research procedures to uncover the social meaning of language consist of laboratory experiments or systematic recording of natural situations; they both yield descriptions of speech styles and reactions to them. Speech situations may be arranged in the laboratory or be simply noted as they happen in everyday life. In both cases, although the description may be preceded by a statement of hypotheses predicting the relationships to be demonstrated, it is often followed by "after-the-fact" interpretations and speculations about what the described events may mean and how they are best to be explained. In other words, what "theory" do they support or suggest?

The social psychologist is able to control, in laboratory experiments, certain characteristics of the participants, such as their ages, educational level, language proficiency, and ethnic identity. However, many other characteristics (perhaps more significant) may be left uncontrolled: the motivation of the participants, their truthfulness, their capacities to report on their feelings, their beliefs, their aspirations, and their political views. Triandis (1977) commented on problems of methodology that are encountered when we try to compare the performance of carefully selected groups in the laboratory: "Controls tend to make the samples unrepresentative and to imbalance them on many variables of which we are not aware" (p. 283). It will not be possible through experiments to discover much about individuals' memberships at different points of time in actual communities, occupations, or primary groups. These group memberships may be extremely influential in everyday behavior, but for the short period and special conditions of the experiment such effective forces have to be excluded. We cannot be sure of creating the conditions under which the pressures of families, friends, occupations, and social classes tend to influence the use, or reactions to, speech styles. The result is that, at this stage of our research enterprise (and maybe indefinitely), language topics consist of many wide-open questions with a variety of possible answers.

On the other hand, if we only describe speech behavior in natural situations, there may be great difficulties in trying to observe many events happening at once. We may not be able to distinguish one influence from others, all operating at the same time. At least in the laboratory we can try to isolate some of these influences and thus assess their impact more adequately.

So what might be the future research strategies for us as social psychologists? Triandis (1977) offers two constructive paths for social psychology in general, which are appropriate also for studies of speech styles. We can describe very well local populations and particular conditions of language use. We can also develop loose theoretical frameworks and explanatory ideas to help us think about social events and thereby understand them better. We cannot hope, though, to set up a general and totally accurate theory.

Investigators like Fishman, Labov, Lambert, Taylor, Tucker, and their colleagues in North American help us to understand how speech styles and language represent or interact with differences between social groups and classes in conflict. Thus, speech styles are likely to be especially important in affirming both the identification with one's own "in-group" and one's differences from other "out-groups."

Social psychologists whose work we have discussed in this chapter offer us ideas that are mostly at the pretesting stage—still at a rather exciting stage of anticipation, of posing new questions, and, possibly, of finding unexpected and enlightening answers. The great utility of these ideas is that they will, no doubt, provide an important framework for many local investigators of language usage, attitudes, and actions. Speech styles can now become a social-psychological topic in a more explicit fashion than ever before. The message is clear: speech is a key factor to assist us in understanding more about the relations between groups in their particular, actual, and historical context.

REFERENCES

Bernstein, B. 1961. Social class and linguistic development: A theory of social learning. In: A. H. Halsey, J. Flood, and C. A. Anderson (eds.), Education, Economy, and Society, pp. 288–314. The Free Press, New York.

Bernstein, B. 1971. Class, Codes and Control. Vol. 1. Routledge & Kegan Paul, London.

Brown, R. 1965. Social Psychology. The Free Press, New York.

Cole, M., and J. S. Bruner. 1971. Cultural differences and inferences about psychological processes. Am. Psychol. 26:867–876.

Ervin-Tripp, S. M. 1968. An analysis of the interaction of language, topic and listener. In: J. A. Fishman (ed.), Readings in the Sociology of Language, pp. 192–211. Mouton, The Hague.

Ferguson, C. A. 1959. Diglossia. Word 15:325–340.

Fishman, J. A. 1967. Bilingualism with and without diglossia; Diglossia with and without bilingualism. J. Soc. Iss. 23:29–38.

Fishman, J. A. 1971. The relationship between micro-sociolinguistics in the study of who speaks what language to whom and when. In: J. B. Pride and J. Holmes (eds.), Sociolinguistics. Penguin Books, New York.

Fishman, J. A. 1972. The Sociology of Language. Newbury House, Rowley, Massachusetts.

Giles, H., and P. F. Powesland. 1975. Speech Style and Social Evaluation. Academic Press, New York.

Greenfield, L. 1968. Spanish and English usage self-ratings in various situational contexts. In: J. A. Fishman (ed.), The Measurement and Description of Language Dominance in Bilinguals, Seventh Progress Report. Yeshiva University, New York.

Hess, R. D., and V. Shipman. 1965. Early experience and the socialization of cognitive modes in children. Child Dev. 36:869–886.

Kloss, H. 1966. Types of multilingual communities: A discussion of ten variables. Sociol. Inquiry 36:132–145.

Labov, W. 1972. The study of language in its social context. In: P. P. Giglioli (ed.), Language and Social Context. Penguin Books, New York.

Lambert, W. E., 1967. A social psychology of bilingualism. J. Soc. Iss. 23:91–109.

Lambert, W. E. 1973. Culture and Language as Factors in Learning and Education. Paper presented at the 5th Annual Learning Symposium on "Cultural Factors in Learning" at Western Washington State College, Bellingham, Washington.

Lambert, W. E., and G. R. Tucker. 1972. Bilingual Education of Children: St. Lambert Experiment. Newbury House, Rowley, Massachusetts.

Lambert, W. E., and G. R. Tucker. 1976. Tu, Vous, Usted: A Social-Psychological Study of Address Patterns. Newbury House, Rowley, Massachusetts.

Mackey, W. F. 1968. The description of bilingualism. In: J. A. Fishman (ed.), Readings in the Sociology of Language, pp. 554–584. Mouton, The Hague.

Peñalosa, F. 1975. Chicano multilingualism and multiglossia. In: E. Hernandez-Chavez, A. D. Cohen, and A. F. Beltrano (eds.), El Lenguaje de los Chicanos, pp. 164–169. Center for Applied Linguistics, Arlington, Virginia.

Robinson, W. P. 1972. Language and Social Behaviour. Penguin Books, New York.

Saha, L. J. 1978. The 'new' sociology of education and the study of learning environments: Prospects and problems. Acta Sociol. 21:47–63.

Tajfel, H. 1962. Social perception. In: G. Humphrey and M. Argyle (ed.), Social Psychology Through Experiment. Methuen, London.

Taylor, D. M., and L. M. Simard. 1975. Social interaction in a bilingual setting. Can. Psychol. Rev. 16:240–254.

Taylor, I. 1976. Introduction to Psycholinguistics. Holt, Rinehart & Winston, New York.

Triandis, H. C. 1977. Interpersonal Behavior. Brooks/Cole, Monterey, California.

Chapter 7
SOCIAL PERCEPTION
IN CHILDHOOD

Kenneth A. Hill

One of the most important components of normal development is the ability to perceive and interpret the actions and psychological states of other people. The acquisition of language, the learning of skills modeled by parents and teachers, all the many occasions in which the behavior of others is responded to, evaluated, predicted, or merely "understood" entail at least some proficiency at social perception.

Fortunately, the vast majority of children in all cultures are to some degree "social animals." In fact, children often seem more than ready to attend to other people around them. This readiness, which becomes manifest early in infancy, has led a number of writers to suggest that social orientation is in some manner innate to or "wired-in" the nervous system (see Bell, 1968). This issue is discussed later.

However, normal social interaction, even of the sort involving children, requires much more than mere orientation. The child's perceptions of others must serve him somehow; they must be adequate to the social task at hand. If a father is growing angry, the child must perceive and interpret the signs of that emotion appropriately. If a peer has not understood something a child has said, the signs of puzzlement must signify a necessity for rephrasing the utterance. With age, the child becomes increasingly competent at perceiving the feelings, motives, and dispositions of others and using those perceptions with facility in the course of social interaction.

Thus, it can be seen that social perception is paramount to social development. That is indeed the theme of this chapter. For the theme to be fully appreciated it will be necessary to define the concept of social perception more specifically and to compare it to nonsocial perception. We outline in this chapter the course of the development of social perception through childhood. Finally, the relationship between social perception and some indices of socialization and moral development is discussed.

WHAT IS SOCIAL PERCEPTION?

Psychologists who write about social perception tend to agree on at least one point: "perception," when appearing after the word "social" or "person," is usually being used in a very loose way. Sometimes social perception is used to refer to a relatively simple phenomenon, such as identifying an emotion from looking at a photograph, or to a much more complex and "cognitive" process, such as inferring another's total personality from a limited number of behavioral cues. Almost always it is used in a somewhat different manner than when reference is being made to the perception of objects or things.

How, then, does *social* perception compare to *object* perception? Let us first consider their similarities. Both kinds of perception involve the sensory apparatus, often more than one modality at a time. A food is smelled and tasted; a friend is seen and touched. From these examples, a second point of similarity is apparent: some sort of information is received about the object of our perception. The characteristics of the friend are quickly grasped and he is recognized (perhaps much less so for a casual acquaintance), and a food is recognized as pudding or kidney pie according to its stimulus features. Thus, the act of perceiving both things and people involves a categorizing process; perception involves the use of labels and categories. To put it another way, perception means sorting out the "raw data" of sensory experience. It is a process, however, that allows for varying degrees of sophistication. An experienced adult may label a subtly patterned facial expression as "sanguine" or "jaundiced," or an inexpensive wine as a "charmingly pretentious Beaujolais."

The categorizing process is one way in which the act of perception imposes structure on the environment. A second way, which also refers to persons and things, is called *perceptual constancy*. A round table seen from the side presents an elliptical image on the retina but is nevertheless "seen" as round. A person who has been standing near you walks toward the horizon. His image on your retina consequently grows smaller, but you do not "see" him shrinking. Both table and person remain constant in shape and size. There are, in fact, many kinds of constancies, but they all seem to involve a tendency to grasp the *invariant* features of the environment, that is, those features that remain "the same" despite momentary transformations. Invariance means stability. An environment without stability is constantly fluctuating and is therefore unpredictable. It is also uncategorizable and unknowable.

While perceptual constancies seem to develop very early in life, there is much evidence that infants are not able to maintain one especially important kind of constancy. That is, when an object in view is momentarily out of view, the infant behaves as if the object no longer existed. For example, he immediately loses interest in a toy that is put behind a blanket. This perceptual constancy is called *object permanence* and usually appears by the end of the first year. Development of object permanence depends upon the development of *memory*, and it is an excellent example of the fact that perception has a *temporal* dimension as well as a spatial one; information about objects and people is received and organized over time. We see below that the temporal dimension is especially important in the case of social perception.

Also during the first year the infant is able to recognize its mother and to distinguish her from other people—a perceptual constancy of no small importance. Schaffer (1971) has aptly described the immensity of the task that confronts the infant, who is so new to the business of perceiving people:

> The infant must not only learn the characteristics which distinguish the mother from other people but he must also conserve her in the face of all the perceptual transformations likely to affect her appearance in different encounters. Sometimes she will be seen at a distance and sometimes close by; on some occasions she will appear full-face and on others in profile; she may have her curlers in and her teeth out, be with or without her spectacles, have or not have a hat, be wearing different clothes on different occasions and perhaps even different coloured hair—and yet must still be recognized as mother (p. 98).

The discussion so far has focused on some similarities between the perceptions of objects and people. Both involve the sensory apparatus, the organizing and categorizing of sensory information, and the determining of invariant features. Of primary interest, however, are the *differences* between the two kinds of perception.

One of the most unique features of social perception is the tendency to consider people as causal agents. Objects are not usually afforded this special status. A rock shattering one's window leads to a search for the human agent "responsible." Of course, one might wonder about further causes bearing on the culprit's toss, but the causal chain is not normally traced very far. Perceivers usually stop at the "reasons" behind human action as cause enough. Since reasons are not directly visible, a perceiver must estimate or infer them from the cues that *are* observable, such as the physical characteristics of the other person, his behavior, or other relevant aspects of the situation.

Social perception, therefore, involves the drawing of inferences and the making of suppositions about the behavior of others. Moreover, if we find ourselves making the same inference regarding the same individual on two or more occasions (for example, "He means to hurt me"), we are likely to attribute some relatively stable disposition to that person ("He is aggressive"). By attributing a disposition, we are assuming that there is a probability that a person will behave in a particular manner in similar situations; we are rendering the other's behavior predictable.

Of course, there are hazards involved when attributing underlying dispositions on the basis of observable cues. For one thing, it seems that perceivers are all too ready to generalize from one disposition to others. Presumably, we all have "implicit personality theories" about what traits go together, and we therefore may construct a whole personality from the perception of only one trait, the way an anthropologist might attempt to build a model of a cave man from a fossilized jawbone. This tendency is found in what is called the *halo effect*, which occurs when an initial evaluation of someone, favorable or unfavorable, leads to the inference of a whole cluster of traits that are consistent with that evaluation.

A related process is called *stereotyping*, which is the inclination to label others according to preconceived categories. Usually, stereotyping proceeds from the observation of one particularly salient characteristic, such as sex, race, and nationality. Often, traits that are considered undesirable within a group are readily attributed to "outsiders," such as when individuals of another race are labeled "lazy," "dirty," or "unreliable." Stereotyping extends to occupations as well; for example, the reader is invited to conjure images of construction workers, policemen, and librarians. The tendency toward generalization, which is so highly subject to error, represents the perceiver's attempt to impose order and structure on the social environment.

A further quality of social perception that distinguishes it from the perception of things is the perceiver's tendency to *assume similarity* with the object of perception. An important component of "knowing" others is assuming that their underlying states are similar to our own when particular behavioral cues are present (for example, smiling or crying). However, assuming similarity is also subject to error, especially when the perception is more complex than the recognition of common emotional states. Often one may "project" motives or intentions to others that are mistakenly generalized from one's own personality.

Finally, the temporal dimension is particularly important to social perception. The forming of impressions of others constitutes a process of receiving information about the other over time and fitting the information into relevant categories, but not all information is given equal weight in the overall impression. In fact, in many situations early information tends to structure the impression, which may be resistant to change, by later disconfirming information. For example, someone described as "smart, artistic, awkward, and faultfinding" in that order will usually receive a more positive evaluation than when the adjectives appear in the reverse order. First impressions do seem to persevere, as common sense informs us. The disproportionately high impact of early information is called the *primacy effect*.

At this point, a word should be said about *accuracy* in social perception. At one time, psychologists thought it desirable to identify types of people who are particularly accurate at perceiving other people. Conceivably, such knowledge would be beneficial toward selection and training in professions where social perception is particularly important (e.g., clinical psychology). Thus, two subjects in an experiment would have some brief interaction with each other and then fill out personality inventories both for themselves and for how they thought the other might answer them. "Accuracy" was then defined as the degree of match between the responses predicted for the other and how the other actually responded.

Unfortunately, while the matching procedure may lead to useful information about the *processes* in social perception (that is, how information about others is organized and interpreted), as a measure of *accuracy* such a procedure is practically worthless. The problem, which is much too complex to be covered here in detail, is that the biases discussed above (assumptions of similarity, halo effects, stereotyping) do not merely introduce error into social perception, they also allow for much naive or questionable "accuracy." For example, a perceiver with a strong tendency to assume similarity will get a high accuracy score when the other is in fact similar. To conclude that he is therefore a good "person perceiver" is obviously gratuitous. Also, predictions made from mere information *about* the other person (e.g., knowing that he is a graduate student) tend to contribute more to the overall accuracy score than does actual interaction with the other. In fact, such *stereotype accuracy* (the ability to

label people according to personality "types") may be negatively correlated with *differential accuracy*, sensitivity to individual differences.
For these reasons, the study of accuracy in impression formation has
proved to be one of the most challenging problems in social
psychology.

To conclude this section, we define social perception as the
process by which the individual presumes to know the psychological
states, motivations, and dispositions of other people. Such a process
depends on the learning history of the perceiver plus his ability to discriminate and attend to relevant cues; we have already mentioned, as
well, the role of memory. Moreover, it should be apparent that social
perception entails the use of thought or cognition: information
processing, inference, categorization, and attribution are all involved
to some extent. Thus, to describe the course of age-related changes in
social perception, we shall have to consider factors related to attention
span, memory, learning experiences, and perceptual and cognitive
development.

INFANT SOCIAL PERCEPTION

As suggested earlier, social perception begins in infancy. Exactly when
it begins depends on the criterion one accepts as evidence that the
infant is responding specifically to social stimuli. Three criteria have
been studied extensively: the gaze, the cry, and the smile.

Regarding the gaze, infants from the first hours of life prefer gaz-
ing at the stimulus characteristics of the human face over other
stimuli, such as newsprint. A number of investigators have proposed
that the face presents the infant with an optimal level of complexity
and is therefore more attractive than nonfacial stimuli. Others,
however, suggest that infants respond specifically to "faceness" per se
rather than complexity, which would make the gaze a technically more
social behavior. For example, four-month-old infants prefer a drawing
of a face over a "scrambled" face of comparable complexity. This
research is consistent with Bell's (1968) hypothesis that infants are
born with a certain degree of social orientation. However, whatever
the basis for the infant's preference, the result will usually be the
same: the infant gazes at people who are in proximity to it.

There is evidence that infants can discriminate a number of facial
expressions. It has been shown that three-month-old infants can distinguish an expression of surprise from one of happiness, and sometimes
from one of sadness. Infants of that age may not yet be able to discriminate between happiness and sadness. However, this research area

is new, and methodological differences between studies make it difficult to generalize about results.

Regarding the cry, infants less than two or three days old will cry upon hearing the cry of another infant, but will cry much less often to a simulated, computer-generated "cry" (Sagi and Hoffman, 1976). This cry-elicited crying has been labeled "empathic distress," and it is possible that such rudimentary empathy may be innate (which is also consistent with Bell's hypothesis mentioned above).

Infants are not so selective at such an early age about what they smile at; any interesting object, especially if it is moving, can elicit the infant's smile. However, babies as young as four months respond to a wide range of distinctly social stimuli with the "social smile," with much less smiling at nonsocial stimuli. Some months later the social smile is reserved for familiar faces only. Thus, it appears safe to assume that stimuli emanating from persons normally acquire their social meaning for infants by the age of four months, if not before, if the smile is used as a criterion.

THE RECOGNITION OF FACES

It would seem obvious that facial recognition is an essential component in the development of social competency. Yet, surprisingly little research has been performed on children's ability, past infancy, to recognize faces. Existent research indicates that memory span, the degree of familiarity with the perceived face, and even the race of both the perceiver and the perceived, affect recognition. In general, it seems that memory for faces may not reach the adult capacity until 11 or 12 years.

For example, one study found that recognition ability for unfamiliar faces improves through middle childhood until about 11 years (Feinman and Entwisle, 1976). It was also found that black children were more adept at recognizing whites than whites were at recognizing blacks. However, such racial differences were considerably smaller for children of an integrated school who also lived in an integrated neighborhood. The authors suggested two possible explanations, which are not incompatible: persons may be more attentive to facial cues of a member of a higher social status, and blacks may have more exposure to white faces, especially on television, than whites have to blacks. The latter explanation seems more likely, in this author's view, but neither the status nor the exposure explanation seems adequate to account for another interesting finding of this study: there was an overall and highly significant tendency to recognize female faces more easily than male faces, whatever the race. Moreover, this tendency was especially evidenced by female perceivers! It seems that considerably more research will have to be conducted before we approach an understanding of the factors involved in children's facial recognition.

THE PERCEPTION OF EMOTIONS

The perception of the emotional experience of others has been a subject of social psychological study for the past century, if not longer. Despite the large research literature on the topic, the processes by which perceivers label the emotions of others are not well understood. The central problem is that it is not clear what perceivers are responding to when they label another's emotional experience. Expressive cues from the other, the particular emotion to be labeled, and the situation to which the other is responding all affect the perceiver's ability to infer emotions. Moreover, all these factors appear to interact with the age of the perceiver.

Consider first the methodological problems in the area. One common tack is to show subjects photos or drawings of faces and to require them to identify the emotions portrayed. However, in real life, perceivers tend to rely heavily on situational contexts as well. In fact, the more information about the situation that is available, the more accurate and reliable are judgments about the emotions perceived. Is the solution then to provide ample information about the situation surrounding the emotional experience? Probably not. The problem here is similar to that involved with measuring accuracy in a personality description. Simply, if a situation is provided, perceivers often assume that the other's emotional experience is similar to what the perceiver's would be in that situation. Thus, the actual expressive cues of the other may not play into the attributed emotion. Such criticisms have been levied specifically at studies purporting to find accurate emotion perception in young children by having them identify the feelings of hypothetical children undergoing certain experiences, such as attending a birthday party or breaking a toy. These studies report that children as young as three years can identify happiness and sadness, and, to a lesser extent, fear and anger. Again, no conclusions can be reached from these studies about *how* children arrive at such judgments. Moreover, it seems that young children are so affected by the situation when identifying emotions that they may not notice when the actor's expression is incongruent with the situation, such as sadness at a birthday party. Hoffman (1977) has concluded from a review of the literature that both sexes appear equally adept at identifying emotions, but that girls may be more inclined than boys to rely on situational cues rather than on facial cues.

Although not directly involving emotion perception, a recent and innovative study attests to the young child's sensitivity to the expressive facial cues of the mother (Abramovitch, 1977). In that study, four-year-old children were able to determine whether their mothers were conversing with friends or strangers merely by watching videotapes of their mother's faces. Although it is not clear what cues the children were using, they were presumably more subtle than the clues typically involved in experiments on children's emotion recognition. This study indicates clearly that children need not rely on situational cues, but can accurately infer aspects of situations from viewing facial cues.

One limiting factor in the research on children's emotion perception is that, with few exceptions, cues have been restricted to pictures of facial stimuli. Very little research has been conducted on other cues, such as vocal ones. In a recent study, subjects between the ages of five and twenty viewed sequences of film (with sound) and determined whether a particular sequence was the same or different from the episode preceding it (Girgus and Wolf, 1975). Three kinds of cues were provided: vocal (happy or angry), bodily movement (approach or avoidance), and facial expression (smiling or frowning). Not surprisingly, the authors reported increasingly more accurate responses with higher age, with younger children making most of their errors by answering "same" when the episodes were in fact different. Of more interest is the finding that vocal cues were the least difficult to discriminate, with bodily movements and facial expressions increasingly more difficult to discriminate. Thus, it may be that research restricting emotional stimuli to facial expressions is underestimating the competence of young children at perceiving emotions.

Hebb (1946) argued that even the *sequence* of expressive cues may be crucial in determining what emotion will be perceived. For example, a smiling face following a grimacing one may be perceived as indicating a different emotion (e.g., relief) than when it is seen in isolation. The sequence of expressions may be especially important when children are doing the perceiving, as young children seem to be much affected by *recent* stimulus information in other areas of social perception, for instance, in making moral judgments. However, neither memory span nor attentional processes have been directly investigated in the context of children's emotion perception. Thus far, the only conclusions that can be drawn with some confidence are that children as young as three or four can label some emotions of others, especially joy and sadness, but that they are more reliant than adults on situation cues when doing so.

MORAL JUDGMENTS AND THE PERCEPTION OF INTENT

A striking thing happens when people are asked to rate the attributes or behavior of others, and children are no exception: they invariably and often immediately evaluate the person according to a good-bad dimension. Children's tendencies to evaluate others have been studied extensively in the context of moral judgments, and we will give it separate consideration in this section.

The central issue is as follows: when and why does the child consider an actor's intent rather than the consequences of his actions when making a moral judgment? In other words, does the child judge others as "bad" according to their bad intentions or according to the "badness" of their actions, intended or not? For instance, a child of six tends to evaluate others by the severity of their behavioral outcomes rather than by their motives. An implicit and much more general issue is how the child comes to be socialized into a legal system that emphasizes the intent of accused wrongdoers and where "responsibility" and "culpability" are standard courtroom considerations. On the other hand, in contrast to this interest in moral judgments of negative acts, some researchers have also been interested in the consideration of intent in the child's evaluation of *good* or *kind* acts. This latter focus coincides with much recent interest in children's positive or prosocial behavior (e.g., helping, sharing, and cooperating).

Undoubtedly the major impetus for research into children's moral judgments was an early book by Piaget (1932) called *The Moral Judgment of the Child*. Piaget presented pairs of stories to individual children about hypothetical boys and girls involved in acts leading to negative consequences. The child was then asked which of two actors had been "naughtier." This is one well-known pair of the stories Piaget used:

A.   A little boy who is called John is in his room. He is called to dinner. He goes into the dining room. But behind the door there was a chair, and on the chair there was a tray with 15 cups on it. John couldn't have known that there was all this behind the door. He goes in, the door knocks against the tray, bang go the 15 cups and they all get broken!

B.   Once there was a little boy whose name was Henry. One day when his mother was out he tried to get some jam out of the cupboard. He climbed up on to a chair and stretched out his arm. But the jam was to high up and he couldn't reach it and have any. But while he was trying to get it he knocked over a cup. The cup fell down and broke (p. 123).

Piaget found that children under eight years almost invariably chose *A* above as the "naughtier" of the two; that is, they made their judgments according to the *consequence* of the act rather than the actor's *intentions*. He found, on the average, that children were about nine or ten years old before they based their judgments on intentions; for example, they chose Henry in story *B* as the naughtier child. In fact, it has been shown in more recent research that, the more *severe* the consequences of unintended acts, the more severe the judgments by young children.

Why should the child ignore an actor's intentions and evaluate him according to the severity of the consequences? Piaget proposed that it is because the young child has an *objective* concept of responsibility: what is "good" or "bad" is what is rewarded or punished, respectively, and not what the actor meant to do. Ironically, parents often teach objective responsibility to their children. "The average housewife," writes Piaget, "will be more angry over 15 cups than over one, and independently, up to a point, of the offender's intentions" (p. 133). However, Piaget adds that "most parents draw a distinction which the children precisely neglect to make: they scold, that is, according to the extent of the material damage caused by the clumsy act, but they do not regard the act itself exactly as a moral fault" (p. 134).

Therefore, it is not that the child is *incapable* of inferring intentions, but rather that he has not learned to consider them relevant to moral judgments. The child responds inflexibly to moral situations, judging acts according to the simple and objective criterion of their results rather than initiating the considerably more complex process of assessing the underlying motivations.

What, then, happens to the child such that about age eight or nine he begins spontaneously to consider intentions? According to Piaget, the child's social life takes an interesting and very important turn around this time: the child becomes oriented to the peer group. Piaget described peer interaction, perhaps somewhat idealistically, as *cooperation among equals*. Cooperation, along with the *mutual respect* that it entails, makes children sensitive to the psychological states, including the intentions, of others. The child thus reaches a higher stage of moral development during middle childhood.

Researchers working in Western and non-Western cultures have corroborated Piaget's stages. However, the particular age at which children make the transition to the higher stage is uncertain and may depend upon how the child is tested, whether or not the child is given training in the consideration of intent, and the specifics of the moral acts to be judged.

For example, it has been found that many six and seven-year-olds will consider intent if the stories are shown on videotape rather than merely read to them. There is also much recent evidence that the reliance by young children on consequences can be practically nullified if the intentions are stated *after* the consequences rather than before. This *recency effect*, to which young children are particularly suscepti-ble, is a factor to consider in practically all areas of children's social perception.

It has also been found that young children can be "trained" to consider intent rather than consequences in a very short period of time. This would seem to argue against any stage-like or "cognitive-developmental" interpretation of children's moral judgments, that is, one that views the change toward considering intentions as indicating a comprehensive restructuring of the child's moral beliefs over time. However, the implications of the training studies for moral develop-ment remain controversial, as these studies are interpreted by some as only instilling in the child transitory and artificial response "sets" that have little bearing on the child's moral world.

Finally, there is a growing body of evidence indicating that children consider bad intent when making moral judgments before they consider good intent. That is, children who have begun to make moral judgments of naughtiness according to actors' bad intentions may nevertheless continue to judge goodness according to conse-quences rather than good intent (Hill and Enzle, 1977). The reasons for this lack of appreciation by the young child for good intent appear to be complex. First, he apparently does not understand what good-ness means apart from obedience to parental expectations. Piaget sug-gested that parents are typically more concerned with bad or disobedient behavior than with teaching the child the more subtle con-cept of good that is not merely the opposite of bad. For example, it has been found that children under eight years almost invariably define good as the absence of bad behavior, but older children tend toward definitions stressing the feelings and welfare of the benefici-aries of good acts.

Given this rather lopsided moral education by parents, how does the child ever come to evaluate good acts according to prosocial intent? As a prerequisite, the child must acquire a new meaning for the word "good," one that is itself prosocial and is independent from notions of obedience, rather than merely the opposite of "bad." Only then can the child understand what "trying to do a good thing" means. Again, Piaget proposed that the child acquires the more advanced concept of good through peer group cooperation and mutual respect. With a growing sensitivity to others' psychological states, the child comes to understand the golden rule; what is good is what benefits other people. For Piaget this was an admittedly idealistic distinction: the "morality of good" and the emphasis on obedience or "doing one's duty" are not always separated in even the mature adult's mind.

PERSONALITY DESCRIPTION

What do children do when they are asked to describe other people? One of the first things they do is to *evaluate* them. Children include much additional information besides how "nice" or "mean" they perceive others to be, but what else they say will depend upon a number of factors, especially the age of the child doing the describing. For example, there are age differences in the sheer *number of traits* attributed to others, the tendency to perceive underlying *psychological* characteristics as well as overt physical traits, the *preciseness* of trait descriptions, and the *uniqueness* perceived in others.

However, a factor that should be considered first is how the child goes about describing others. Should the child be asked to fill out a series of bipolar scales (each of which allows the child to indicate a point along a continuum between two extremes, e.g., intelligent and dumb), which are provided by the researcher? Or should the child be allowed to use whatever descriptions come to mind? There are advantages and disadvantages to both methods, but we look first at the rating scale technique. There is usually no problem in persuading anyone to use the scales. In fact, researchers are often amazed that people of all ages will unhesitatingly rate others on dozens of scales after only five or ten minutes of contact with the ratee! The problem has to do with relevancy to the persons using them of the particular scales involved. For example, it might not occur to a rater to describe someone according to a "humble-proud" dimension if it were not included on a questionnaire. On the other hand, the rater may prefer one or more dimensions that are *not* included. The "impression" that emerges from an array of scales may therefore be questionable in its meaningfulness to the rater.

With the free-description method, most of the problems of relevance are overcome. Its major disadvantage, especially when compared to rating scales, is that it is often difficult to compare the reponses between two or more perceivers who supply their own descriptive terms. However, free descriptions are especially useful when individual differences among perceivers, including age, are of interest.

In fact, a great deal of useful information about children's person perception has been uncovered recently by researchers using the free-description method. The most noteworthy general finding, which coincides remarkably well with children's moral judgments, is that the age of eight years consistently emerges as a critical turning point in children's descriptions of others. In one study, which included eight age groups between 7 and 15 years, the most important differences in social perception occurred between children 7 1/2 and 8 1/2 years of age (Livesley and Bromley, 1973). When describing people they knew seven-year-olds focused on physical characteristics, used relatively few trait descriptions, and were particularly evaluative. Older children, however, were more inclined to focus on covert, psychological characteristics, used many more trait descriptions, and were not as evaluative. Descriptions used by older children became more differentiated and precise. For example, where a seven-year-old might describe someone as "nice," older children would use a word like "considerate" or "helpful," etc. Older children were also more sensitive to regularities in others' behavior over time and were therefore more inclined to infer stable dispositions and values based on such regularities. Finally, the older group was also more inclined to focus on the person's impact on other people, a finding that coincides with the developing interpersonal orientation of middle childhood.

Peevers and Secord (1973) focused on children's perceptions of *uniqueness* in others, that is, their tendency to describe others in a manner that clearly differentiates them from the perceivers themselves or the settings in which the others are known. Kindergarten children were inclined to differentiate others only very superficially, such as by appearance or possessions, or by how much the child liked or disliked the person (the evaluative factor again). Many of the descriptions of this youngest group were, in fact, *undifferentiating* ("He lives up the street," or "She's a friend of Sally's"). Older children were considerably more differentiating in their descriptions, including mention of *interests* ("He wants to be a lawyer"), *abilities* ("He gets straight A's"), *values* ("She's a liberal"), and *feelings* ("He feels insecure"). It was also found that the use of highly differentiating descriptions increased sharply between 8- and 12-year-olds and kept increasing at a high rate thereafter.

There were also significant age differences in the *frame of reference* the children adopted in describing others, that is, the degree to which the perceiver was personally involved in the descriptions. A high proportion of the descriptions by younger children, especially kindergarteners, were oriented toward the perceiver. For example, this is one kindergarten boy's response:

> Well, he kind of scares me. He has a monster act. He's such a silly boy. And his mom teaches me piano lessons. He rides bikes with me, but his bike is bigger than mine. (Interviewer: "Is there anything about him that you don't like especially?") He talks mean words to me, and sometimes he's mean to me, and that's all (Secord and Peevers, 1974, p. 129).

Children of all age groups, especially the older children, gave a high proportion of *other-oriented* descriptions. Such descriptions require an objective and impersonal stance toward the person described. For example, one 16-year-old girl talks about a friend:

> She's quiet and shy and she doesn't like to talk too much. She's really intelligent, especially in languages and English—she catches on really quickly. She's unathletic and likes to read. She's the romantic type who likes all the Victorian novels—you know, sitting in castles and having people row up and play songs under the window. And that's what she is like (Secord and Peevers, 1974, p. 129).

The research discussed so far in this section focused on children's perceptions and descriptions of *familiar* people. It indicates quite clearly a growing sensitivity with age toward the unique, often subtle, personal qualities of acquaintances. Not as much is known about how children describe *unfamiliar* people. Are they in fact subject to all the biases described earlier that the adult perceiver is heir to? Unfortunately, it appears they are.

For example, three-year-olds already show a *halo effect* in regard to physical attractiveness: other children seen as attractive are assumed to be friendly and unaggressive, while unattractive children are expected to be antisocial (Dion, 1973). Children also acquire the culture's *stereotypes* at an early age. For example, ethnic stereotypes begin to emerge by age four in most children.

Sex-role stereotypes are also acquired at an early age. In one study, the majority of a sample of kindergarten children perceived males as "adventurous," "dominant," and "ambitious" (among other traits) and females as "emotional" and "soft-hearted" (Williams, Bennett, and Best, 1975). Seven-year-old children were even more in agreement about such descriptions and added "confident" (males) and "dreamy" (females) to their stereotypes. Overall, it was found that the male stereotype seems to be learned earliest and, moreover, that both sex-role stereotypes are shown by girls as much as by boys.

Social Perception and Socialization

Up to this point, we have been solely concerned with how the child perceives and describes other people. Almost nothing has been said about how the perception of people affects social interaction. Here, we cannot attempt a complete description of the role of social perception in the interaction process. However, in this section we briefly examine the relation of social perception to one especially important area of children's social behavior: the socialization process. Specifically, children's prosocial behavior and the inhibition of aggression are discussed.

In an earlier section, we mentioned the necessity for the child to learn to consider an actor's intent when judging his actions. Not only will perceived intent affect a child's judgment of, for example, naughtiness, but it should affect subsequent social interaction with the other as well. Here we shall consider another important form of social behavior where intent affects both a judgment and a response: *aggression.*

First of all, an inflicted injury is not normally judged to be true aggression unless it was *intended*; accidental harm is more correctly labeled as carelessness or negligence. In fact, adult victims will retaliate according to the intentions underlying an aggressive act rather than the actual degree of harm inflicted. For obvious ethical reasons, experiments on children's retaliation after injury have not been conducted. However, at least one study has examined children's hypothetical reactions to intended and accidental provocations (Shantz and Voydanoff, 1973). Boys nine years old and older reported that they would retaliate much more for intended rather than accidentally inflicted harm. Boys in the younger (seven-year-old) group barely made such a distinction and reported that they would retaliate almost as much for accidental provocations as for intended ones. If such self-reports are any indication of actual behavior under comparable circumstances, then it appears that perception of aggressive intent rather than harm or injury per se may begin to determine retaliation at about eight years of age.

Other studies, however, indicate that young children at least understand different *kinds* of intentions and judge aggressive acts accordingly. For example, Rule, Nesdale, and McAra (1974) reported that children as young as preschool age judged hostile aggression to be more wrong that "prosocial" aggression (protecting others from harm). The authors suggested that parents may be inclined to emphasize the distinction to young children between antisocial and prosocial aggression. Corporal punishment is perhaps tacitly viewed by parents who use it as positive or prosocial and they justify it to their children as such.

Thus, it appears that an important factor in the socialization process is the lesson that judgments of and responses to aggression are at least partly determined by the aggressor's intentions. Hypothetically, this should result in fewer occasions of retaliation to accidental injury.

The child's inference of an actor's intent represents a highly cognitive process, and, indeed, some psychologists are convinced that cognitive development and moral development go hand in hand (Kohlberg, 1969). However, such views risk de-emphasizing important emotional components of social perception and the possible motivational role that emotion may have in moral behavior. An important and positive motivational role of emotion involves the concept of *empathy*.

Despite problems of definition and measurement, many psychologists believe that empathy is a fundamental component of positive social interaction. Recent discussions of the topic seem to agree that empathy is a twofold process: it involves *both* the perception of the positive or negative emotional state of another person *and* a resultant experience of a similar emotion in the perceiver. Without the latter component emotion perception would just as easily serve an unsympathetic, or even sadistic, perceiver as an empathic one.

When the emotion is *negative* (e.g., distress), the empathic perceiver is presumed to be motivated to terminate the aversive conditions impinging on the other (e.g., by helping), thereby alleviating the suffering of both perceiver and perceived. It has been proposed that one's empathic response to another's distress is aroused because of past experiences of associating others' emotional behavior with one's own distress. The perception of others' distress cues thus comes to elicit similar emotional responses in the empathizer. The factor in empathy that is most likely to be affected by the *age* of the perceiver is the initial perception of the emotional state of the other. As the child grows older, he may become more adept at inferring another's emotion from subtle expressive and situational cues. Many adults, in fact, can empathize with an unseen other merely by imagining the other's situation.

When the empathized emotion is *positive* (e.g., joy), the perceiver is presumably motivated to reinstate the conditions that led to the positive emotion. For example, one study found that elementary school children would donate money to the "needy" after watching a generous role model express pleasure after donating (Midlarsky and Bryan, 1972). Theoretically, watching a model experience a positive emotion leads to "vicarious" reinforcement to the observer: the child experiences all the joys of giving without actually having given. If positive empathy is in fact reinforcing to the child, vicarious or not, he will perform similar acts of generosity in the future in order to recapture the "warm, happy feeling."

Besides prompting a prosocial response in the child, such as helping or sharing, it seems that, under some conditions, empathy may also prevent or inhibit negative behavior, such as aggression. In one study, six- and seven-year-old boys who received high scores on a test for empathy were rated as relatively unaggressive by their teachers (Feshbach and Feshbach, 1969). On the other hand, low-empathic boys were rated as significantly more aggressive. Apparently, children who tend to empathize with the negative emotional experience of victims of aggression are less likely to initiate aggressive acts themselves.

Thus, it should come as no surprise that the development of empathy is regarded by many as an essential factor in the socialization of the child. Without an acute emotional involvement in the experience of others, there is merely indifference or, at best, an ethic based on social expediency rather than on humanitarian concern. Although the world could probably function well enough without empathy—indeed, many individuals may be unaggressive or even "generous" for strictly egotistic reasons—it is doubtful that the social bond would be complete without the adhesiveness that empathy provides.

CONCLUSION

This has been a survey of current work, and much important research has necessarily been omitted from discussion. On the other hand, many of the studies that have been discussed are very recent and, as yet, difficult to assimilate into earlier research. It is still too soon to assess the implications of some studies for other, seemingly contradictory, ones; many of the recent findings need first to be replicated (i.e., reconfirmed in subsequent research). Researchers working on problems related to children's social perception frequently focus on a specific behavior (e.g., smiling in infancy or the recognition of emotions) without extending their research horizons very far. Comparison of studies and the drawing of generalizations is therefore difficult and perhaps premature.

As is typical in the early stages of any scientific enterprise, most of the research in the area is strictly *descriptive*, and a comprehensive and satisfactory theory of the *development* of social perception has not yet been formed. The key word in the last sentence is "satisfactory," because a number of interesting theories have been offered but later have been disconfirmed or proven unsatisfactory. Even the results of descriptive studies, which attempt only to "map out" the course of children's social perceptions rather than test hypotheses, are often quite tenuous. For example, slight changes in testing methods in later studies sometimes reveal striking precociousness. It has proven to be a risky endeavor indeed to assert that a child of a certain age cannot perform a particular adult-like behavior; children are full of surprises.

REFERENCES

Abramovitch, R. 1977. Children's recognition of situational aspects of facial expression. Child Dev. 48:459–463.

Bell, R.Q. 1968. A reinterpretation of the direction of effects in studies of socialization. Psychol. Rev. 75:81–95.

Dion, K. K. 1973. Young children's stereotyping of facial attractiveness. Dev. Psychol. 9:183–188.

Feinman, S., and D. R. Entwisle. 1976. Children's ability to recognize other children's faces. Child Dev. 47:506–510.

Feshbach, N. D., and S. Feshbach. 1969. The relationship between empathy and aggression in two age groups. Dev. Psychol. 1:102–107.

Girgus, J. S., and J. Wolf. 1975. Age changes in the ability to encode social cues. Dev. Psychol. 11:118.

Hebb, D. O. 1946. Emotion in man and animals: An analysis of the intuitive process of recognition. Psychol. Rev. 53:88–106.

Hill, K. A., and Enzle, M. E. 1977. Interactive effects of training domain and age on children's moral judgments. Can. J. Behav. Sci. 9:371–381.

Hoffman, M. L. 1977. Sex differences in empathy and related behaviors. Psychol. Bull. 84:712–722.

Kohlberg, L. 1969. Stage and sequence: The cognitive-developmental approach to socialization. In: D. A. Goslin (ed.), Handbook of Socialization Theory and Research. Rand McNally Co., Chicago.

Livesley, W. J., and D. B. Bromley. 1973. Person Perception in Childhood and Adolescence. John Wiley & Sons, New York.

Midlarsky, E., and J. H. Bryan. 1972. Affect expressions and children's imitative altruism. J. Exp. Res. Personal. 6:195–203.

Peevers, B. H., and P. F. Secord. 1973. Developmental changes in attribution of descriptive concepts to persons. J. Personal. Soc. Psychol. 26:120–128.

Piaget, J. 1932. The Moral Judgment of the Child. Routledge & Kegan Paul, Boston.

Rule, B. G., A. R. Nesdale, and M. J. McAra. 1974. Children's reactions to information about the intentions underlying an aggressive act. Child Dev. 45:794–798.

Sagi, A., and M. L. Hoffman. 1976. Empathic distress in the newborn. Dev. Psychol. 12:175–176.

Schaffer, H. R. 1971. The Growth of Sociability. Penguin Books, New York.

Secord, P. F., and B. H. Peevers. 1974. The development and attribution of person concepts. In: T. Mischel (ed.), Understanding Other Persons. Roman and Littlefield, Totowa, New Jersey.

Shantz, D. W., and D. A. Voydanoff. 1973. Situational effects on retaliatory aggression at three age levels. Child Dev. 44:149–153.

Williams, J. E., S. M. Bennett, and D. L. Best. 1975. Awareness and expression of sex stereotypes in young children. Dev. Psychol. 11:635–642.

Chapter 8
THE DEVELOPMENT OF CHILDREN'S COMMUNICATION SKILLS

Kenneth A. Hill

EGOCENTRISM IN CHILDHOOD

Few would deny that the use of language is a distinctly *social* phenomenon. Yet, developmental psychologists are frequently struck by the apparently *nonsocial* quality of young children's speech. For example, consider this "discussion" among several Swiss six-year-olds, who are commenting on some drawings they have made:

Lev: "It begins with Goldilocks. I'm writing the story of the three bears. The daddy bear is dead. Only the daddy was too ill."

Gen: "I used to live in Saléve. I lived in a little house, and you had to take the funicular railway to go and buy things."

Geo: "I can't do the bear."

Li: "That's not Goldilocks."

Lev: "I haven't got curls."

This conversation was one of many recorded by Piaget (1959, p. 58) in a seminal investigation of children's language. It exemplifies what Piaget calls a *collective monologue*, in which each child seems to "think out loud" about his ongoing activities, with little apparent intention to communicate information to others. Technically, collective monologues do qualify as social behavior, because the presence of other children often serves as a stimulus for such talking, and, perhaps more importantly, because there is usually a semblance of *turn taking*, a desirable characteristic of adult conversations. However, the actual communication in the collective monologue, as the phrase suggests, is minimal.

Why does the young child engage in such an apparently inadequate form of verbal interaction? According to Piaget, it is because of the child's *egocentrism*, or his inability to distinguish his own point of view from that of other people.

To appreciate the role of the concept of egocentrism in developmental psychology, we shall need to describe Piaget's classic "three-mountains" problem. Children were individually shown a miniature landscape of three mountains of different sizes and asked to identify the view "seen" by a doll having a different perspective. A child indicated the doll's view by selecting the appropriate photograph from several photographs taken from different angles, one of which was the child's own perspective of the landscape. It was found that children under six years were inclined to select the photograph representing their own point of view rather than the doll's; they were therefore egocentric.

Thus, according to Piaget, young children cannot *decenter*, or imagine a point of view that is different from their own. Piaget saw egocentrism as a natural stage in early cognitive development wherein the child is unable to clearly differentiate himself from others. The young child *assimilates* stimuli emanating from other people, especially verbal stimuli, into his ongoing thoughts and activities. This inability to decenter leads children to engage in the collective monologue, because it does not occur to them that different topics are being discussed! Also the child does not feel any need to communicate, because he assumes that others already *know* what he knows anyway.

The young child's egocentric confusion of his own knowledge with that of others is perhaps best revealed in failures of *reference*. For example, Piaget (1959) explained the function of a water tap to one child, with the aid of labeled diagrams. He then required the child to repeat the explanation to another child, who, of course, had not been present during the initial explanation. The following is the first child's explanation (interjected with Piaget's comments):

> The water can go through there (points to the large pipe in Figure 1 without designating the exact spot, the opening) because the door (which door?) is above and below (the movable canal *b*, which he does not show) and then to turn it (turn what?) you must do so (makes the movement of turning fingers but without pointing to the handles *a*). There, it (what?) can't turn round (i.e., the water can't get through) because, the door is on the right and on the left. There because the water stays there, the pipes can't get there . . . and then the water can't run through (p. 103).

In this "explanation" the child has not defined terms (doors and pipes) and is inexact about what his words refer to, especially in his use of the demonstratives *it* and *there*. In summary, it is apparent that the child has not considered the listener's needs. The child seems to confuse his own, private knowledge with what is public knowledge.

SOCIALIZED SPEECH

The next stage in language development, according to Piaget's analysis, is *socialized speech*. It is at this point that the child's utterances appear to be communicative, as well as appropriate to the listener's point of view. This stage signifies the emergence of genuine dialogue.

Piaget maintained that peer interactions among children tend to discourage egocentrism. The child is "disciplined by cooperation" to coordinate the often conflicting points of view of playmates with his own, thus acquiring a "rational system of reference" for thinking about the world. Mature reasoning, toward which the child strives, is relatively objective. In fact, Piaget observed that conversations between a child and a peer were typically more mature than those between a child and an adult. The following is a conversation between two three-year-olds, which, despite its primitiveness, shows some effort toward "mutual understanding and the sharing of viewpoints":

Hans: "Ruth, look up, there is the railway that goes to heaven."
Ruth: "No, there aren't any railways up there."
Hans: "But there are railway lines."
Ruth: "No, there aren't any railway lines up there. There are no railway lines in heaven. God doesn't need any railway lines."
Hans: "Yes he does . . ." (Piaget, 1959, p. 247)

To summarize, Piaget's theory addresses the complex relationship between cognitive and social development. Initially, the child's thoughts are "preverbal," or without word content. As language is acquired, thinking becomes permeated with words and sentences, but overt speech is egocentric and nonsocial; to repeat Piaget's phrase, the child is merely "thinking out loud." As egocentrism declines, language becomes increasingly more social. Moreover, thinking itself becomes socialized, as the child is now able to address himself from the perspective of another—a prerequisite for internal "dialogue." Indeed, logic itself is a dialogue of sorts.

In a later section we evaluate Piaget's theory in the light of recent evidence. However, we first discuss some of the large amount of research subsequent to Piaget's that largely supports his theory of children's communciation skills.

RECENT RESEARCH ON
CHILDREN'S EGOCENTRIC COMMUNICATION

Imagine the following situation. Two children are sitting at a table in a psychology laboratory, facing each other, but unable to see one another because of a barrier in the middle of the table. Both have an identical set of stimulus pictures before them. The pictures are like doodles and do not resemble anything without considerable use of the imagination—that is the point of the experiment. One child is to describe a particular picture so that the other child can correctly pick it out. The following, often quoted interchange between two four-year-olds captures the flavor of "egocentric" communication (remember, the children cannot see each other):

Speaker: "It's a bird."
Listener: "Is this it?"
Speaker: "No."

Experiments like these by Glucksberg and his colleagues (1975) support Piaget's ideas about young children's difficulties in what we call *referential communication*. These experiments have shown that children do not usually attain a 50% success rate on such tasks until they are about 12 years old.

Children seem to do better as listeners than as speakers, and if an adult is in the role of speaker (describing the pictures), the child tends to do quite well at identifying the correct picture. While it is likely that the speaker's role is merely the more difficult one, such a finding is also consistent with Piaget's discussion of verbal interaction between parent and child. That is, while a parent may readily grasp a young child's rather idiosyncratic (and egocentric) manner of expression—and not try to induce him to speak less egocentrically—the child is continually trying to interpret more complex and sophisticated language from parents. Thus, language comprehension outstrips production.

Other research on children's referential communication observes the response of the speaker when the listener indicates a failure to understand the message. When an adult speaker hears "I don't understand what you mean" from a listener, the message is usually elaborated and improved. Children, however, tend to repeat the same message or merely remain silent. Younger children are particularly unresponsive to other forms of feedback indicative of communication failure, such as facial expressions of puzzlement. It seems that the only way to get an improved message from a child is to make an explicit request for one, such as "Please tell me more about it."

It is important for success on a referential communication task that the speaker be sensitive to the relevant and nonrelevant features of the referent (the object to be identified) and its context (expecially objects with which the referent may easily be confused). A referent does not have any particular name by which it can always be identified. A coin in an otherwise empty pocket may be a dime, but the same coin in a pocketful of dimes must be referred to, for example, as a 1931 Mercury Head.

Thus, after considering the whole context of stimuli, the child must select the relevant, distinctive features of the object, and adjust his message accordingly. A criticism made recently by Gelman (1978) is relevant here. She pointed out that other research has shown that the young child has difficulty merely identifying such distinctive features, regardless of whether or not they have to be communicated. Thus it may be that children have problems with such tasks not solely because of their egocentricism, but because other requirements of the task are too difficult for them.

A task devised by Flavell (1968) uses an interesting picture technique. A child is shown seven consecutive pictures that illustrate a story about a boy walking along a sidewalk (Picture 1) who suddenly appears frightened upon seeing a dog (Picture 2); the boy begins to run (Picture 3), approaches a tree (Picture 4), climbs the tree with the dog nipping at his heels (Picture 5), stands upon a branch as the dog walks away (Picture 6), and sits in the tree, eating an apple, with the dog having disappeared (Picture 7). Only pictures 2, 3, and 5 depict a threatening dog. Without these particular pictures, an entirely different story is depicted—a considerably more tranquil one about a boy walking down a street, climbing a tree, and eating an apple.

After the child has heard the original, "mean-dog" story, the three critical pictures are deleted, and the child is asked to tell the new, four-picture story as it would appear to another person coming upon the pictures for the first time. Does the child interject details of the first story—in which the boy's motivations are decidedly different—into the second story despite the absence of the corroborative pictures? It depends on the age of the child. There was evidence that the younger subjects (second and third grades) were inclined to embellish the new story with motivations unique to the old one. For example, when asked to tell the second, four-picture story, one child responded:

> Well, this—this boy was walking down the street whistling, and he noticed this apple tree and *obviously wanted to get an apple* so he climbs up it and he noticed a dog *and, uh, well I presume he'd stay there until the dog would go away* and then finish up eating the apple (p. 80; italics original).

Flavell proposed that the ability to inhibit knowledge of the original story and to grasp how someone else would interpret the four-picture sequence is a measure of role-taking skills. More than just communication ability, role-taking refers to the child's general social and cognitive development—as, indeed, does Piaget's concept of egocentrism. Role-taking involves not only the awareness that others have a different perspective but also a need to take others' points of view and the ability to assess or infer additional characteristics of the other that are relevant to the situation (for example, the listener's motivations or ability to understand). Finally, role-taking requires that the child *coordinate* the (inferred) perspective of the other with his own during the interaction process. Role-taking is thus seen by Flavell as an important component of general social competency.

Another of Flavell's role-taking tasks illustrates the interrelationship between social and cognitive development. A child is shown two cups turned upside down on a table. One cup has a nickel glued on its bottom (which is therefore visible to the child); the other cup has *two* nickels showing. The cups are then lifted, revealing that they each cover the same number of nickels as displayed on the cups. The child is told to remove the money from inside one cup, whichever he chooses, before another person enters the room. The other person will be allowed to select one cup and keep any money it contains. It is the child's task, therefore, to fool the person by removing the money he thinks the person will select. Moreover, the child is told that the person *knows* he is going to be tricked.

In this study, the experimenter is not interested in the particular cup from which the child chooses to remove the money, but in the underlying *strategy* reported by the child. We can see all the components of the role-taking process here. The child must realize that the other person has a different perspective on the game, and that he needs to take that perspective into account in order to "win." Moreover, the child must be able to make a relatively sophisticated assessment of the other's knowledge—especially the fact that the child's own thoughts and motivations can be an object of the other's thinking. Finally, the child must *coordinate* the two reciprocal points of view, each of which takes the other's motivations into account. For example, an adult's reasoning might resemble the following pattern: "I'll leave the money under the dime cup, because *he* will think I'll leave it under the nickel cup, because *I'll* think he will choose the dime cup . . ." Thus, the chain can be continued indefinitely. It should come as no surprise that evidence for such *recursive* thinking was rare in children younger than nine or ten, increasing only gradually with age thereafter. The younger children tended to ignore the information that the other person knew he was going to be fooled. These children often assumed that the other would merely choose the dime cup because "He'll get more money."

Although, as we indicated, the chain of recursive thinking can be continued ad infinitum, recursiveness in spoken language is limited by *communicability*. For example, one sometimes gets the impression that some of the sentences uttered by reflective adults fall just short of being *too* recursive, such as, "Sometimes I think you believe that I don't understand how you feel about me."

SUMMARY: THE CONCEPT OF EGOCENTRISM

The role-taking tasks devised by Flavell seem far removed from Piaget's "three-mountains" problem, and only vaguely related, at best, to Glucksberg's communication tasks. Nevertheless, many psychologists, particularly of the cognitive-developmental school, have proposed that all such tasks and indeed all socially relevant behavior are facilitated by declining egocentrism and an increasing perspective-taking ability in the child. Thus the concept of egocentrism is an elegant theoretical construct: it is presumed to explain a great variety of psychological and behavioral phenomena, including the child's inability to conceive of another's spatial orientation, to take the other's role, or to communicate effectively.

An important criterion for a good theory is that it should generate research. By this standard, Piaget's theory of egocentric speech has proved to be excellent; indeed, most of the research discussed in the remainder of this chapter is influenced by Piaget's ideas. A second criterion is that the theory should be testable. That is, it should be possible to specify the conditions under which the theory could be proved inadequate or even false. Again, the egocentrism hypothesis has been a good one, as a number of methods for testing egocentric speech have been devised. Finally, a third criterion is how well the theory survives such empirical investigation. By this criterion the egocentrism hypothesis does not fare so well. That is, a surge of recent studies with children suggests quite compellingly that the cognitive and communicative skills of the young child—even the toddler—have been very much underestimated.

We shall now briefly review some of those studies, while suggesting some alternative explanations for children's poor performance on perspective-taking tasks. We shall also review two hypotheses that have been proposed as alternatives to the egocentrism explanation of social development.

PERSPECTIVE-TAKING RECONSIDERED

It is likely that young children fail the "three-mountain" task for reasons other than egocentrism. If the task is simplified, children as young as three often behave nonegocentrically. For example, if the mountains are covered by a box and the child views first one perspective and then one from the opposite direction, the experimenter can rotate the landscape to present identical perspectives on both viewings. Under such conditions, many preschoolers show bewilderment that the scene should be the same, a finding that clearly indicates that the children have expectancies for different scenes from different perspectives (Shantz and Watson, 1970).

Why does the child fail the three-mountain task when the task requires choice of the correct perspective from an array of alternatives? Research suggests that the young child must infer the correct right-left orientation of another person at a time when most children have barely learned to match their own shoes with the appropriate feet. Thus if the child is allowed to *rotate* the landscape to indicate the other's perspective, rather than selecting among various photographs, even three-year-olds will frequently choose the correct perspective (Borke, 1975).

Indications of perspective-taking ability in young children are even more apparent if the task is further simplified. For example, it has been shown that most preschoolers will have little difficulty with the following task. The child is shown a card containing a different picture on each of its two sides. Then the child is asked both, "What do *you* see?" and, "What do *I* see?" The latter question taps the child's perspective-taking skill, although at a very rudimentary level, as the child must be aware that the experimenter cannot see the child's side of the card, but rather sees a picture that the child for the moment cannot see. The task is simplier than the three-mountains problem because the child has only one alternative perspective rather than several or more to choose from; the right-left orientation is not a factor, and therefore cognitive skills over and above perspective-taking ability are minimized.

Other research demonstrates that young children can apply their perspective-taking skills to tasks that are most distinctly social. For example, most four-year-olds can correctly infer which of two other people does not share knowledge of a "secret" if one had both eyes closed during the relevant event.

While it has been shown conclusively that the young child can take the perspective of others in a variety of situations, we can also ask if the child goes a step further and incorporates such inferences into the communication process. Although, as we have mentioned, earlier research indicated that the child cannot do so, the research we now review indicates that the young child is a remarkably competent communicator.

COMMUNICATION SKILLS IN PRESCHOOL CHILDREN

One of the first studies to demonstrate nonegocentric communication in young children was conducted by Maratsos (1973). A child was seated at a table containing a number of toys. The experimenter sat on the opposite side of the table and introduced the task as a game in which the child was to indicate which of several toys the experimenter was to place into a toy car. Half of the children were told, in addition, that the experimenter would close his eyes while the children made their selections. These children represented the "blocked-vision" group, while the remaining half were the "normal-vision" group. Of interest, of course, was how well the blocked-vision children would describe the toy they had selected, in comparison with the normal-vision group. Children in the normal-vision group, especially three-year-olds, often merely pointed to the selected toy: a gesture that was indeed adequate for its visibility to the experimenter. However, the children in the blocked-vision group hardly ever relied on pointing to communicate their choices; they attempted to describe the toy to the experimenter (who, unknown to the child, was, in fact, peeking in order to check for pointing).

A further finding in this study warrants mentioning. When the toys from which the child was to choose were *identical* (and therefore identifiable only by specifying their spatial location), children in the blocked-vision group greatly decreased the adequacy of their communications. Thus, the children seemed to behave egocentrically when in fact their poor performance was caused by sheer task difficulty.

This finding echoes Gelman's criticism of the Glucksberg tasks discussed earlier.

Maratsos' findings of nonegocentric communication in young children have been replicated a number of times by studies that have varied the experimental procedures a great deal. For example, it has been shown that four-year-olds will "talk down" to a two-year-old (that is, use more simplified grammar), while using longer sentences and more complex language to an older listener (Shatz and Gelman, 1973). No less remarkable is a study showing that three- and four-year-olds will "tailor" their communications to an adult listener according to whether the listener is knowledgeable or naive in regard to a conversation that occurred *one week earlier* (Menig-Peterson, 1975).

Why had so many previous investigators concluded that the young child's communication skills are limited by egocentrism? We have already suggested that the tasks devised to measure such skills may have been too difficult in some respects. However, we suggest that task difficulty may be only part of the story. It is a well-known and rather poignant comment on all scientific endeavor that what one discovers depends largely upon what one is looking for, and developmental psychology is no exception. A concluding statement by Menig-Peterson is highly instructive:

> In the present study, an investigator looking simply at the children's verbalizations to the naive listener would have ample support for claiming that the children were making a lot of egocentric mistakes. On the other hand, by looking at how their verbal productions differed relative to different listener needs, it is clear that appropriate tailoring of their communication occurs (p. 1018).

It has been noted by some perceptive writers that an indication of Piaget's genius lies in his interest in children's *errors* in reasoning (see Brainerd, 1978, for an excellent review and critique). For example, in a task on the conservation of liquid quantity, most six-year-olds believe that water poured directly from a low, wide glass somehow becomes "more" when poured into a tall, narrow glass, despite the fact that they have witnessed the transformation. The surprisingness of this judgment, to an adult, is confirmed whenever it is demonstrated for students in introductory child development. Invariably, an incredulous sophomore will try to persuade the child that his perceptions are misleading him.

Piaget is the single most influential theorist in developmental psychology today, and generations of graduate students have been trained in Piagetian research, including the conservation task just mentioned. Because Piaget's theory of cognitive development proposes *qualitative* changes between stages of development (that is, differences in kind rather than degree), it has been necessary to show that the child of a particular age *cannot* think in a fashion comparable to that occurring in later stages. The emphasis, therefore, tends to be on the young child's cognitive limitations. The earlier work on children's egocentrism reflects that emphasis.

Nevertheless, we have reviewed research indicating that the young child is, on the contrary, quite capable of considering the listener's point of view during the communication process. This research is representative of a recent surge of interest in the young child's cognitive abilities rather than limitations (see Gelman, 1978). In a later section we look at studies indicating important experiential factors in the development of the child's perspective-taking and communication skills. Presently, we take a brief look at studies that have examined the young child's total communication competency beyond perspective-taking. Nowhere is it more apparent how much the concept of egocentrism has underestimated the child's social skills.

COMMUNICATION AND SOCIAL COMPETENCY

Egocentrism as it has been discussed by Piaget and others is seen as a factor that impedes social interaction. Early social development is assumed to proceed without the benefit of effective perspective-taking ability or communicative intent. However, other developmental psychologists have proposed quite a different hypothesis: that children's talk serves rather as a *tool* for exploring and learning about social interaction. By using language, the child learns how to get and maintain the other's attention, to make requests, demands, commands, promises, and excuses, how to praise, insult, and even manipulate the other as effectively as possible. Language is thus seen as an important *facilitator* of social development rather than a phenomenon that necessarily follows along behind it.

A study by Garvey and Hogan (1973) illustrates this change of focus. Children between 3 1/2 and 5 years of age were tape-recorded as they conversed in dyads. The conversations were subsequently scored for various indices of "social speech," that is, how well the children's utterances were adapted to the speech or behavior of the partner. The experimenters were especially interested in dialogues suggesting that the children were "in focus" or engaged in a mutual activity (e.g., discussing a toy of common interest).

The results showed that every dyad, even those consisting of the youngest children, were mutually engaged and in focus during much of their interaction. Social speech seemed to be the rule rather than the exception. In fact, the experimenters found many instances when the primary focus of activity was not some toy or perceptible object but conversation itself. The authors gave the following example—a boy and girl contemplating the future:

Boy: "If I grow up my voice will change and when you grow up your voice will change. My mom told me. Did your mommy tell you?"

Girl: "No, your mommy's wrong. My voice, I don't want it to change. Oh, well."

Boy: "Oh, well, we'll stay little, right?"

Girl: "No, I don't want to. I *want* my voice to change. I don't care if it changes."

Boy: "*I* care." (p. 565)

The results, in fact, showed more than mutual engagement. There were many instances in which children used language to secure the social involvement of the partner with what is called the *summons-answer routine*, a device that not only suggests substantial communicative intent but also suggests the ability to use at least one of the many conventional ploys common in adult conversations. The summons-answer routine consists of an opening word or phrase intended to get the attention of the partner (e.g., "Hey, you"), followed by the answer (frequently "What?" or "Yeah?"). By answering, the second person has indicated his availability for verbal interaction, while the first person is committed to having a "reason" for the opening summons.

One example cited by Garvey and Hogan suggested considerable mastery of the routine, as it was playfully manipulated to introduce a joking insult as the reason for the summons.

Boy: "Do you know what?"

Girl: "What?" (Pause)

Boy: (Grins, then laughs before speaking.) "You're a nut."

Girl: "What? What? What's a nut? What?" (Both laugh simultaneously, girl dashes threateningly at boy, shrieking the final "What?") (p. 566)

While this study indicates a great deal of social speech and mutual engagement, a further analysis by Garvey (1974) on the same children's play behavior goes even further in suggesting remarkable role-taking skills. The following excerpt, involving two boys, illustrates that social play involves *shared imagination* in which the course of the play episode is developed mutually. Moreover, and especially important, the roles are *complementary* and *consistent* (recall the hypothesis that the young child egocentrically confuses roles).

X: "OK, dinner is ready. Now what do you want for dinner?
     (turns to Y)
Y: "Well . . ." (indecisively)
X: "Hot beef?"
Y: "OK, hot beef."
X: "Coffee, too?"
Y: *"No I'm the little boy. I'll have some milk."* (p. 174; italics
     added)

It seems clear from the studies just discussed that communication skills begin to emerge before the age of three. In fact, the third year (i.e., age two) has been identified as a time of particularly rapid growth in such skills. In one recent study, the communicative behaviors of three two-year-olds were videotaped and recorded over the period of a year (Mueller et al., 1977). Generally, the children showed a highly significant improvement in the ability to elicit a verbal response to their utterances from their playmates. The experimenters were particularly interested in the antecedent factors conducive to successful communications. For example, it was found that children learned to adjust the content of their speech to the listener's activity rather than to their own. Also, they learned to speak when they had the listener's attention rather than when he was occupied with something else.

Thus, it appears that effective communication skills, including perspective taking, may develop along with early language acquisition itself. While the young child is learning, very rapidly, the vocabulary and grammar of the native tongue, he is also learning how to apply language to everyday, social activities. Indeed, it is frequently commented by researchers working with young children that they seem to enjoy verbal interaction for its own sake, a conclusion that should come as no surprise to most parents.

That young children show clear evidence of communicative intent has led some developmental psychologists to suggest that children are born *sociocentric* or oriented toward social interaction (see Chapter 7). Thus, social development, including the learning of language, is presumed to be greatly facilitated by the child's innate preparedness to engage in social interaction. As such, the sociocentric hypothesis is radically different from the egocentrism hypothesis, which presents the child as basically "asocial" at birth and somewhat resistant to socialization in his early years because of an absence of role-taking skills and communicative intent. While a number of research studies seem to be consistent with the sociocentric hypothesis, it is nevertheless not a particularly "good" hypothesis considering all of the criteria discussed earlier; that is, it is doubtful that it could ever be conclusively proven wrong if it is in fact so. At the same time, it could be argued that acceptance of the sociocentric hypothesis could deter investigation of experiential and environmental factors conducive to social development (including communication skills). For example, an extreme (but frequently encountered) version of the sociocentric hypothesis is that individual differences in "sociability" are inherited; therefore, one need not bother looking too closely for child-rearing practices (for example) that may be correlated with sociability.

Nevertheless, in the next section we take a look at research indicating how perspective-taking and communication skills may in fact be learned. We also discuss some rather compelling evidence for the role of experience on the development of individual differences in such skills.

EXPERIENTIAL FACTORS IN COMMUNICATION DEVELOPMENT

A number of studies have examined the possibility of directly training the child to improve his communication effectiveness. While the evidence is not exactly straightforward, it seems to favor the affirmative: training does seem to facilitate the requisite skills if the tasks involved are suitable to the child's age level. However, while such evidence provides optimism for those educators interested in improving deficient communication skills in children, it does little to suggest how children actually acquire the skills in their natural development. The reason is simple enough: outside of teaching word meaning, few parents directly tutor their children on the rules of language use (recall Piaget's observation, mentioned earlier, that the parent is likely to tolerate "egocentric" speech rather than correct it). Probably we will only discover more about these experiential factors in children's communication effectiveness by carrying out studies that approximate "real world" language development.

However, one recent "training" study is worth discussing. Whitehurst (1976) examined the social learning approach to the acquisition of communication skills. Briefly, this approach proposes that children learn such skills (as they learn many complex behaviors) by observing and listening to models, especially high status adults such as parents. According to social learning theory, a major part of children's language acquisition involves imitation of the words, speaking styles, and even the rules of grammar that they normally encounter.

Thus, Whitehurst (Study 2) exposed a number of six-year-olds to both "good" and "bad" models of communicative efficiency. With each individual child, an adult male played a game wherein the adult indicated which of a collection of overturned cups covered a marble. The cups varied in size, color, and other markings, and no two cups were identical. Thus, it was always possible to discriminate verbally any particular cup from another, although some discriminations were more difficult than others, because some cups had characteristics in common (for example, small and blue) with only one distinguishing feature (for example, spotted or striped).

Children seem to have considerable difficulty in determining which of the stimulus characteristics of an object makes it unique. Indeed, Whitehurst had discovered earlier (Study 1) that there were almost no differences in such abilities in children ranging from kindergarten to fourth grade. However, other factors made the older children's communications more effective. First, messages that were incomplete and uninformative (for example, "blue," when both cups were blue) dropped drastically after kindergarten. Second, older children tended to use "redundant" messages, which contained the distinctive feature plus one or more nondistinctive features (for example, "blue and spotted," when only "spotted" was a distinguishing characteristic). Older children therefore got their messages across at the expense of word economy.

Thus, in the modeling experiment, some of the six-year-olds heard a series of messages from the adult that were incomplete and ambiguous (bad-model condition), while others heard messages that were efficient and not redundant (good-model condition). A control group of children was not exposed to modeling. Afterward, it was the child's turn to communicate to the adult. Did the children imitate the models' communication styles? To a considerable degree, yes. The bad model group of children were especially inclined to give ambiguous messages, compared to controls. While the good model children did not show a significant increase in the crisply efficient messages to which they were exposed, they did nevertheless deliver more redundant messages, which, as we mentioned, get the job done. It therefore appears that children will attempt to imitate the communicative styles of adult models—even styles that are ineffective.

While in some important respects the Whitehurst study addresses the issue of how communication skills may develop (or fail to develop) in normal childhood, it would be hazardous to generalize too far. For one thing, in the pursuit of good experimental control, the study is highly artifical and "unnatural"; the model, for example, was a stranger to the child, and the tasks were not like anything communicated about in the "real world." The optimal research strategy would be to go from the laboratory study, such as the one just discussed, to the child's natural environment to see how well the experimental evidence is supported by observations in the field. Conversely, further hypotheses derived from such field observations can be tested in the laboratory under more controlled conditions.

Do children in fact imitate the communicative styles of parents, both good and bad? The answer is a qualified yes, as other factors besides imitation seem to be important in the development of communication competence.

For example, a study by Bearison and Cassel (1975) addressed the hypothesis that *person-centered* rather than *status-centered* families are conducive to the development of good communication effectiveness. In person-centered families, behavior expected of the child is justified by parents in terms of others' feelings and preferences; children are given "reasons" for complying, frequently stressing the logical consequences of alternative courses of action. On the other hand, in status-oriented families appeals are made to role expectations when controlling the child's behavior; for example, "Do it this way because I said so," or "Obey your teacher because she's in charge." Such appeals are relatively simple, arbitrary, and insensitive to individual needs and motivations.

In the Bearison and Cassel study, the mothers of a number of white six-year-olds were questioned about what they would say to their children in various hypothetical situations, most of which pertained to verbal discipline. The protocols were then scored for person- versus status-centeredness, and the children were identified accordingly. As a measure of communicative effectiveness, the children played a game in which they had to tell two other players, on separate occasions, about the rules. One listener could see the child, the other was blindfolded. The experimenters could then compare the relative communicability of messages delivered by children having different family orientations.

The results were remarkably unambiguous When the listener could see, there was little difference between the groups. When the listener was blindfolded, however, the person-centered children scored much higher than did the status-oriented children on all five measures of communicative effectiveness. Thus, the person-centered children gave the blindfolded listener more useful information, used fewer inadequate referents, used more words in general, but with fewer demonstratives (*this*, *that*, *there*, *it*), and gave richer descriptions of the game materials.

Bearison and Cassel reasoned that person-centered appeals encourage the child to coordinate listener-speaker perspectives, an argument that has very much in common with Piaget's explanation for the demise of egocentric speech (discussed earlier). Both approaches propose that egalitarian social experiences in early childhood are conducive to mature social development in general and communicative effectiveness in particular. However, while Piaget pinpointed peer group cooperation as the source of such development, Bearison and Cassel identified the family—judging from their research design, particularly the mother. While the results of their experiment lend cogent support for emphasizing mother-child interaction, a study performed by Hollows and Cowan (1973) in Norway supports Piaget's emphasis on the peer group.

In the latter study, children between seven and nine years of age were selected from three Norwegian social settings: a medium-sized town, a small village, and an isolated farm community. Children of the farm community proved to be considerably delayed in the development of their role-taking and communication skills, compared to the the children from the other environments. The only apparent differences between the environments relevant to social development were the opportunities available for children's peer interaction: children of the isolated farm community rarely played games with others of the same age. On the other hand, the investigators reported that these children did receive much social stimulation and support from their mothers, although it is not possible to determine from their report whether it was person- or status-centered, as described by Bearison and Cassel. Nevertheless, a comparison of the two studies just reviewed suggests that both parents and peers are an important influence in the development of the child's communication skills.

In addition, other potential factors have been identified. It has been shown, for example, that *bilingualism* may facilitate a sensitivity to the other's needs during the communication process. Young English-speaking children in Montreal who were immersed in French language instruction performed better on a communication task than children not taking French (Genesee, Tucker, and Lambert, 1975). The investigators suggested that exposure to a second language may have made the bilingual children acutely aware of possible difficulties in communicating, as well as giving them some practical experience in dealing with such difficulties.

Another factor in the development of communication skills is social class. A number of studies have reported that middle-class children are better communicators than are lower-class children. However, there are at least two problems with identifying social class per se as a determinant of communicative skill. The first is that many of the language "deficiencies" of lower-class children have proven to be more apparent than real (see Chapter 6). White social scientists, for example, have notoriously underestimated the language skills of lower-class blacks. In fact, instances have recently been uncovered in which black English is more specific and informative than standard English. Considerable caution is therefore warranted until much more research evidence is accumulated.

A second problem is more substantive, as it has to do with the concept of "social class" itself. Historically, social scientists have had much difficulty defining social class by other than arbitrary criteria. The problem is particularly acute in North American society, where it is not uncommon for individuals to have high status by one criterion (education) but low status by another (income). "Social class" tends to be a rather diffuse, catch-all concept that may mask a variety of factors, some of which may be directly related, while others may be only indirectly related or even irrelevant to communication skill. This is not to say, of course, that social class should be of no interest to the psychologist. Rather, once social class *is* positively correlated with communication skills (and note our caution about premature conclusions), the next step is to determine which of the many variables associated with social class are responsible for the relationship.

CONCLUSION: THE COMPETENT COMMUNICATOR

We have reviewed a number of studies that indicate that, contrary to earlier research, young children are not without communicative intent and the cognitive ability to use language effectively in social interaction. Also, they seem to have a sufficient degree of perspective-taking ability, so long as tasks appropriate to their age level are involved.

We should not overstate the case. There are certainly limitations to the young child's communicative ability. Relatively poor sensitivity to nonverbal feedback seems to be one such limiting factor. In addition, Flavell (1977) has speculated that young children lack the cognitive ability to analyze a message objectively for its adequacy; that is, they have trouble thinking about a message (and thereby editing it for a listener's needs) before actually sending it. Such a limitation should also hamper the child's ability to rephrase an utterance when asked to do so.

Lastly, we should not overlook the obvious: effective communication, in addition to sufficient linguistic and cognitive competence, depends upon considerable *knowledge about life* as well. How else, for example, are the sentences, "The teacher yelled at the student because he was lazy," and "The teacher yelled at the student because he was irritable," saved from ambiguity? No small amount of classroom experience is involved, to be sure. Thus, children just learning to use reference words, such as pronouns and demonstratives, would seem to have a formidable task before them, for the border between clarity and ambiguity in language use is often determined by assumptions of plausible human motivations, or by what is loosely referred to as "common sense." How the child acquires such common sense and learns to apply it to language use would seem to be a significant component in the development of communicative competence.

REFERENCES

Bearison, D. J., and T. Z. Cassel. 1975. Cognitive decentration and social codes: Communicative effectiveness in young children from differing family contexts. Dev. Psychol. 11:29–36.

Borke, H. 1975. Piaget's mountains revisited: Changes in the egocentric landscape. Dev. Psychol. 11:240–243.

Brainerd, C. 1978. Piaget's theory of intelligence. Prentice-Hall, Englewood Cliffs, New Jersey.

Flavell, J. 1968. The Development of Role-Taking and Communication Skills in Children. John Wiley & Sons, New York.

Flavell, J. 1977. Cognitive development. Prentice-Hall, Englewood Cliffs, New Jersey.

Garvey, C. 1974. Some properties of social play. Merrill-Palmer Quart. 20:163–180.

Garvey, C., and R. Hogan. 1973. Social speech and social interaction: Egocentrism revisited. Child Dev. 44:562–568.

Gelman, R. 1978. Cognitive development. In: M. R. Rosenzweig and L. W. Porter (eds.), Annual Review of Psychology. Vol. 29. Annual Reviews, Palo Alto, Calif.

Genesee, F., G. R. Tucker, and W. E. Lambert. 1975. Communication skills of bilingual children. Child Dev. 46:1010–1014.

Glucksberg, S., R. H. Krauss, and E. T. Higgins. 1975. The development of referential communication skills. In: F. D. Horowitz (ed.), Review of Child Development Research. Vol. 4. University of Chicago Press, Chicago.

Hollos, M., and P. A. Cowan. 1973. Social isolation and cognitive development: Logical operations and role-taking abilities in three Norwegian social settings. Child Dev. 44:630–641.

Maratsos, M. P. 1973. Nonegocentric communication abilities in preschool children. Child Dev. 44:697–700.

Menig-Peterson, C. L. 1975. The modification of communicative behavior in preschool-aged children as a function of the listener's perspective. Child Dev. 46:1015–1018.

Mueller, E., M. Bleier, J. Krakow, K. Hegedus, and P. Cournoyer. 1977. The development of peer verbal interaction among two-year-old boys. Child Dev. 48:284–287.

Piaget, V. 1959. The Language and Thought of the Child. Rev. Ed. Routledge & Kegan Paul, Boston.

Shantz, C. U., and J. S. Watson. 1970. Assessment of spatial egocentrism through expectancy violation. Psychonom. Sci. 18:93–94.

Shatz, M., and R. Gelman. 1973. The development of communication skills: Modifications in the speech of young children as a function of listener. Monographs of the Society for Research in Child Development, 38(5)(Serial No. 152).

Whitehurst, G. J. 1976. The development of communication: Changes with age and modeling. Child Dev. 47:473–482.

Chapter 9
ETHOLOGY
Animals and How They "Speak" to One Another

J. A. Darley

Most animals have to coordinate various activities among themselves. This coordination comes about in many ways. A foraging ant leaves a scent trail of pheromones that other ants can follow to locate a food source. A male robin sings, indicating to other robins that this is his territory. A male spider presents a female with a dead insect wrapped in a cocoon as part of its mating ritual. All these behavioral patterns serve to bring about a response in another animal. Other ants go directly to the food. Other male robins stay away from the singer's territory. The female spider accepts the gift-bearing male for a mate. All these patterns communicate information. These signal systems serve as the "language" for the various species.

Animal "languages" are not restricted primarily to sound, as in humans, since several sensory mechanisms can be and are used. A domestic dog "speaks" in a number of ways: by barks, snarls, and whines; it urinates on posts, bares its teeth, flattens its ears, and wags its tail. All these actions communicate information to other dogs. The use of a variety of sensory mechanisms in communication is also recognized in humans. Much work has been carried out in recent years on nonverbal communication. These studies are concerned with the understanding of body movements and eye contact, and with the examination of actions such as laughter, grief, and other emotional responses that transmit information either along with or in the absence of speech. No real functional difference exists in any means of communication, whether it be visual, tactile, olfactory, or auditory. They all serve to communicate information, however crude or imprecise it may be.

The best-developed language is of course human speech. Its precision and accuracy are probably unparalleled in the animal world, with the possible exception of dolphin communication. Dolphins seem to have a complex mechanism for receiving and sending sounds, but little is known about dolphin "language." It is often argued that language is not the correct term to use for the signal systems of various species, since we think of it in human terms with its nouns, verbs, syntax, grammatical structure, and, above all, its "ideational" component, that is, the part language plays in planning and thinking ahead (Hebb and Thompson, 1968). For these reasons, "communication mechanism" or "signal form" are better terms to describe the diversity of communication types used by other species to transmit information.

The science that examines animal communication is ethology. This discipline is concerned with the study of animal behavior in its natural habitat. Ethologists examine the organization, the origins, the physiological bases, the genetic background, the evolution, and the functions of behavior.

Two approaches to animal behavior have developed over the last 40 years. Ethologists largely of European origin, with biological backgrounds, formed one approach, and the American comparative psychologists formed the other. The approaches used for study were diametrically opposed. Ethologists examined many species of animals under conditions as natural as possible and focused on unlearned or instinctive behavior, its survival value, and its evolution. Comparative psychologists were concerned mainly with learning, and conducted their experiments for the most part in laboratories, using such equipment as mazes and Skinner boxes. Most researchers used the rat as an experimental animal and worked toward the establishment of laws of learning behavior to describe how reward, punishment, and practice affected learning proficiency. The two schools developed independently for some time, mainly because of language differences. Much of the early work in ethology was published in German by writers like J. Von Uexkull, Konrad Lorenz, and Niko Tinbergen. Tinbergen moved from Leyden to Oxford University and publications subsequently appeared more frequently in English journals. Disagreement between the two approaches to animal behavior developed. Psychologists pointed out that ethologists were virtually ignoring the effect environments had on altering behavior, and ethologists countered that comparative psychologists knew nothing about normal behavior, because the latter studied animals under abnormal conditions. Also, they pointed out that laws of behavior were unlikely to be understood if they concentrated on just one species, the rat. Fortunately, both sides benefited from the arguments and altered their techniques to minimize the deficiencies found in their approaches.

The considerable overlap in interest between the psychologist concerned with animal behavior and the biologist concerned with ethology led to a degree of merging of these disciplines. This is reflected by the training and presence of ethologists in both biology and psychology departments at many universities. In addition, ethological interest has extended in recent years to studies of primates and humans to determine the biological roots of human behavior, a preserve once restricted to psychology. The combined interest of the psychologists and biologists led to the rapid growth of ethology. This expansion has extended to other disciplines, such as anthropology and sociology, which adopted ethological techniques and presented such courses as primate and human ethology and sociobiology.

Why do psychologists, anthropologists, and sociologists, members of disciplines concerned with humans, study animals? This old question continues to arise at regular intervals, for two main reasons: first, a lack of knowledge of the close knit physiological and structural interrelationships between humans and many animal species and, second, human vanity. The latter reason is supported by the existence of cultures and religions that argue that humans are unique beings bearing few, if any, ties with animal species. The question of "continuity" between humans and animals is not raised in medical science when research is conducted on liver, heart, or lung transplants in pigs or dogs. It is well known that pig and dog physiology, organs, and immunity systems are very similar to human counterparts. However, the continuity question is repeatedly raised if comparison of mental properties or behavioral systems between humans and beasts are made. The lack of acceptance of continuity of mental activity appears odd considering that brain structures are very similar in humans, chimpanzees, monkeys, dogs, and dolphins, to name a few. To suggest there are fundamental differences in mental activities when there are similar mental organs seems absurd. Certainly the degree of development can be questioned, since humans have larger and more complex brains than most species. However, the basic structure of mental processes must be similar. The continuity question also appears in comparisons of behavior. This arises from the mistaken belief that all behavior is plastic and can be shaped through learning experiences. This is not true, since "innate" or "inborn" behavior is as stable in the genetic makeup as any other genetic based structure, such as muscle, bones, and organs. Innate behavior, such as a smile, a temper tantrum, or an expression of grief through crying, is so stereotyped it is immediately recognized by all humans regardless of race or locality. Learning certainly permits a wide variety of behavior patterns, but the underlying mechanisms for learning are stable. The same learning task can be presented to a dog, a rat, or a chimpanzee. The means by which the task is learned is similar or basic to them all. As Boice (1976) points out, "The Darwinian notion of mental continuity between animals and man was a great prod to modern scientific psychology, specifically to an emphasis in America on learning in animals as evidence of subhuman consciousness." This continuity of systems is the reason why animal studies are valid approaches to the understanding of human behavior.

ETHOGRAMS

The first step in an ethological study is to make an accurate description of behavior patterns. A catalogue or "ethogram" of all behavior patterns of an animal is made. In ideal conditions the animal is observed, photographed, filmed, and recorded over all stages of its life. This permits a full description of all possible behavioral patterns for the species. Behavioral units are selected that are constant in form, such as walking, barking, or staring. Each of these patterns are described in detail. An accurate description commonly requires the use of movie camera or videotape to record every detail using slow motion and stop action as aids for analysis.

Often animals are observed in captivity. These observations have to be examined carefully, because abnormal environments often lead to abnormal behavior. Wolves in cages, for instance, frequently pace back and forth along the same path for hours on end. This pacing, a major behavior element in captive wolves, is never seen in wolves that are free. It seems that suppression of opportunities to explore and engage in the normal activity of wild wolves leads to this stereotyped pacing of the caged animals.

An observation of the unusual behavior shown by isolated rhesus monkeys in cages led to the classic work by Harry Harlow on social deprivation. By isolating monkeys from their mothers and siblings from birth, he noted they showed abnormal behavior when placed in social situations with other monkeys. They showed abnormal levels of fear, shrinking into corners, and clasping themselves with their arms. If one touched another accidentally, this often resulted in a vicious attack. A mother reared in isolation refused to nurse a newborn, sat on top of the shrieking youngster, or picked it up by a leg and bashed it against the floor. Monkeys raised in normal groups showed none of the aberrant behavior.

Unusual behaviors have been observed in many species in confined situations. Steps must be taken to ensure that the ethogram for a species includes the normal elements of behavior not those brought on by confinement.

DEVELOPMENT

A second step toward understanding behavior is to look at its development. How does a particular pattern first present itself? There are two basic ways. An animal can imitate the actions of a parent or sibling and through this learning process develop the pattern. This is the way Harlow's monkeys developed their maternal behavior. If reared with a normal mother, the daughter, in turn, became a normal mother to her young (i.e., nursing, protecting, and providing comfort). However, a female isolated from its parents during its development to maturity did not show normal maternal behavior when she had her first youngster. The youngster was abused, was prevented from suckling, and was ignored when distressed. The lack of opportunity to learn normal maternal behavior prevented its development in the mother reared in isolation. An interesting observation of this mother with subsequent young was that she developed more maternal behavior as time went on. It appeared that her young were, in a sense, teaching her. Their persistence in nursing and approaching her in spite of the number of times she flung them away gradually overcame the mother's adverse reaction. Presumably it took less effort to allow the baby monkeys to suckle and cling to her fur than it took to continually brush them away. With each subsequent youngster she became a "better" mother. In this case the development of this behavior arose through learning that came about from an unexpected source, namely, her own young.

The second way in which behavior develops is in the absence of learning. The pattern is "inborn" or "innate" in origin. A mallard drake reared in isolation from other ducks makes all the duck sounds of a normal drake. In addition, the isolate performs the normal species-specific "displays," for example, courtship postures and threat postures. The isolate can also swim, walk, and fly normally. As this individual has had no opportunity to imitate, by observing or hearing others, these behaviors must be innate. However, it must be pointed out that the displays are not performed at appropriate times or directed at the correct object. In normal courtship and threatening situations, no response is made by the isolate. At other times, when no ducks are nearby, the isolate might launch into a series of courtship displays, turning in tight circles, directing the displays toward its own tail, or pecking viciously at its own foot. The isolate, in the absence of the appropriate learning, directed the displays at itself. Thus, in mallard drakes the manifestation of the behavior patterns is inborn but the proper time of presentation of a pattern depends on learning. The combination of the innate and learned aspects results in the correct behavior occurring at the correct time and in the correct situation.

In what circumstances does specific behavior first appear as the individual animal grows up? When does a male puppy begin to mark its home range by urinating like adult males? (This behavior serves to communicate to other dogs by means of the urine scent the boundaries of the home range or territory of this male. Wolves mark their home territories in a similar fashion.) Newborn pups of both sexes urinate in the manner of adult females, i.e., squatting down with outspread legs before releasing the urine. When the gonads of the male pups begin to produce testosterone, an abrupt change in urination behavior occurs. They lift one leg and urinate in small amounts on posts, walls, and trees, as adult males do. This behavior can be precipitated by injecting testosterone into the pups before normal maturation. The circumstances around which this behavior develops are thus linked with gonad maturation.

Curze (1935) showed how pecking accuracy in chicks improved as they matured. Experimental chicks were kept in the dark for one to five days. They were then brought out into the light and allowed to peck at grains of millet. In spite of no opportunity to practice, the older chicks showed more accuracy than the younger ones. Clearly this behavioral ability was caused by maturation.

Hess (1956) established that pecking ability was innate. He mounted prism glasses that deflected vision by seven degrees over the chicks' eyes from birth. The pecking action of these chicks was seven degrees off and did not improve with practice. From experiments like this we see that the development of accurate pecking requires a maturation period and is innate in origin.

MOTIVATION

A third method in the study of behavior is aimed at answering the question of what makes a behavior happen at a particular moment.

Most behavior is organized so that it occurs at appropriate times. For example, a female mallard does not assume the copulatory position spontaneously. Many factors contribute to the control of the time of this action. She does it during the breeding season, in the presence of a specific male, her chosen mate, in response to specific precopulatory displays by her male, at a time just before egg laying, when the eggs can be fertilized. Thus many specific stimuli are required before the copulatory position is assumed: the season, her mate, courtship displays, and the physiological condition of her ova. The study of motivation concerns the search for the specific stimuli necessary for the performance of particular behavior patterns. These stimuli are both internal, such as the physiological state of the ova, and external, such as the presence of the male and the courtship displays.

Internal stimuli

Internal stimuli are examined using experimental techniques incorporating either a specific or a general approach. Specific aspects of behavior, such as hunger, are examined in several ways. Electrodes are inserted into brain centers to monitor what occurs during eating or to activate eating. Fistulas are inserted into the throats of animals so that food eaten is shunted out of the body before reaching the stomach. Alternately, food is shunted into the stomach without passing through the mouth. Nerves serving the stomach wall are severed so that stomach contractions and stomach distention are not recognized by the brain. Through this systematic intervention, those parts of the body involved with hunger and eating can be identified.

Control of general internal stimuli is carried out by varying the period of deprivation. An animal starved for 24 hours reacts more positively to food objects than one separated from food for just a few hours. Differences in the hunger response are established using this technique.

Since internal stimuli play a definite role in activating eating behavior, hunger is called a "drive." Other drives, such as thirst, sex, sleep, and maternal and exploratory behavior, account for many other categories of behavior. Studies of each of these drives indicate many differences among them. Evidence for clear-cut internal mechanisms are present for drives such as hunger, thirst, and sleep. However, inner mechanisms for other drives are not as straightforward. Brain centers have not been discovered that initiate exploratory behavior. Maternal behavior often requires learning experience. Sexual behavior in many species is not dependent on hormone levels in the blood, but glucose or salt balances are directly related to hunger or thirst. These basic differences present some difficulties in the acceptance of the concept of drive for all types of behavior in all species.

Often it is observed that the same stimulus does not lead to the same response. Something has changed within the animal to alter the "threshold" of response. A hungry cat presented with food will behave differently than a full cat. The internal state of the cat, its hunger, lowers the thresholds to allow eating to start. However, the hunger level is not the only variable altering threshold. The attractiveness of the food alters the eating behavior as well. A satiated animal often eats again when presented with a favorite food. Similarly a very hungry animal eats something it normally does not eat. So there is some latitude in what makes eating behavior happen. An unusually strong drive and an unattractive food can release the same behavior, that is, eating, as a very weak drive coupled with attractive food. Differences in thresholds can be generated in sexual behavior. If male mallard ducks are presented with a female after being deprived of females for several weeks during the breeding season, they will exhibit high intensity courtship and compress into a few hours pair formation that normally takes several weeks. Thresholds can be lowered so far that mallard drakes isolated from birth from all animals will perform courtship activities toward their own tails, circling repeatedly during the performance.

Clearly the internal stimuli that make behavior happen are both complex and variable. The role they play has to be examined for specific behavior and specific animals. Internal stimuli for thirst, hunger, and sleep appear similar in many species. This is not true for sexual, maternal, and exploratory behavior.

External Stimuli

A second method of examining motivation is used in naturalistic studies and concentrates on the external stimuli associated with a behavior pattern. The circumstances surrounding the occurrence of a pattern are described in detail. With the observation of many repetitions of a pattern, the specific stimuli occurring in conjunction with it become clear. In the example of the mallard duck adopting the copulation posture mentioned earlier, the external circumstances were: breeding season, presence of her mate, and male performance of precopulatory courtship patterns. Using this technique, the external stimuli associated with particular patterns are recognized.

External stimuli are also examined experimentally using deprivation techniques. A cat isolated from food for variable periods is exposed to a variety of stimuli, such as food smells, the sight of different food objects, live mice, dead mice, or dog chow. Thus, different aspects of hunger behavior can be examined through the design of the experiment. Does the smell of food elicit the same response as the sight of food? Does a live mouse elicit the same behavior as a dead mouse? These questions can be answered using these techniques.

The normal sequence of ethological study begins with the observation in the natural state and proceeds to experimental studies. In the wild, the male stickleback fish develops a red belly during breeding season. The function of this red belly was clarified by Tinbergen (1951) in experimental studies. He noted that the color red was an important stimulus for aggressive behavior. A crude model with a red underside was attacked immediately, whereas an accurate model without red was seldom attacked. If the crude model was turned over so the red was on top, the stickleback no longer attacked it. Sticklebacks that were raised in isolation responded to the models in the same manner as normally reared sticklebacks. This means responses to the key signals are inborn. Thus, the key stimuli for attack by male sticklebacks are the cues "red below." The structures in an organism that respond to this type of stimuli have been called the "innate releasing mechanism," or the IRM.

Turkey hens respond to sound cues. They will mother any object that gives the cheeping call of turkey chicks, including a speaker cone that emits recorded cheeps. Deafened hens, i.e., hens in which the IRM cannot be triggered, will kill most of their young because of their inability to respond to the call that signifies chicks.

Herring gull chicks normally peck at their parents bills to receive regurgitated fish to eat. Models of the parents' heads and bills indicate that one with a red circular patch similar to the one found in adults releases a stronger peck response than models with different colored patches or those with no patch. Surprisingly, a thin red rod with three rings releases more responses than an accurate copy of the head and bill of a normal parent. This exaggerated response has been observed in other situations as well. An oystercatcher, when presented with a giant model of an egg, prefers it over its own normal-sized one. These stimuli that release a stronger than normal response have been called "supernormal" stimuli.

Releasing mechanisms are not all innate. Mallard ducks reared by humans perform courtship behavior toward humans rather than toward other ducks. In the cichlid fish, "Astatotilapia" males that have had experience with females will not court models of females. However, the males reared in isolation will court very crude models, including a wax ball attached to a glass rod. The males learn to recognize females and are not confused by good models of real fish. If they have no opportunity to learn, they are easily confused by crude models.

External releasing mechanisms have considerable significance, especially for animals that breed within a year from birth. It is essential to communicate by means of key stimuli, e.g., courtship cues, in an inborn fashion because there is often little or no opportunity to observe courtship in progress. The parents courted before the offspring were born and could not serve as models. Yearling animals may learn during the first breeding season, however, that any failure to communicate or any delay lowers chances of breeding. Animals with a built-in signal system are going to be more successful. Recognizing each other, recognizing parents, feeding situations, eggs, and many other cues all improve an individual animal's chances to survive and to pass on its genes to its offspring.

The role of external stimuli in initiating a behavior is easier to determine than the role of internal stimuli. They often can be examined with simple experiments, e.g., those that use models to imitate releasing stimuli, or deprivation experiments, which demonstrate how lack of learning opportunities alters behavior. External stimuli coupled with behavior are the "words" of animal signal systems. A hungry herring gull chick "speaks of its hunger" by pecking the red spot on its parent's bill; the parent responds to the message by regurgitating food, which the chick eats.

STAGES OF BEHAVIOR

There are three basic stages of animal behavior: appetitive, consummatory, and refractory. A hungry cat that is searching for a mouse is showing the *appetitive* stage of eating behavior. The cat eating the mouse is showing the *consummatory* act of eating. Following the consummatory act the cat typically will not eat for a time. This time span is called the *refractory* period. In the sexual behavior of dogs, the male shows appetitive behavior in response to the smell of the bitch in "heat." This attracts males from long distances. The consummatory act is copulation, then the males retire during the refractory stage, in spite of the fact that the bitch is still receptive. The thirst drive typically releases a similar sequence. the search for water, drinking to satiation, and refraining from drinking. Chimpanzee females without young show a very high interest in new born members of a group. They attempt to hold, fondle, or touch the newborn, in spite of the mother's usual attempts to prevent their contact with her newborn. This could be interpreted as the appetitive aspect of maternal behavior. The appetitive state continued over extended periods of time because the mother prevents the consummation of the behavior by withholding her young from these females.

Each of these three subdivisions of animal behavior is also examined from a motivational point of view. The internal stimuli and the external circumstances in which they occur are determined using the techniques described earlier.

EXPRESSIVE BEHAVIOR

Not all behavior patterns serve as communication devices. A cat roused from sleep stretches its body before it moves off. This same cat humps its back and hisses at another animal. In the first instance, although information about the cat is communicated to an observer, the cat is not consciously signaling another animal. In the second situation, it is signaling that it is angry. The latter type of behavior is grouped under the term "expressive movements."

Since expressive movements function to communicate information, often conspicuous structures and conspicuous behavior are used. Courting male peacocks fan their huge ornate tail and perform a dance before potential mates. Angry dogs snarl and adopt a stiff-legged posture, with shoulder hair raised and teeth bared. Courting ducks display bright plumage and strange movements, such as pumping the head up and down, swimming in half circles with head extended, rearing the body and flicking water at another duck, and pointing to bright feather patches with the bill.

Many expressive behaviors develop through a mechanism ethologists call "ritualization." Through this process a piece of behavior adds or enhances a signal or communication function. Marking a home area with urine, observed in many species of mammals, probably developed through this process. The urine deposits signal the presence of another animal. Deposits around an area signal the territory perimeter. Marking by urine has been refined in dogs and wolves. Small amounts are deposited by lifting the hind leg and urinating on scent posts at a nose-high level. In this way the urine supply can be spread around an extended perimeter at optimum levels for detection. Thus a normal body function took on the signal function of territory marking. Female mallards perform a ritualized action called "inciting" in which they rhythmically point over their shoulders with their bill while following their male. The bill is often directed in the general direction of another male and signals to the male she follows that he is her choice as a mate. In sheldrakes this same pattern is less ritualized. The female points at another duck, then attacks it, returns to her mate, and points over her shoulder at the other duck again. Through the process of ritualization, the mallard has dropped the attack components and has just retained the signal aspect of the behavior. In the female lesser Antillian grackle a particular display in the process of ritualization has two very different functions. This display is the typical soliciting posture adopted by the female before and during copulation. She crouches down, trembling her wings, she elevates her tail to a vertical position, and then lifts her head, with the beak vertical, while she utters a quiet peeping call. The male normally responds to this signal display by copulating with her. This exact same posture, however, is adopted in different circumstances, namely when intruders appear near the nest area. In this situation her male attacks and chases the intruders away. When this action is completed, the female resumes her normal activities. However, her male sometimes is confused by this posture and begins his precopulatory approach to her, with feathers fluffed and wings outspread. The female rewards this response with a peck or two, and the male retreats and chases off the intruders. This posture appears to be in the process of ritualization. There is a clear separation of function but the separation of form has not taken place, as can be seen by the male's confusion when it is performed.

EVOLUTION OF BEHAVIOR

How do the many complex and elaborate behavior patterns come about? Ethology examines this question from an evolutionary perspective; that is, the laws of evolution have operated to shape behavior just as they have operated to shape body forms. Animals that showed behavior patterns that gave them an advantage over others were more likely to live and raise young than those that did not have these patterns. Over many generations the genes of animals with advantageous behavior persisted and disadvantageous genes decreased.

Behavior, unlike bones, cannot be buried in sedimentary deposits to form a fossil record of development. How can evolutionary evidence on behavior change be accumulated? Three avenues exist. One is to study closely related species to see the similarities and differences. Variations found in a specific behavior, such as inciting in female ducks, just discussed, provide insight into how the pattern evolved. The evolution of courtship display in phasianid birds, e.g., the domestic rooster, ring-necked pheasant, impeyan pheasant, peacock pheasant, and peacock, indicates that the display originated with the food call. The rooster scratches at the ground, steps back, and pecks at the ground while giving food calls. The hen rushes over to look for the food, and the male courts her. The ring-necked pheasant male shows similar behavior. The impeyan pheasant also pecks at the ground, but once the female approaches, the male bows toward her, spreading the tail and wing feathers and moving the fanned tail rhythmically forward and back. The peacock pheasant, with more conspicuous wing and tail plumage, pecks at the ground like the others. When the female approaches, he bows with spread wings and tail feathers and moves his head back and forward toward the female. The last component appears to be ritualized pecking. The courtship pattern of the peacock drops some elements and exaggerates others. The male spreads its huge ornate tail, vibrates the feathers, and steps backward. The fanned tail is bent forward and he points his beak down. The female runs forward and pecks in the area the beak is directed. Thus the feeding elements are abbreviated, and the use of the tail through its size, pattern, and vibration is enhanced. Knowledge of the other species reveals the intermediate steps in the origins of the very ritualized behavior of the peacock.

A second means of studying the evolution of behavior is to observe carefully the development of patterns in the young animals. Young male peacocks include scratching and pecking in early courtship displays. As they mature, these elements disappear. Just as embryonic development provides clues about the evolution of the body, embryonic development of behavior provides evidence of evolution of behavior.

A third means of studying the evolution of behavior is to look at similar existing species that occupy similar habitats. If conditions are similar to those of ancestral forms, some understanding of ancestral behavior can be obtained. This is one of the reasons why primate behavior has attracted so much interest in recent years. Jane Van Lawick-Goodall (1971) has provided fascinating information on many aspects of the growth and social development of chimpanzees, a semi-arboreal species that spends considerable time on the ground in mixed social groups. Studies of baboons by DeVore (1963, 1965) provide information of social interactions of a species living in savanna regions of Africa. Many of the environmental conditions in which chimpanzees and baboons find themselves are similar to those that human ancestral forms probably occupied millions of years ago. The behavioral responses of the chimpanzees and baboons to these conditions may provide insight into the precultural behavior of humans.

FIXED-ACTION PATTERNS

In observing animal behavior it is noted that many actions are very stereotyped. A mallard duck in Europe shows identical behavior patterns to a mallard in North America. These stereotyped behavior units are called "fixed action patterns." Fixed action patterns, or FAPs, are innate, or not learned. They may appear in newborns, e.g., the suckling response in mammals, or they may appear at sexual maturity, e.g., courtship display in ducks.

FAPs include, as the term indicates, a rigid sequence of actions. This sequence of actions, once started, continues automatically even if inappropriate conditions are present. Dogs about to lie down turn in circles, making scratching movements on the ground surface to prepare it before actually lying down. This scratching occurs regardless of the bedding surface. The dog will scratch at a concrete floor just the same as it would at straw bedding. Similarly, cats normally defecate on earth then bury the feces by scratching the surrounding earth over them. In unusual situations, such as on a hard surface, or a very soft surface, such as "Kitty litter," the same sequence occurs. However, in the former the cats continue to scratch ineffectually at the hard surface, and in the latter they continue to scratch long after the feces are covered. In both cases, the fixed behavior continues in an inappropriate situation.

Many fixed action patterns include a taxis or orientation element. A frog turns toward an insect before it flicks its tongue out to capture the prey. The "taxis" element is the turning aspect of the frog's behavior and the FAP is the tongue flick. If the egg of a grayleg goose is moved to a point outside the nest, the goose will roll it back in, using the underside of its bill. The "taxis" element is in the control of the egg. As the egg rolls unevenly toward the nest, the goose makes suitable adjustments with her bill to keep the egg's path more or less straight. If the egg is removed after the FAP starts, the bill is brought straight back to the nest; i.e., the taxis element is left out.

How can an experimenter establish that a particular behavior is inborn or not learned? Ethologists conduct what is called deprivation experiments. An animal is raised in isolation from other members of its species. In this way, it is impossible for this individual to learn or imitate the behavior of others. Any species-specific behavior patterns this individual exhibits must then be innate or inborn.

Eibl-Eibesfeldt (1961) investigated prey catching in polecats. He reared a number of polecats in isolation, then presented a live rat to individual polecats. When the rat ran away, each polecat immediately chased and seized it in its mouth, shaking it in a stereotypic fashion. Thus prey catching in polecats must be innate.

Certain aspects of singing in the American white-crowned sparrow are innate. Marler and Tamura (1964) placed newly hatched young males in soundproof enclosures. When the birds matured, they all sang simplified songs characteristic of their species. These songs must be inborn, since the birds had no opportunity to learn them.

It should be pointed out that, although the elements of various behavior patterns can be considered to be innate, this does not mean learning has no role. A goose reared by a human directs its behavior displays toward humans rather than toward other geese. The initial attacks on rats by the polecats of Eibl-Eibesfeldt's (1961) studies were often ineffective. They bit any part of the rat, from the head to the tail. Only after some experience did they learn that the nape of the neck was the correct area of attack. Although the white-crowned sparrows in Marler and Tamura's (1964) study sang recognizable songs, the diversity of the songs was not that of normal birds. They discovered that if the young birds heard songs of adult males during the first three months of life they sang the songs of the birds they heard. Although they had an innate ability to sing, they required learning experiences to attain the diversity of song found in normal birds. A male cichlid, mentioned earlier, will court a wax ball if it has no previous experience. However, after courting cichlid females, if will no longer respond to models. Therefore the appearance of fixed action patterns is often due to combinations of learned and innate factors.

ANIMAL COMMUNICATIONS

The range of animal communication shows enormous variation in form and complexity in different species. These differences reflect species needs. A male songbird that defends a territory typically has a small display language. It sings to attract a female and to advertise its presence on its territory to other males. It may adopt a threat posture at territory boundaries held in common with other males, and it may have a courtship posture for its female. Because there is little interference from others in the territory there is little need for a complexity of signals.

In a species that has many social contacts, a much more complex system develops. If competition for food, mates, and other reproductive requirements are to take place in relative harmony, intentions of individuals in the group must be clear. Social species, that hunt in packs, such as wolves, show many more expressive patterns than the fox, which hunts alone. A courting mallard drake in a mixed group of males and females must do many things to attract and hold a mate. He must attract and maintain her attention while courting to allow time for bond formation to take place. All these activities occur while other males are trying to do the same thing. Because of the competition in social situations, spectacular plumage and displays have evolved in males of different species of ducks. Their communicative system, compared to that of a typical songbird, is much broader and more elaborate.

Different systems often reflect the different habitat in which animals are found. Birds that see each other frequently, such as gulls, seabirds, and waterfowl, use visual signals, whereas birds in heavy tree cover rely more on songs that penetrate thick cover for some distance. Nocturnal mammals, which cannot rely on sight, use smell, marking territories with urine or scent glands. In other words, various species can communicate their presence to others by using the most effective sensory system.

Certain species, those with large brains, such as porpoises and chimpanzees, seem capable of communicating information of a much more refined nature than that communicated by other animals. Dolphins use sound to "see," especially in turbid water conditions. In addition they emit high-pitched rapid bursts of sounds in order to communicate to one another. They appear to have a hearing and brain capacity exceeding ours, allowing them to recognize these rapid sound bursts, which we can differentiate only when they are slowed down on audiotapes. Not only do they recognize these sound bursts, but also they analyze the sonar information, which is simultaneously striking the ear.

Early attempts to communicate with chimpanzees were disappointing because of the approach used. Chimps were reared with humans who tried to teach them the human words for milk, cup, mother, etc., with little success. However, success altered dramatically when symbols and sign language were taught to the chimps. A chimpanzee named Sarah, taught the use of symbols to represent words, made up new sentences such as "Mary give Sarah apple," "Mary wash apple," and "Debby cut banana." The chimpanzees used the word symbols in new ways to communicate information to the experimenters. They asked for food, for a drink, or asked to be taken for a walk. They lied to the experimenter, claiming that someone else broke a cup. They even taught sign language to other chimpanzees.

Similar successes occurred with dolphins. Experimenters tried to teach human words to the animals, with better success than with chimps, but the results were disappointing all the same. The second phase of using symbols instead of human sounds has not yet been completed. If other indications are correct, once a symbol language for dolphins is devised we may find we have a very intelligent animal capable of communicating complex information.

Our complex language may be the basis for much human success and development, but signal systems in other animals ensure success for their species as well. The complexity varies according to their evolutionary past and was shaped to meet their communication requirements.

Animal research has established that behavior is not a nebulous, constantly changing phenomena. Systems and patterns become obvious after the study of many species. They have fixed action patterns, drives, innate and learned behavior, innate releasing mechanisms, and expressive behavior. Many types of human behavior fit these categories as well. The continuity of animal and human systems of behavior can be seen through these studies. Because human behavior is more complex and variable than that of any other species, its roots and framework are not always clearly seen. Its very complexity makes analysis difficult. Animals, with their limited behavioral systems, permit easier analysis. Once behavioral systems are understood in other animal species, we can look for similar systems in humans.

On the other hand, we should not confine our interest just to the similarities between human and animal behavior. As Carolyn Sherif (1976) points out, "We should study those human behaviours that are distinctive to human beings with as much care and as great interest as those that are not. Otherwise we reduce the problems of human behaviour to those that are directly comparable to behavior of other animals. Thereby we eliminate most of the significant problems for social psychology" (p. 147). Nevertheless, the establishment of the continuity of behavior between animals and humans has provided psychology with a powerful tool for unraveling some of the origins and evolution of human behavior.

HUMAN ETHOLOGY

Communication in humans involves much more than the use of words. Feelings, emotions, and information are conveyed in facial expressions, through eye contact, in body actions, in music, and in dance. Compare a good dramatic performance with dialogue delivered without body actions, with no change in facial expression, with no accompanying music, with no variations in the pitch, loudness, or inflection in the voice. Stripped down to just verbal elements, the communication effect of the performance is severely diminished. A good performance requires excellence in the nonverbal, as well as the verbal, components. To take another example: an audiotape of a lecture actually delivered before a live audience is apt to fall very short of a videotape of the same performance. The expressive movements of the speaker are an extremely important part of the communication.

Silent movies relied almost entirely on nonverbal actions and expressions to convey information. Plots in these movies concentrated on high-emotional and high-activity situations, such as wild chases by the Keystone Cops, trains approaching stalled cars on railway crossings, death, grief, or torrid love scenes. These situations were self-explanatory and required few interruptions by printed dialogue.

In recent years the study of nonverbal communication in humans has attracted the attention of many workers in psychology, sociology, anthropology, and biology. This interest stems from work on animal behavior by ethologists, such as Lorenz, Tinbergen, and Morris. Popular books examining human behavior from an ethological viewpoint, such as *On Aggression* by Lorenz (1966), *The Naked Ape* by Morris (1968), and *The Human Animal* by Hass (1970), have extended this information to a very wide audience. Reaction has been positive in many cases and negative in others. These differing views revolve around the concept discussed earlier concerning continuity between animal and human behavior. Acceptance of a continuity in behavior systems with animals and humans provides insight for some and abhorrence for others. However, scientific evidence accumulated over recent years has helped to sway opinion toward acceptance of some similarities in our behavior and that of some animals. For instance, certain specific human behavior patterns, such as expressions of joy, grief, and anger, are inherited or are inborn, like many patterns in animals. Innate releasing stimuli, such as "infant characteristics" (described in detail later), initiate child-caring responses in humans, just as the red topside marking in male sticklebacks initiates aggression in other male sticklebacks. Many discrete aspects of social behavior parallel those found in primates. A chimpanzee youngster, like a human child, seems to be attached by elastic to its parent when it is investigating its environment: it moves a short distance, plays with some object, returns to the parent, moves off again to play with some other thing, then returns to the parent. This sequence repeats itself over and over again. These exploratory forays are virtually identical in the two species. As the youngsters age, the forays are longer, but contact with the parent is still maintained, sometimes by the youngster's simply turning and waiting until the parent looks his way and sometimes by his returning to the adult. In another social situation, adult baboons and humans show amazing tolerance to infant attempts to wrestle or to initiate contact play with them. These same adults maintain an aggressive or aloof attitude toward other members of their species; the tolerance and playful reaction are unique to adult-infant interactions.

HUMAN EMOTIONS

The important role of emotions in human behavior is underlined by evidence that emotions are inborn and that certain expressions of them are similar to fixed action patterns. If different expressions of emotion are examined in different races and groups of humans, we find a remarkable similarity, in spite of widely divergent backgrounds, rearing patterns, and cultures. Expressions of fear, happiness, humor, joy, grief, surprise, boredom, and astonishment are similar for North Americans, Germans, French, Spanish, South American Indians, New Guinea natives and Japanese, despite some differences in conventional or socialized elements in the expression of these emotions from one culture to another.

These observations suggest there are fixed action patterns structured in the human genetic pattern. This concept is supported by observations of blind-deaf children by Eibl-Eibesfeldt (1970). These children have no opportunity to learn emotional expressions through visual or sound imitation. However, they laugh normally, throwing back their head, opening their mouths, and making rhythmic laughing sounds. They show anger by stomping their feet, shaking their head, and clenching their teeth. Their patterns of crying and expression of grief are identical to those of normal children. These expressions must be inborn, since these children cannot imitate the patterns of other people. The continuance of such expressions in blind-deaf children, however, does not always follow that of normal children. Crying continues at a normal rate, but smiling declines as time passes. Presumably this is due to the reactions these two patterns evoke in the parent. The parent will comfort a crying child and will smile back at a smiling child. For the blind child the smile is not rewarded as crying is, so smiling declines. Thus, the origins of these emotions are inborn but their maintenance requires learning experience.

HUMAN EXPRESSIVE BEHAVIOR

Many behavior postures shown by humans convey information to others, just as expressive behavior in animals does. In addition, many patterns seem to be ritualized. Excitement, for instance, is often shown in a stereotyped fashion. The person stands or jumps up, with the posture of the body forming the shape of an X, the arms and leg extended. Often the hands are drawn toward the body then raised again rhythmically; these movements may be accompanied by shouts. Children, before they can crawl, show a similar posture; lying prone on the floor they extend their leg and arms rhythmically making shrieks and gurgling sounds at the same time. Adults show the excitement posture in sporting events, during a football or hockey game for example, as they leap to their feet cheering when a goal is scored. This pattern has been ritualized for many situations. A wrestler or boxer who wins has hand or hands raised above the head. A referee at a football game signifies a goal by raising both hands over the head. Cheerleaders at football games exaggerate the positions of the arms and legs by using colorful pompoms as "supernormal stimuli" and try to generate excitement by performing repeated patterns of this display. Thus, the ritualized pattern that signifies scoring or winning is derived from an excitement display that is probably innate.

Mouth-to-mouth contact, usually involving exchanging food, is found in many species, including humans. In humans it probably became ritualized to kissing. The origin of this ritualization process can be seen through intermediate stages in other species. Many birds feed their young by passing food or regurgitated food into their mouth. Often in these species the adults perform a courtship pattern that is identical to this feeding behavior. The female bird crouches and "begs" while making a wing-trembling movement similar to that observed in the young. The male responds by passing food to the female, and pair formation takes place. Young jackals cause the adults to regurgitate food by muzzling the mouth area. Wolves and seals mouth one another in greeting displays. Chimpanzee mothers transfer food to their young with their mouths but greet adults by kissing. Bushwomen kiss-feed their babies. In many societies high intensity kissing includes tongue movements into the partner's mouth similar to those necessary for food transfer. Kissing may have developed through the process of ritualization (as described above) in which the function was altered from giving food to showing affection to a child, then to an adult. This transfer of function is similar to that described earlier with peacock courtship, where the original pattern of feeding was altered to a courtship display.

Bowing is another expressive behavior found in most cultures. The extent of the bow can vary from a slight bending of the head forward, to bowing fully from the waist, to the most extreme form, where the person lies prostrate on the ground. This pattern has the common function of indicating subservience, either to other persons, such as monarchs or leaders, or to spiritual beings, such as God, Buddha, or Allah.

These expressive behaviors and many others, such as shaking a closed fist, greeting others at a distance with an open upraised hand, or raising the eyebrows, are just a few of the many body movements that convey meaning in the absence of speech. One just has to see or experience the problem of two people communicating to one another when they speak different languages. Gestures, facial expressions, and body movements usually allow some degree of understanding. Similar actions, although somewhat dampened, serve the same function (in normal conversation with others) by amplifying or clarifying communication.

RELEASING STIMULI IN HUMANS

The success of modern advertising in many instances seems to stem from the use of key "releasing stimuli." These stimuli may be learned or inborn. Attractive adult models or small children are used to hold the interest of spectators while the message is given. The interest of the audience is maintained by the sexual or child-caring response to the actors and not by the soap product or cleaning agent advertised.

K. Lorenz suggested that the child-caring response in humans is released by specific stimuli possessed by the infant. These include round, protruding cheeks, large head in proportion to the body, large protruding forehead, large eyes below the head midline, short, thick legs and arms, rounded body shape, soft elastic skin, and behavioral clumsiness. These cues in the child or in other objects release parental interest. "Parental" is used in its broadest sense, as young children show the same response toward dolls and other objects. Many products, such as comic strip characters, dolls, dogs, and cartoons, possess these cues, which consciously or unconsciously attract interest. All the characters in the comic strip "Peanuts" have huge rounded heads relative to their bodies which have short, thick arms and legs. Mickey Mouse, in addition to the above cues, has huge eyes below the head midline, along with protruding cheeks and forehead, Donald Duck is similar, but, in addition, he is clumsy. Most Disney characters have some combination of the cues Lorenz outlined. The cues are not only present but also exaggerated to such a degree that they elicit a "supernormal" response, which many account for their wide appeal.

Dolls that are considered "cute" contain differing combinations of the qualities Lorenz mentioned, e.g., the large eyes, large forehead, and exaggerated cheeks. Dolls with short, thick arms and legs, a rounded body, and even soft elastic skin also are found. Popular stuffed animals, such as teddy bears, rabbits, and other animals, possess high combinations of the releasing stimuli Lorenz listed. Many fashionable breeds of dogs possess some of these qualities as well. Pekinese, small Terriers, Corgies, and Basset Hounds have large heads, short appendages, and rounded shapes that are considered cute, where as other "functionally" bred varieties, with long legs and sharp features, such as greyhounds, Great Danes, and Afghans, are not "cute". It seems that the high level of interest that people have in some animals, dolls, and forms of entertainment stems from an instinctive response to releasing stimuli associated with infants.

TERRITORIAL BEHAVIOR

A somewhat more complex form of behavior that humans share with other species is territorialism. A common behavioral characteristic of humans is the control of things and space. In many instances, the defense of these involves nonverbal communication. Territory has been defined as any defended area. Later definitions include the degree to which an area is used exclusively by its occupants. This element is included because of variations seen in different animals. One animal may immediately attack any animal that crosses a boundary, whereas another may simply use chemical markers to indicate its border, seldom attacking others.

The term territory has, in fact, been applied to a bewildering variety of situations. The bitterling, a small fish, defends a mussel in which its eggs are deposited. As the mussel moves around the bitterling follows, defending it from other bitterlings. Many songbirds defend large territories, in which they nest, rear young, and gather food. Others, such as bank swallows, may only defend nest sites. Wolves have two forms of territory. While traveling in packs, they may cruise around a hundred-square-mile area, urinating at "scent posts" on the periphery. Adjoining wolf packs mark the same scent posts to indicate their presence. In the spring pairs of wolves break off from the pack and form their own smaller territory, which is marked in the same fashion by the male. The young are born and reared through the summer in this area, then the packs reform. Dragonflies patrol the ponds in which their eggs were laid, driving out other dragonflies. This variety of behavior indicates the difficulty in describing a particular behavior as "territorial behavior." The problem arises from the term territory itself, which suggests that the main item of concern is defense of space. In fact, the defense is not of space but of things. The bitterling is defending the mussel, not the space around it. The songbirds are defending nest sites, food sites, and their young. The wolves are doing the same, and the dragonfly is defending its eggs. This distinction becomes clear in studies of catbirds. Males arrive back on the breeding grounds first, and establish territories by singing and fighting with adjoining males. These territories usually include several thick bushes that are potential nest sites. When the females return, some territory boundaries shift. If the female selects a nest site within the former boundaries there may be few changes. However, if she chooses one near the edge or just outside, a new boundary is formed by the male, extended out and around the nest site. After the eggs are laid and incubation begins, the original boundaries shrink and the nest area becomes the center of a new, smaller territory. When the young hatch and fledge, it changes once again. The young move about through other territories, defended by their parents. Clearly, defense of an area is not the important factor here. The critical factor is defense of certain items: the potential nest site, the nest site, the active nest, and fledglings within the area.

Other species of animals may defend a specific area throughout a season or year. In this situation it is difficult to decide what aspects of the territory are being defended. The concept of territorialism thus shows such a range in variety that a single definition does not apply. The term includes the aspect of defense, but the concept of space or things to be defended has to be examined on the level of the individual species. Also, the methods and mechanisms of defense vary considerably. Clawing bark off a tree by bears, howling by wolves, fighting by dogs, adopting threat postures by many species, and chasing off their competitors are just a few of the actions taken to communicate to others that this is a particular territory.

Again, care is taken to argue that the "continuity" between territorialism in animals and humans is in question. It seems strange that there is such widespread acceptance that humans show territorial behavior, a phenomenon first described and studied in animals. However, arguments are brought forward to show that human territorialism is fundamentally different from animal territorialism. One argument concerns its origin. Territorialism in many animals is accepted as having a genetic basis. Humans, it is argued, *learn* to be territorial. If we consider territorialism in terms of defending things, this becomes difficult to accept. All humans defend things. The degree of defense and the things defended vary considerably according to the age group, the social status, and the culture to which one belongs. The concept of "mine" appears early in childhood, whereas the concept of "sharing" seems to require intensive training. Children become very possessive of toys and home territories, often punishing trespassers with physical and verbal aggression. It is difficult to accept that a concept as universal as territorialism, which appears so early in children, is resistant to change through learning, and is found in closely related primates, has a different origin than its counterpart in other animals.

Other arguments consider the varieties of territory that humans have, compared to animals. Humans have territories in separate areas, such as the home, the office, and the club. We defend children and spouses for a much longer time than most animals. We have cognitive territories. We defend our writing, our films, and our music—products of our thoughts—with copyright laws. Patent rights defend our inventions. Examination of territories of animals also shows much variety. A swan mates for life, but a catbird mates for only a season. A cowbird male defends only its mate, while a robin defends its mate, its territory, its nest, and its young. Many of the differences in types of territory in humans reflects our technological development. The patents, copyrights, and office defense are just a few. We simply have more things to defend. Although the things defended change, the basic concept (defense) remains the same for *all* animal species.

Many actions of humans can be classified as territorial behavior. In western society we protect our cars, houses, bodies, and other goods with insurance, with laws, or through personal confrontation. Each member of a family will have his own chair at the kitchen table. Parents have their bedroom, children have theirs, individuals have their clothes and their belongings. Many items are defended. Personal space may be violated in certain situations, such as in elevators or crowded buses, whereas similar violations in uncrowded conditions lead to either aggression or withdrawal.

Territories are marked in many ways. Hedges and fences can be used around homes to outline property borders. Hostile looks and facial expressions can deter people from approaching areas. In public areas books or items of clothing can be left behind to reserve chairs in libraries or cafeterias. Sommer and Becker (1969) did a study of public territories in a study hall, cafeteria, soda fountain, and university library. In the library they found that people occupied the end chairs on a long table if they wished to avoid others. If they wished to keep others away from the whole table, they occupied central chairs. This latter technique did work to a degree, as people avoided the table if other tables were available. Marking of these territories allowed them to be held in the absence of the "owner." If personal markers, such as a sweater or notebook, were left, the seat remained vacant longer than it did if nonpersonal items, such as library journals, were left. In addition to the markers, students in nearby chairs sometimes defended the unoccupied chairs by telling others, if asked, that someone recently occupied the chair. Similar observations were made in other public situations, such as the cafeteria and soda fountain.

Defensive behavior operates not only within a culture but also between cultures as well. International laws exist for the protection of fish stocks. Treaties exist for protection from aggression by other nations. Major nations engage in never-ending circles of arms growth and improvement of war technology, justifying this as a means of preserving peace. Paradoxically, this is correct. Threats serve to reduce overt aggression. Threat postures serve the same function in animals. A stickleback male adopts a head-down posture when another male approaches his territory. A catbird spreads its body feathers and points its bill up in similar circumstances. A dog stands still-legged, snarls, baring its teeth, and raises the hair on its back. All these threat postures serve to communicate the aggressive state of the individual to others. Usually the threat is sufficient to prevent over-aggression from starting, and thus, it paradoxically reduces fighting.

Territorial behavior in humans is therefore found in many forms, ranging through the personal level to family groups, clubs, and other social units and continuing up to cultural and national levels. Defense also is wide-ranging, from frowns to killing, depending on the situation. Defense of things in our environment by humans is such a pervasive behavior that we have developed comprehensive mechanisms to avoid escalation of aggression to the point of violence. We have verbal and cultural cues that permit us to recognize other territories. A sweater on a library chair, a no trespassing sign, a fence, a locked door, and knowledge of laws are just a few items that communicate the territory of others. Understanding and responding to these cues mean aggression rarely occurs.

CONCLUSIONS

Human language is not the only means we have to communicate to one another. Language is the best tool available for expressing some types of information, but we make extensive use of other communication mechanisms as well. Verbal language, body language, emotional expressions, and other behavioral actions combine in a complex fashion to serve as an integral communications form for humans. Awareness of the integration of these nonverbal elements has developed from studies of communication in other animals. Animals, for the most part, make extensive use of expressive behavior, such as threat displays and other stereotypic postures, actions, and calls to signal to one another. Comparative studies of these revealed certain basic forms in terms of their origins, development, and expression. Once these basic systems were observed it became obvious that many human behaviors had similar characteristics. Human emotional expressions are inherited. We react to "key stimuli" just as other species react to "key stimuli" necessary for their success. We also engage in extensive forms of territorialism. Although our technological environment affects what is defended, the concept of defense remains in a form similar to territorialism in other animals. Actions and actions combined with words form the complex communication systems that humans use. Words and actions cannot be separated, one to be judged more important than the other. They each serve as parts of the whole communication mechanism.

REFERENCES

Boice, R. 1976. In the shadow of Darwin. In: R. G. Green and E. C. O'Neal (eds.), Perspectives on Aggression. Academic Press, New York.

Cruze, W. W. 1935. Maturation and learning in chicks. J. Comp. Psychol. 19:371–409.

DeVore, I. 1963. Mother infant relations in free-ranging baboons. In: H. Rheingold (ed.), Maternal Behavior in Mammals. John Wiley & Sons, New York.

DeVore, I. 1965. Changes in population structure of Nairobi Park baboons 1951–1963. In: H. Vatgberg (ed.), The Baboon in Medical Research. University of Texas Press, Austin.

Eibl-Eibesfeldt, I. 1961. The Interactions of Unlearned Behaviour Patterns and Learning in Mammals. Symposium on Brain Mechanisms and Learning. CIOMS Montevideo. Blackwells, Oxford.

Eibl-Eibesfeldt, I. 1970. The Biology of Behavior. Holt, Rinehart & Winston, New York.

Hass, H. 1970. The Human Animal. Dell Publishing Co., New York.

Hebb, D. O., and W. R. Thompson. 1968. The social significance of animal studies. In: G. Lindzey and E. Aronson (eds.), Handbook of Social Psychology, 2nd Ed., vol. 2, pp. 729–774. Addison-Wesley, Reading, Massachusetts.

Hess, E. H. 1956. Space perceptions in the chick. Sci. Am. 195:71–80.

Lorenz, K. 1966. On Aggression. Harcourt, Brace & World, New York.

Marler, P. and M. Tamura. 1964. Culturally transmitted patterns of vocal behaviors in sparrows. Science 146:1483–86.

Morris, D. 1968. The Naked Ape. McGraw-Hill Book Co., New York.

Sherif, C. W. 1976. Orientation in Social Psychology. Harper & Row, New York.

Sommer, R., and F. D. Becker. 1969. Territorial Defence and the Good Neighbour. J. Pers. Soc. Psychol. 11:85–92.

Tinbergen, N. 1951. The Study of Instinct. Oxford University Press. Oxford.

Van Lawick-Goodall, J. 1971. In the Shadow of Man. Houghton Miffin Co., Boston.

Chapter 10
ENVIRONMENTAL PSYCHOLOGY

Buildings — We Shape Them;
Do They Shape Us?

J. A. Darley

More attention has been focused on the human environment in recent years than ever before. Much of this has been provoked by alarming increases in destructive behavior, such as crime and vandalism. A higher level of crime on a per capita basis is found in cities than is found in rural environments. Is the city environment at the root of these problems?

Natural or country environments are for the most part slowly changing, self-correcting systems. An abandoned farm will return to its original state, growing weeds, bushes, and eventually trees, given enough time. City environments change rapidly and are not self-correcting. An abandoned paved parking lot or cement sidewalk is much more resistant to change and to return to its original state than an abandoned field. In addition, relatively more of natural or cultivated growth disappears in cities as time goes on than disappears in the country. Cities also have large numbers of people in a small area. Perhaps the more or less permanent disappearance of the natural environment and the crowding together of humans have contributed to the high levels of destructive behavior.

Are we genetically prepared for city life? Humans, like all living organisms, are the products of their ancestral environments. These environments have shaped our bodies and behavior through the mechanism of evolution. In the past, humans with physical or behavioral attributes that made them more successful than others in their existing environment were the ones who reproduced and kept their genes in the human gene pool. Humans with physical or behavioral deficiencies were less likely to have young, and their genes were lost from the gene pool. This mechanism, operating over thousands and thousands of generations, shaped us physically and behaviorally into the creatures we are today. Males, with their large muscle masses, were shaped for strenuous exertion. Females were shaped physically and behaviorally for child-bearing and raising. Children were shaped physically and behaviorally to elicit child-caring responses in their parents and siblings. Our behavior and physical structure has been molded by the millions of years of ancestral environment.

This ancestral environment was considerably different from our present environment both physically and socially. Humans lived in small social groups or tribes and maintained their existence by hunting and gathering food. Their living accommodations were often temporary, as they had to move from place to place to obtain sufficient food. At that time most adults spent the majority of their time searching for food. Social ties were very strong within the group or tribe because humans often had to work together to succeed in hunting and fishing expeditions. Groups were restricted in numbers by the amount of food they could collect in the area around their camps. Contact with strangers was limited as populations were scattered, because overlap of hunting and food-gathering areas would lead to starvation.

The hunting environment for our human ancestors probably began as far back as fourteen million years ago. Because evolution is for the most part a very slow process requiring many generations for change in the gene pool, sufficient time certainly was available to shape humans for the hunting-gathering existence. Sufficient time certainly was *not* available to shape humans for our present environment. It is only in the last 10,000 years, or less than 1000 generations, that humans have been free from the hunting existence.

Agriculture began at that time. Cultivation of food supplies and domestication of animals meant that a few individuals could provide sufficient food to feed many. The limiting factor, food, was removed and populations increased.

The social environment radically changed along with the physical environment. People remained in specific areas close to the farmlands and built permanent housing. Thus, the environmental situation today in many ways is diametrically opposed to the environment found earlier. Socially, in Western societies competition between individuals is encouraged and crowding and high rates of contact with strangers is common. Physically, there is reduced contact with the natural environment and more permanent ties with a specific area, house, apartment, or town. The nomadic hunting in close cooperation with a limited number of other humans no longer exists for most present-day individuals.

Many of our present-day behavior patterns reflect ancestral roles. These have sometimes been interpreted as responses to our biological roots. In Western cultures hunting and fishing are almost exclusively a male preserve, as they were for ancestral humans. Male cooperative groups, such as clubs and sporting teams, are common. Spectators at baseball, hockey, football, and soccer matches are predominantly males. These are so popular that outstanding players command huge salaries, often receiving more than the leaders of the countries they live in. The popularity of these activities may be rooted in biological needs or drives.

As urbanization continues, "back to nature" trends increase in intensity and volume. This activity ranges from the current vogue for blue jeans (the traditional wear for country dwellers), organic gardening, natural food diets, and camping, to desertion of the city to subsist on marginal farms, self-supporting communes, commuting to work, purchasing a country retreat, and many others.

Camping popularity, for instance, has increased dramatically. In the United States the number of people who use the wilderness increased from 5% in 1946 to 15% in 1967. What are the psychological needs that are satisfied by this behavior? The commonest response is that camping allows a change in role from one of the spectator to one of the participant. It is psychologically rewarding to cope with the elements relying on one's own ability. When camping, there is a change from the typical urban behavior, and cooperation with other campers is observed and expected. Family ties are strengthened at campsites. Camping also provides a situation for new role playing, where pioneer roles can be acted out: hunting, fishing, cooking with primitive facilities, and chopping wood. The ever growing popularity of camping may be a reaction against the urban environment, because roles are simplified and social communities are reduced in size.

Not only are people obtaining relief from urban stress by temporary or permanent absence, but many are working hard within the cities to reduce the scale of urban structure and change. Attempts to preserve historic buildings have met with considerable success. Modern high-rise buildings dwarf humans in size, obscure views, and eliminate sunlight; historic buildings and houses seldom do. Human perspective is lost in the deep valleys of concrete, brick, and glass seen in many downtown areas of cities. Environmental groups, working to prevent the spread of this form of architecture into residential areas, have been given wide public support. Municipal government has also responded to the extent that the present Mayor of Toronto has attempted to prevent high-rise development in downtown Toronto and to encourage people-oriented structures and activities. His success is shown in the change in the Toronto city environment. Municipal leaders' attitudes are beginning to change from the old standard of "How much taxes will a new building generate to pay for the other required facilities?" to "How will the proposed structure add or detract from the human needs of the city dwellers?"

Another trend we see in Western cultures as population levels increase is a *focusing on oneself*. As the significance of an individual diminishes in the presence of millions of other humans, increased concern and energy are devoted to establishing a stronger self-image. Eastern spiritualism, transcendental meditation, primal therapy to express individual emotions, mind expanding drugs, personal psychoanalysis, and many other forms of narcissistic behavior can be interpreted as a means of strengthening the personal self-image or understanding oneself better.

The question concerning our genetic preparation for city life cannot be resolved. We have not had sufficient time to adapt biologically to our new environment. However, our genetic makeup for the hunting-gathering tribal environment *may* provide sufficient plasticity to include the new environment. Many of the activities of urban dwellers include bits of behavior that mirror activities of our hunting ancestors. Perhaps these, the upswing in "back to nature" activities, widespread preservation, the cleaning of the environment, and the humanizing of cities, will be sufficient to curb the destructive activities we engage in. Humans have succeeded in surviving widely divergent natural environments, ranging from the Arctic to the desert regions; urban settings may be conquered as well.

Humans have altered their environment to an extent seen in no other organism. After the development of farming, which enables a few people to feed many, the people, freed from the food collecting role, turned their ingenuity to technological development. Success has been so great that we are now dwarfed by our own technology. This is especially evident in city cores, which have become groups of sky-scraper office buildings interspersed with a variety of transit systems. The offices house the machinery and the people to run various facets of our technology. The transportation permits people to get to and from the office or stores where technical products and services can be obtained. Residents of these core areas tend to leave. In the Manhattan section of New York, for instance, half of the population has left since 1905. Few people wish to live in city centers.

Transportation has increased in priority to the point where two-thirds of available space in Los Angeles core areas is devoted to the automobile (roads, services, and parking). Lewis Mumford (1961) wrote, "The time is approaching in many cities when there will be every facility for moving about the city and no possible reason for going there." In spite of the increase in transit systems, efficiency has declined to the point where it is more expensive to move an orange from the West Side of Manhattan to the East Side than it is to bring it from Florida to New York. The priority of transportation has reached the point where a planning report for Los Angeles described the pedestrian as the major obstacle to free traffic movement. It is factors and attitudes like these that contribute to the depersonalization of city environments.

Does crowding contribute to the increased crime rates and social breakdown? Let us examine some conclusions presented by Booth and Walsh (1973). The highest rates of juvenile delinquency are found in the highest crowding density situations, using number of people per room in dwelling units to measure crowding. Similarly, crimes of homicide and civil disorder, such as riots, were correlated with high levels of crowding, again using the person-per-room measure of density. International aggression seems to have been strongly related to person-per-acre population measures. These recent observations suggest that population density may be associated with juvenile crimes, homicide, and violence.

It should be pointed out that crowding has to be considered relative to particular cultures. What is considered crowded by North American or English standards is not crowded by Chinese standards in Hong Kong. Densities in Hong Kong are ten times the maximum permitted by the London County Council for Greater London. The Housing Authority in Hong Kong thinks nothing of densities of 2,000 people per acre in 16-story public-housing units. Six people live in apartments of 210 square feet. Two hundred people per acre is the *maximum* for the city of London. Different cultural mechanisms exist to permit different levels of population density. In Hong Kong, Michelson (1970) and Mitchell (1971) noted, Chinese cope with the high levels of crowding with their styles of family functioning, social organizations, and other cultural means.

Mental and physical illness also have been correlated with population densities. Galle et al. (1972) demonstrated correlations between mortality and mental-hospital admission rates. In addition, a higher level of psychosomatic illness, anxiety, and tension is found in crowded homes (Marsella et al., 1970).

Certain housing environments can contribute to high rates of juvenile deliquency and crime. In a study of social behavior and public housing, Newman (1973) noted that high levels of crime and vandalism can be caused by such factors as building design and site layout. He discussed design and layout in terms of "defensible space," which is defined as an area enclosed by barriers, such as houses and fenced yards, or areas controlled through other factors, such as facilities used by limited specific groups. Shared entrances and areas allowing surveillance, such as a courtyard used by a small number of units, are considered as defensive areas. Criminal activity is discouraged in these areas because of the group cohesion, mutual aid, and surveillance that results from this kind of arrangement.

High-rise buildings have proportionately less defensible areas than low-rise buildings. They have several entrances that are used by large numbers of people, because many more live in the building. Stairwells, elevators, and hallways are considered public areas and have limited surveillance. It is in these areas where most crime and vandalism is found. Grounds around high rises are usually much greater in extent than those around small buildings. This decreases surveillance opportunities as well as weakening territorial feelings by the inhabitants. Low-rise dwellings are conducive to a stronger territorial sense. Residents know more neighbors and at the same time exercise a more defensive attitude toward their outside living space. In examining felony rates on a per capita basis for four categories of building height, the rate for the shortest (two or three floors) was approximately half that for the tallest (16 floors or more). Newman (1973) attributes much of this to the anonymity in the high-rise buildings. Residents can seldom distinguish other residents from nonresidents so criminals can come and go with little chance of being identified.

A classic example of failure of high-rise public housing is the Pruitt-Igoe project in St. Louis. In spite of an acute shortage of housing, people refused to remain in the project. Some of these buildings were demolished after occupancy of only 19 or 20 years. Reasons for the project's failure included high rates of crime and vandalism, poor opportunities for social contacts, isolation from the surrounding community, and poor admininstration.

This dramatic failure, with its huge cost losses, has affected the development of new housing. In San Francisco a low-cost project has included consultation between architects and potential users. This allowed the architects to determine the needs of a group of people they know little about. In addition, the economic limitations were spelled out for the users. The resulting design consisted of two-story duplexes designed to emphasize privacy for individual families. Semiprivate areas, such as gardens, were included to encourage interaction between families. In this project, the physical setting and the social setting were considered together as a vital requirement to ensure user satisfaction.

A number of general observations have now been made on the effect urban living has on humans. For example, Milgram (1970) pointed out that many of the characteristic qualities of city life can be considered to be adaptations to urban "overload." He reported that on his first arrival in New York he was caught in pushing crowds, people bumped into him without apology, drunks on the street were stepped over without a glance, and he observed two people actually fighting for a cab. Why do humans behave differently in the city than they do outside the city? In the city, Milgram suggests, humans are bombarded with too much information. If they responded to everything they encountered, their own lives would be chaos. In response to this overload situation, adaptations take place, priorities are set, and choices are made. City dwellers become acquainted with fewer people than rural inhabitants and maintain more superficial relationships even with these acquaintances. They disregard drunks or people sick on the street. Social contact is reduced by such devices as unlisted telephone numbers, telephones off the hook, or a scowling face to discourage others from speaking. These city responses protect individuals from overload but at the same time separate them from their social environment.

Social responsibility in cities is also restricted. It ranges from refusal to become involved in desperate situations to withdrawal of common courtesies, such as offering a lady a seat. An example of the former occurred in a suburb of Queens in 1964 when Katherine Genovese, coming home from a late night job, was stabbed many times over a long period of time. Thirty-eight residents of her neighborhood witnessed some part of the attack. However, nobody responded to her pleas for help. No one called the police until she was dead.

This event was examined by Milgram and Hollander in "The Nation." They observed that friends are not formed in cities on the basis of physical proximity. Miss Genovese had many friends, but they were all miles away. Second, her cries for help were not *directed to a specific* person, so none felt obliged to respond. Another factor in the adaptation to city life was called "collective paralysis," that is, each felt someone surely would have telephoned the police. This observation has been supported by laboratory studies of bystander intervention. In a situation where smoke was coming into a room, it was noted that the larger the number of bystanders the less likely it was that any would respond to the potential emergency (Latané and Darley, 1969).

It is not just lack of concern for others that lowers bystander intervention; nonintervention is a rule of urban life because emotional privacy is a difficult commodity to find in such a crowded environment. For the individual, it is hard to tell whether a response by a bystander would be seen as interference or as the proper response to a critical situation. If husband and wife are quarreling on a city street, at what point should a bystander interfere? The city produces greater tolerance in ethics, dress, and behavior, and this tolerance extends to withholding aid for fear of annoying the participants. The importance of this emotional privacy is indicated by the fact that Chicago police responding to calls about domestic quarrels have a higher probability of getting killed than on any other police duty.

Urbanites also have a higher fear of physical vulnerability. Studies where students asked to use the telephone in cities and small towns indicated that significantly more were allowed into the house in small towns than in the city (Altman et al., 1969). In the city, 75% of the people communicated by shouting through closed doors; as opposed to in towns where 75% opened the door. This fear in urbanites could account for some of the reserve that they exhibit.

Anonymity is another factor that also alters the behavior of urbanites. Someone involved in a car accident who leaps out to scream at the other driver does not do so if the other driver is a friend. Thus, in a small community where everyone knows each individual, behavior is moderated by this fact. In a large city, where most people are strangers, these behavioral restraints are not present. This was shown clearly in a study of car vandalism. In an observational study by Zimbardo (1969), two cars were left 64 hours on public streets, one near the Bronx campus at New York University and the other in the small town of Palo Alto near Stanford University. The license plates were removed and the hoods raised. The New York car was stripped of all movable parts within a day and reduced to a wreck in 3 days. The Palo Alto car was not touched, and one individual even lowered the hood when it started to rain. Zimbardo attributed the difference in behavior to social anonymity in the Bronx, although the socioeconomic composition of the surrounding population may have had something to do with it.

VANDALISM

What factors lead to the high levels of vandalism we observe in cities today? Anonymity is an important factor. Individuals who know they are unlikely to be recognized can vandalize with relative impunity. High-rise, family-unit buildings often have high levels of property destruction. One of the parents' common complaints in these units is that they cannot supervise their children. A mother working in a tenth-floor apartment cannot see her child playing in a ground-level playground or elsewhere in the building. Other tenants rarely know the children or the parents and thus have no effective control over their behavior either directly or indirectly. If the child wishes to go to the toilet, he is less likely to go up ten floors to his apartment than to use the closest secluded area, such as the elevator or stairwell.

Sommer (1974) suggested that a "hardening" of our environment, both physically and behaviorally, could be a reason for increased vandalism. It could be that humans react to the inhuman environments by defacing or destroying them. (In California, restrooms in city parks have vandal-proof fixtures installed. Advertisements for these fixtures show a man attacking a toilet with a sledgehammer!) A recreation director of parks in California described measures to cope with the problem of vandalism: new recreation buildings are made of concrete blocks, rather than brick or wood; there is no exposed plumbing, fixtures are cast aluminum covered with hard epoxy; picnic tables are made of concrete and are embedded three feet into the ground. A similar trend is found in childrens' playgrounds in school yards, which may be covered with asphalt, be surrounded with steel mesh walls containing heavy steel, and have concrete playground equipment. In cities like Los Angeles most of the area around buildings is covered with asphalt or concrete roads and parking lots. In addition to this, in Los Angeles the river bed is lined with cement! Subways are made of concrete or are faced with hard glazed tiles. Gray or dark green subway cars, with their hard, uncomfortable seats, are designed with surfaces to resist vandalism. In an official report to the Mayor of New York by Ervin Galantay (1967), the subway environment was described as "the world's most squalid environment."

No one should be surprised that these public environments are subjected to attack by vandals. The large-scale, multicolored slogans painted on subway cars in New York are often far more attractive than the cars themselves. The cat faces painted on the large sewer covers draining into the Los Angeles river are improvements on an otherwise stark, cement-lined river bank. These impersonal surroundings are given a human touch only by the graffiti that appear on them.

Alternative explanations to vandalism have been cited, such as envy, deprivation, and anger. These all have to be considered as possible bases to the widespread vandalism observed today.

Sommer points out that public attitudes are "hard" as well. For example, prison officials usually recommend single cells for inmates, which permit better control, increase privacy and personal dignity, protect weaker inmates, and reduce homosexual attacks. Nevertheless, the officials who publicly support this may be accused in the press of "coddling convicts." The minimum effect that imprisonment should have on an individual is that he leaves no worse than when he entered, but this is unlikely to be the case with the present system. As a further example, plans for attractive public housing often meet with strong opposition in North America. Why should taxpayers reward the poor with good housing? The resultant poor quality housing is just another indication that people do not really care for those on welfare. Poor workmanship is only one of the many problems involved in public housing.

Many slums for welfare communities are found in city core areas where certain advantages exist. Rents are low and transportation costs are minimal, since people can walk to nearby facilities. The community can provide considerable social interaction, as most people have common problems and strong neighborhood relationships. These relationships are major sources of resident satisfaction. Many residents have spent much of their lives in the area and consider it their home. Studies in some slums have shown that the majority of the inhabitants like living in the area, a fact that probably surprises most middle-class people. New public housing creates new problems and usually leads to considerable distress. For example, rents may still be low relative to other accomodations but they usually are higher than previous rents. Moreover, new public housing is put on the cheapest land available, far from the downtown areas. Transportation is usually difficult, so that getting groceries or going to work becomes a problem. Situations have arisen where welfare agencies had to provide money to purchase cars so recipients could go to work. People removed from their former community are often separated into different subgroups and in some cases have been assigned houses in new public housing in alphabetical order. This means the social fabric of the former community is completely torn. Old friendship groups, one of the major sources of residential satisfactions, are destroyed. Under these circumstances, it should be no surprise to see anger released through vandalism.

Hard environments and attitudes are found in student life as well. College dormitories and classrooms seem to be designed by architects to be somewhat uncomfortable so that students will not fall asleep. Study guides recommend straight-back chairs with no cushions. One typical statement reads "Do not read in bed as concentration will lapse" (Sommer, 1974). There are no studies to indicate that this is true. Few people would choose an uncomfortable chair to read a newspaper or magazine at home—why should the student be forced to do this? Often there are strict rules against students' hanging posters on walls, and this requires constant supervision to enforce. The reason cited is that removing posters damages the paint.

Similar situations are found in most working environments. People are not allowed to personalize their working area. Federal government office regulations prevent workers from hanging anything on walls, having plants or flowers, or rearranging furniture without permission. It is argued that employees are imposing their standards on others if they hang up a painting or make their areas more attractive. No one extends this argument to the employer who exposes everyone to the government-issue gray desks and bookcases and the picture of the President and agency director hanging on the wall. In fact, this is a well-known policy used in management training to combat individual favoritism. Thus, impersonal working conditions are not simply an oversight; these are carefully planned.

DESIGN: WHAT CAN BE DONE?

In the case of family high-rise living discussed earlier, either additional facilities should be made to allow for alternatives to traditional techniques of child-rearing and supervision, or housing facilities closer to traditional forms should be made available. Supervised playgrounds and day-care centers could be alternatives to parent supervision in high-rise or family units above ground levels. If this is not possible, low-rise developments would permit normal parent supervision.

The East Bay Municipal Park District in California was plagued by vandalism of the restrooms. Rather than attempting to make them more vandal resistant, they hired an amateur artist. He painted murals of nature scenes including mountains, trees, and grass on the outhouses. They have been free of vandalism since they opened (Sommer, 1974).

Additional planning is required to soften the concrete cities, using trees, grass, and flowers where concrete is not necessary. Unnecessary concrete in school yards and playgrounds can be eliminated. Britain is finding that "adventure" playgrounds are proving very popular with the children. Piles of boards, ropes, and nails are available. Some children build assorted structures or tear them down, while others dig holes and play games with and around things they designed and built themselves. Social skills, motor skills, and high personal involvement all develop in this playground environment (Hayward et al., 1974). This presents a striking contrast to the under-used asphalt playgrounds with steel equipment found in many North American communities.

Differences in subway systems seem also to show the effects of different environments on attitude and behavior. According to Galantay (1967), the squalid New York subway systems encourage littering. He asked, "How can you discourage litter in a huge litter bin?" Graffiti and vandalism levels are high. In contrast, the subway in Montreal has attractive stations and cars. Litter is put into litter bins; vandalism and graffiti levels are very low. In spite of these observations, taxpayers' attitudes are difficult to change. Efforts to make the Toronto subway more attractive through the installation of huge murals and sculptures by local artists met with strong resistance, as reported by recent newspaper articles. How could the subway commission consider squandering public monies on art for the subway system? This public outcry led to the suspension of the project.

In planning for public housing, serious consideration should be made to improve existing areas for the present inhabitants on the same site. This will permit us to preserve the advantages of existing services and at the same time to maintain the social fabric of the community. It must be recognized that the house itself is not the only factor of major importance. Suitable services should be available and attempts should be made to plan for the community as a unit.

In village dormitories at the University of California, the administration dropped their rule against wall posters and permitted the students themselves to paint their walls if they wished. The cost of painting (Hart, 1970) dropped to one-fifth of what it was (per room), as professional painters' wages were no longer necessary. In addition, instead of all rooms, only one in ten needed painting each year. Scratches and marks on old walls were covered by new posters. Through planning, new dormitory walls are made of soft cork or burlap over wood so that the students can hang whatever they wish. Similar changes can take place in work environments. Employees should be given the opportunities to personalize their working space. Additional costs for attractive, colorful furniture and surroundings are small, and the return is likely to be high in the psychological satisfaction of employees who realize that the administration is concerned for their welfare. Obviously, this is to be preferred to an impersonal approach in employer-employee relationships.

The argument by Sommer (1974) that the environment is "hardened" through semipermanent physical changes such as roads and high rises as well as through regulations in working and living environments is a plausible one. Such factors could be the basis of some of our present-day social problems, such as vandalism. According to Sommer, frustrations created in the impersonal environment explode into the destruction of property and the "personalizing" of problem objects with graffiti!

CITY STRUCTURE

What features of cities enhance peoples' satisfaction with urban life? The answer to this is of major concern, as most of the world's population lives in cities. Little information is currently available on the subject. Kevin Lynch's (1960) discussion in the *The Image of the City* makes a case for "legibility." A city whose parts are readily recognizable is more satisfying than one where an urbanite is frequently disoriented. Lynch interviewed citizens of several cities to determine what mental image they had of their cities. In addition, he had observers map these cities, gauging the "image strength" of various parts. From these studies he concluded that there were five principal elements that contributed to the image of the city: paths, nodes, edges, districts, and landmarks.

Paths are the elements used by most people to organize the image. These include streets, railroads, subways, and walkways. *Nodes* are junctions or centers of activity, ranging from transportation nodes where subways or bus lines intersect to enclosed shopping areas, including many shops under one roof. *Edges* are barriers to movement, such as railways, water edges, or borders of development. These are used by many to form a mental map of the city. *Districts* are sections of the city with a common feature, such as shopping or residential concentrations. *Landmarks* are used as points of reference and include such things as towers, historically significant buildings, statues, etc.

Cities with sufficient numbers of these elements provide a degree of comfort not only for the long-term dwellers but for people who visit the cities for short periods. People can maintain their orientation in this type of city with considerably less stress than in cities where one section looks much like another. In addition to the practical advantage of a city with a strong image, psychological effects could also be of importance. A city, or even an area, with a strong image or "personality" is more likely to be viewed as an attractive place to live than the faceless bland areas many people inhabit.

The environment of sound or noise in cities has also been examined. Evidence suggests that hearing is a more important psychological perception than sight. Studies of people who had suddenly become blind or deaf indicate that deafness has a much more severe effect than blindness. The deafening resulted in deep depression, feelings of loss, sadness, loneliness, paranoid tendencies, and lack of alertness.

Studies of sound in a city have been conducted to determine those sounds perceived as attractive or unattractive. Subjects were pushed in a wheelchair through a variety of districts of Boston, recording their perceptions of the city. Three groups were taken on the same path, one group was blindfolded, another had earplugs, and the third group was free to hear and observe. In this fashion, the sound environment and visual environment were examined separately by Groups 1 and 2 and were combined for Group 3.

The results showed that the preferred sounds were those that were quiet but informative, "people-sounds," such as conversation, whistling, and echoes in alleys and narrow streets. Nature sounds were rated highly, such as birds in the park or water sounds at the wharf. Sounds of cars and trucks were very annoying when close or moving, as they masked every other sound. However, subjects liked cars idling and liked traffic sounds at a distance. "Vision only" subjects had different perceptions of the same environment. The city appeared "surrealistic in its peacefulness' with the moving things appearing to float by. The city seemed sad and lacking contrast. They found more imperfections in the environment than other subjects. They described the waterfront as a very ugly place, with its openness, inactivity, and shoddy buildings. It appears that city planners should give strong consideration to controlling the impact of sounds in the city in order to provide an attractive environment in which people can live. Attempts should also be made to improve the visual environment. These should not only apply to new structures but to old buildings as well.

Satisfaction in residential areas has also been examined by Zehner (1972). His study of different suburbs with well-educated, well-to-do residents indicated that there were five general factors that contributed to residential satisfaction: neighborhood density, accessibility of facilities, house, social compatibility, and quality of neighborhood maintenance. A very important factor was neighborhood density. High levels of satisfaction came from people in the least dense neighborhoods. These provided the quietest environment with the most privacy. Facility accessibility was important for families with children, but it was not a feature correlated with neighborhood satisfaction. Social compatibility was important, although this did not mean that people interacted frequently with neighbors. The highest correlation with satisfaction came from neighborhood maintenance. Good maintenance of lawns, houses, and flowerbeds led to high satisfaction, and poor maintenance led to low satisfaction.

Observations on neighborhood satisfaction have also been made in an urban slum in Boston's West End. This area had a relatively stable population, with 55% either being born there or living there for 20 years or more. Only 10% disliked living in this slum, with 15% neutral and 75% positive. Two major factors were correlated with neighborhood satisfaction: first, the feeling that the areas outside the houses were important integral parts of the home environment, and second, the social ties or relationships with neighbors. People who held a strong feeling of belonging to a particular neighborhood also expressed feelings of familiarity and security and were very positive toward this area. People with considerable social contacts with other West End residents also expressed high satisfaction levels. Although those with kinship ties expressed higher satisfaction levels than those with high levels of nonkinship social contacts, the latter maintained high levels of neighborhood satisfaction as well. Moreover, there was considerable variation existing, as people with few social ties also liked the neighborhood. Many considered the area outside the houses as a contiguous part of the dwelling, and they had a feeling of belonging to an area rather than to just a home. In considering these observations it was noted that these results do not necessarily apply to all slum areas. Slum districts contain considerable differences in structure and ethnic composition, which could have some impact on attitudes about environment.

In cities some interesting cultural patterns have developed. A basic social institution found in the American black culture is the block club. Clubs normally include two blocks of residents along one side of the street. This social unit is used to maintain the area, clean up vacant lots, pave alleys, plant grass, sponsor Christmas lighting programs, and prevent landlords from overcrowding tenants. If a family does not comply with the rules of the block club, it is forced out. All adults are responsible for encouraging good behavior as well as for disciplining children in the club who do wrong. This is a sharp contrast to white communities, where child-rearing standards are controlled by the family. When blacks are moved to high-rise housing, the block club ceases to function because of the physical differences in housing layout. The results are a dramatic decline in social interaction between neighbors and a rapid increase in juvenile delinquency.

Middle-class whites are responsible for most planning of changes in the environment. Such changes are usually based on their own standards and on their own interpretation of what is necessary.

However, people must recognize that their standards are not the only ones. Different ethnic groups and different socioeconomic groups have developed behavior mechanisms to cope with their environments. These mechanisms have to be considered when changes in their environment are to take place. Once this has been done, perhaps we will see a decline in the social pathology that now seems to be increasing at alarming rates in city environments.

REFERENCES

Altman, D., M. Levine, M. Naden, and J. Villena. 1969. Trust of the stranger in the city and the small town. Unpublished research, Graduate Center, City University of New York.

Booth, A., and S. Walsh. 1973. The effects of crowding. A cross-national study. Paper presented at American Psychological Association, Montreal, Canada.

Fried, M., and P. Glercher. 1961. Some sources of residential satisfaction in an urban slum. J. Am. Inst. Plan. XXVII(4).

Galantay, E. 1967. Space time in Montreal. Nathan, May 1, p. 560.

Galle, O. R., W. R. Gove, and J. M. McPherson. 1972. Population density and pathology: What are the relationships for man? Science 176:23–30.

Hart, R. 1970. Room painting in the Residence Halls. Unpublished report, Davis Housing Office, University of California.

Hayward, D. G., M. Rosenberg, and R. R. Beasley. 1974. Children's play and urban environments. Environ. Behav. 6(2):131–168.

Latané, B. and J. M. Darley. 1969. Bystander "apathy." Am. Sci. 57(2):244–268.

Lynch, K. 1960. The Image of the City. MIT Press, Cambridge, Massachusetts.

Marsella, A. J., M. Escudero, and P. Gordon, 1970. The effects of dwelling density on mental disorders in Filipino men. J. Health Soc. Behav. 11(4):288–294.

Michelson, W. 1970. Man and his urban environment: A sociological approach. Addison-Wesley, Reading, Massachusetts.

Milgram, S. 1970. The experience of living in cities. Science 1167(3924): 1461–1468.

Mitchell, R. 1971. Some social implications of higher density housing. Am. Soc. Rev. 36:18–29.

Mumford, L. 1961. The city in history. Harcourt, Brace & World, New York.

Newman, O. 1973. Architectural design for crime prevention. National Institute of Law Enforcement and Criminal Justice, United States Department of Justice, Washington, D.C.

Zehner, R. B. 1972. Neighborhood and community satisfaction: A report on new towns and less planned suburbs. In: J. F. Wohlwill and D. H. Carson (eds.), Environment and the Social Sciences: Perspectives and Applications. American Psychological Association, Washington, D.C.

Zimbardo, P. G. 1969. The human choices: Individuation, reason, and order versus deindividuation, impulse, and chaos. In: W. J. Arnold and D. Levine (eds.), Nebraska Symposium on Motivation. University of Nebraska Press, Lincoln.

Chapter 11
CONCLUSIONS
Open Questions and Controversies

J. K. Chadwick-Jones

NEUROPSYCHOLOGY

In the chapter "Brain and Behavior: Recent Topics in Human Neuropsychology" (Chapter 3) we selected research evidence that illustrates neuropsychological approaches to the investigation of what particularly characterizes humans: language, handedness, cerebral dominance, and, ultimately, the experience of the self.

Several main points emerged from this discussion. First of all, we saw that the human brain, compared to the brains of all other animals, has the largest amount of neural tissue in the cortex and has developed the most efficient cross-communication system, the corpus callosum. The evolutionary story was once more picked up at the end of the chapter when we looked at research that addressed itself to the emergence of the self. We briefly looked at work with nonhuman primates and retarded humans, using self-recognition as the minimal condition necessary for the experience of self. Severely retarded humans seem not to experience a clear sense of self. Most nonhuman primates do not have the ability to recognize themselves, although the great apes are evidently an exception. The assumption underlying this type of research is that, with the evolution of the brain, something happened to make possible the experience of self. The normal human being, in contrast to the severely retarded human and to most nonhuman primates, has a sense of self that is unitary over space and time. We say that the "I" stays the same although all else changes. In some people, however, the brain is damaged, and the experience of the self is fractionated. This suggests, at the very least, that the experience of the self is associated in some way with brain processes.

What other conclusions can we draw from human neuro-psychological research? Basic to our understanding of human complex abilities is the concept of lateralization of functions, especially where language, handedness, and visuospatial functions are concerned. These have been explored with brain-bisected patients. The research has shown that whether an individual "knows" or "does not know" something depends on which side of the hemisphere is engaged in the processing of the information in question. The most perplexing results occur when the hemisphere that is normally involved in the task is not able to partake in the execution of the task.

An area where there is much room for speculation and future work is that of conscious and unconscious processes. We touched only briefly on this topic when we discussed the example of the female patient whose left and right hemispheres were alternately exposed to a picture of a nude pinup. The concept of consciousness must be clearly distinguished from the concept of self. Still, the concepts are closely related, and research work often bears on both. The double-mind theory, for example, assumes that the self (which is a *conscious* self) can be localized in the left hemisphere. This assumption fits well with what we find in research with bisected patients. It also fits well with what we know happens all the time with "normal" humans, who may do things without "knowing why." Why is it that we are not more knowledgeable about our unconscious and cannot know more about it even following conscious "probing"? Is it just that the right hemisphere does not "feed into" the left? Or is there active suppression of information, as psychoanalytical theory would have it? How would such suppression, which can be very particular and subtle, take place, physically? These are the kinds of questions that the double-mind theory would have to answer. What seems clear is that real progress in the understanding of the self will depend on how well we can bring together the two disciplines of neuropsychology (where the objective study of brain-behavior relations is primary) and clinical psychology (where the reporting of experience is a fundamental part of the methodology).

SEX ROLES

The study of the psychology of sex roles is fraught with difficulty and controversy. The following are some of the reasons for this. Historically, there has been a substantial amount of experimenter bias in the selection of research problems, in the methodologies used, and in the interpretation given to research findings. This bias usually worked to strengthen, by adding a "scientific" foundation, preconceived stereotypes of male and female behavior. For example, to document the biological basis of sex differences in aggression and in nurturance, investigators typically selected only those animal species in which the behavioral pattern fitted the preconceived notion, ignoring species for which this pattern did not hold. The evidence does not show that there are *no* biologically based differences between males and females with respect to these two behaviors, but the situation is probably more complex than many thought.

A second area of difficulty stems from the emphasis on males and females as *groups*, rather than as individuals, in the study of sex differences. The large variability between individuals, which is perfectly normal and is to be expected, tends to be forgotten. In the popular culture this leads to a solidification of stereotypes and an unhealthy readiness to label as immature, or sick, or somehow odd, an individual who cannot be fitted into the group norm.

Also, it should be noted that the emphasis on sex *differences* has perhaps had a detrimental effect. The similarities between men and women are so great, it is curious that the scientific interest has been in those small areas where the "otherness" of the other is highlighted, but this is a historical problem that is being resolved.

In the future, investigators of the psychology of sex roles will look first and foremost at the flexibility and variability of individual expression regardless of sex. For many, the concept of *androgyny* (from the Greek *aner*, a man. and *gyne*, a woman) has become of paramount importance. An androgynous person is not a unisexual person, as depicted in the mass media, with a certain hairstyle and wardrobe. This notion is equally a stereotype. Rather, someone is androgynous who can think and act in ways that can no longer be tagged as male or female but as simply human, appropriate to the human context.

The exploration of the human potential outside the sex-role boundaries has to start from early childhood. Chapter 3 does not attempt to summarize the vast research literature on the development of sex-roles, acquisition of sex-typed behavior through modeling, and identification with same-sex parents and peers. However, it is obvious that if the future should bring about changes in our attitudes toward sex-typed behaviors, these changes must occur both within the family as well as within society as a whole. It is one thing for parents to provide a relatively non-sex-typed environment for their own children and quite another for these children to *remain* non-sex-typed in society as adolescents and adults if this society remains polarized in its sex roles.

SEX DIFFERENCES AND SOCIAL BEHAVIOR

Women tend to speak more correctly than men and, as we see in Chapter 4, strive harder for correct pronunciation than men do. More than this, in different kinds of tasks and in varied situations, women seem to be more competent verbally. We have considered some alternative explanations including women's greater sensitivity to the stigma of incorrect speech and to its consequences in the face of social-class evaluations. It could be that women have learned to use speech more effectively through necessity under the pressures of dependency, but there is also evidence that females tend to be more fluent, more capable verbally, than males of their equivalent social group.

Up to now research has confirmed that women opt for high-prestige speech forms. When it comes to explaining why this is so, the researchers can do no more than suggest questions that have yet to be answered.

Eye contact studies reveal that in social situations women look more and give more attention to visual cues. These studies are consistent with the hypothesis that women need more feedback about the reactions of other people (because they are less powerful than men). However, this evidence takes us no further toward resolving the speculations listed above, although it indicates the kind of question we should ask.

The patterns of female speech in loudness and pitch are shown to be more expressive and dynamic than the patterns of male speech. Are women actually more expressive, or do they learn to be? Are women sex-typed as both expressive *and* unstable? The female characteristic of expressive speech could be the result of social conventions; it could be similar to the rule that permits women to weep openly when they are sad, although men are supposed to mask their sadness, or to the rule that allows men to show their anger, although women must mask their irritation with a smile. There are many instances where such social training operates. Boys are encouraged at an early age to be more interested in public affairs than girls, just as fathers are supposed to be more interested in politics than mothers. Biological structures, described in Chapter 3, blend with a host of social influences, but the sex-role training of boys and girls goes much deeper than this. In trying to obtain a better view of the depth of these socialization practices, we get some help from Freudian theories. Of course, Freudian theories are controversial. There is not doubt that they have many weaknesses, but we cannot deny their persistence and apparent explanatory power. They are influential in some feminist movements, a rather unexpected development for those of us who tend to reject Freud as a male chauvinist. The advantage of Freudian theories for feminists is that they provide greater understanding of how children are socialized into the patriarchal system.

Evidence from a variety of quarters indicates the strength of the movement for change in women's position in society. A review of experimental studies of conformity points to behavioral changes even since 1970.

The possibilities of change in occupational and marital roles of male and female are discussed, and we note the argument that solutions to discrimination may come out of current pressures to undermine the patriarchal family as a socializing agent.

SOCIAL PSYCHOLOGY

Recently there has been much discussion among social psychologists concerning the use of experimental research. Some of these research designs have been criticized for being trivial and, on top of that, for being less objective than was earlier thought. The results of experiments may be biased in unsuspected ways (as was mentioned in Chapter 5). As research results are published more widely, the student population (from whom experimental volunteers are drawn) becomes more sophisticated about what experimenters attempt to do, and this may affect their performance in experimental tasks. Other possible limitations are mentioned at the end of Chapter 6.

It is evident, therefore, that generalizing from experiments should be undertaken cautiously. It is less likely now than it was during the 1960s that social psychologists will believe that their experiments are the ultimate refinement at the apex of scientific advance. It is more likely that a variety of approaches—observation of everyday behavior, interviews, as well as experiments—will be seen as equally valid parts of the same general search for better understanding.

The experiment rightly remains the classic teaching method, allowing students to share in the practical problems of scientific control, to relate research to theory, to attempt statistical treatment of data, and to gain experience in the new computer techniques of analysis. However, some students and psychologists will feel that these are only preliminaries to going out and slaying a few real dragons.

LANGUAGE AND SOCIAL BEHAVIOR

In our discussion of language in its social context, we describe research studies of bilinguals and of the rules that people follow when they switch from one speech style or dialect to another, and we consider the structure of domains or situations where different speech codes are appropriate for each.

One outstanding question remains. What is the behavior that changes with code-switching? If there is a change of language, what other aspects of individual or group behavior also change? When these questions are answered by research, we will understand more fully the social functions of language—functions that social psychologists have only recently, although successfully, begun to study as a major topic.

Possible changes in personality traits as a bilingual changes from one language to another have been suggested, but we can, as yet, offer no more than hints at the extent and nature of these changes.

We discuss attempts to apply social psychological theories to the individual's choice of speech styles in interpersonal contacts. Here the research approach can focus on the particular conditions of language use in a specific context. At the same time this approach allows the testing of theoretical ideas.

Another aspect of language codes that has received slightly more attention is the study of social class and speech forms. Considering the viewpoints available about "restricted" (lower-class) and "elaborated" (middle-class) codes, we see that the newer evidence does not support such a rigid classification, since it now appears that the "restricted" code may be just as complex and effective. While this does not remove the social stigma attached to nonstandard codes (as mentioned in Chapter 4) nor avoid the element of higher prestige in the standard speech variety, it does detach the notion of deficiency from the non-standard codes.

A different example of higher and lower speech codes is found in the language minorities of North America, where individuals are often multilinguals rather than bilinguals and have to navigate their speech through various standard and nonstandard codes as well as between major languages. Our illustrations of this group are the Acadian and Chicano minorities, who share similarities in their language situation. Here again there are many possibilities for research, either by experiment or by observation of speech behavior in everyday life.

CHILD PSYCHOLOGY

Although the idea is increasingly popular, many psychologists would still disagree that the child comes into the world with innate social tendencies. Some argue that an infant becomes attached to his mother only because she is associated with the satisfaction of primary needs, such as feeding and warmth, and that it is all a matter of reinforcement. It has been shown, for example, that the social smile can be "extinguished" in infants who are exposed to grim-faced adults who do not return the smile.

Those who argue for the social-animal approach typically do so from an evolutionary or ethological perspective (see Chapter 9). For example, the infant of prehistoric times who was not person oriented—especially toward the mother—may have been less likely to survive the threat of predators and other emergencies. Natural selection favors those children who stay near their mothers.

After studying research on child development we can consider other questions that are raised by the findings. How do children learn stereotypes at an early age? Many parents try to avoid exposing their children to negative attitudes, for example toward ethnic minorities. The same parents are often chagrined to discover that their children have acquired precisely these prejudices.

Why are children (and adults for that matter) apparently so ready to *evaluate* other people? Research has consistently shown that evaluation according to a good-bad distinction is the single most important factor in people's judgments—for many nonsocial as well as social stimuli.

One further question: Does egocentric speech really disappear as the child becomes an adult? Some writers suggest that adults are at risk egocentrically all their lives. Speaking under pressure, or while anxious, sometimes leads adults to forget the communicative needs of their listeners.

Chapter 8 focuses on the role of spoken language in the communication process. However, almost nothing is known about how children acquire nonverbal communicative skill (body language). The nature-nurture issue is raised in this area of child development also. Psychologists have presented evidence that very young infants will move rhythmically to the sound of speech, suggesting that the infant may arrive already prepared to use expressive movements during the communication process.

ETHOLOGY AND ENVIRONMENTAL PSYCHOLOGY

The biological roots of human behavior are beginning to be unraveled. Many decades of continued research will be required to develop a comprehensive understanding of the degree of importance genetics have on shaping human behavior. Ethology has provided a framework by which the innate factors of human behavior can be examined.

Using the techniques we have discussed in Chapter 9, a systematic approach can be made.

Continued animal study will also be necessary if the various systems of behavior are to be examined in sufficient detail. Animals provide oportunities for manipulation and experimentation that are not possible with human subjects. By studying primates, we can find parallels in their forms of behavior that give additional insight into the behavior that may have existed before our human technology arrived.

The results of ethological studies of human behavior, giving further understanding of where we fit into the animal world, will probably generate considerable interest and controversies, because beliefs developed over many centuries may be difficult to reconcile with the new data.

The role of environmental psychology in planning for the future appears to be vital. We face a rapidly changing environment in the urban setting. It has become obvious from environmental studies that the immediate environment, building and housing facilities, and the structure of cities have a profound effect on human behavior. The current environment can affect the rates of crime, vandalism, health, and general feelings of satisfaction. If this is the case, then future planning at the individual level, in housing and apartment design, and for groups, in playgrounds and in cities, will be indispensable.

Index

Aggression, as sex-typed behavior,
    41–43, 45
Animal(s)
  behavior
    appetitive, 156–157
    consummatory, 156–157
    evolution of, 158–159
    refractory, 156–157
    ritualization of, 157–158
    stages of, 156–157
    stereotyped, 160–161
  behavior development in, 151–152
  behavior motivation in, 152–156
    external stimuli, 154–156
    internal stimuli, 153–154
  communication in, 147–163
  expressive behavior in, 157–158
  fixed-action patterns in, 160–161
  and humans, continuity between,
    149–150
  interspecies communication,
    possibility of, 162–163
  territorialism in, 168–171
Aphasia, 21–22
  recovery from, related to
    handedness, 24
Arcuate bundle, 22
Astereognosis, 30

Behavior
  hormonal influence on, 36–39
Bilingualism, 85–89
  in Acadians, 99–100
Brain
  bisection, 26
  Broca's area, 21
  cerebral cortex, 16–17
    functions of, 18–19
  cerebral dominance in, 21–22
    for speech, linked with
      handedness, 23–25
  contralateral control of body, 21
    defined, 19
  see also Split-brain(s)

cross-communication in, 20
evolution of, 16–17
forebrain, 16
function, defined, 17–18
functions, lateralization of, 19,
    26–29
gyrus, 17
ipsilateral control of body-half,
    defined, 19
left hemisphere, functions
    lateralized to, 24–25, 26–29
lobes, 17
paired structure of, 19–20
prenatal sexual bias in, 36–39
right hemisphere, functions
    lateralized to, 24–25, 26–29
structure of, related to function,
    17–19
Wernicke's area, 21
Buildings
  effect of, on behavior, 180–181
  see also Environment

Cerebral cortex, 16–17
Child psychology
  research questions for, 196–197
  see also Children
Children
  communication skills in, 135–137
    development of, experiential
      factors of, 140–144
    and competency in, 137–140
  egocentric communication in,
    130–133
  egocentrism in, 127–129, 133–134
  moral judgments made by,
    116–119
  perception of intent by, 116–119
  personality descriptions made by,
    119–122
  perspective-taking skills in,
    134–135
  socialized speech in, 129–130
  social perception in, 107–124

Chromosomes, role of, in
    determining sex, 33–34
Cities
    effect of, on behavior, 175–182
    see also Environment
    structural factors that enhance
        satisfaction with, 187–190
Codes, use of, and social status,
    90–92
Code-switching, 89–90, 97–98
Commissure, defined, 20
Corpus callosum, evolution of, 20
Crowding, effect of, on behavior,
    179–180

Dextrals, see Handedness, right
Diglossia, 85–89
    in Acadians, 99–100

Emotion(s), perception of, 114–116
Environment
    "hardened," effect of, 183–185,
        186–187
    influence of, on behavior, 175–182
Environmental design, to prevent
    vandalism, 185–187
Estrogen, 35
Ethograms, 150–151
Ethology
    defined, 148
    research questions for, 197–198

Facial recognition, in development of
    social competency, 113–114
Female, embryologic development of,
    33–39
Feminism, 60–63
Fissure, 17
Forebrain, 16

Gyrus, 17

Halo effect, 121
    defined, 110

Handedness, 22–23
    and cerebral dominance for speech,
        23–25
    development of, 23
    lack of counterpart to in animals,
        22
    left, origins of, 24–25
    mixed, 22
    right, prevalence of, 22
    see also Brain, cerebral dominance
        in
Hermaphroditism, progestin-
    induced, 36, 38–39
Hormones, role of, in sex
    determination, 34–39
Human(s)
    and animals, continuity between,
        149–150
    brain bisection in, 26–29
    emotions, importance of, 165
    ethology, 163–165
    expressive behavior, 166–167
    releasing stimuli in, 167–168
    territorialism in, 168–171

Language
    brain area(s) governing, 21
    domains of, 95–96
    as facilitator of social
        development, 137–140
    forms of address, 92–94
    and personality, 94–95
    and social behavior
        research questions about,
            195–196
        theories about, 97–98
    and social status, 90–92
    and social stereotypes, 100–103
    see also Bilingualism; Codes;
        Code-switching; Diglossia;
        Speech
Left-handedness, see Handedness

Male, embryologic development of,
    33–39
Marriage, changing nature of, 66–68

Men
  social status of, 60–61
  see also Language; Sex differences;
    Sex-typed behavior
Mullerian-inhibiting substance, role
  of, in sex differentiation, 35

Neuroanatomy
  defined, 17
  see also Brain
Neurophysiology, defined, 17
Neuropsychology
  conclusions drawn from, 191–192
  defined, 17
  research questions for, 192

Object permanence, 109

Patriarchy, 60–62
Perception, 29–31
  see also Social perception
Perceptual constancy, 108
Primacy effect, defined, 111
Progesterone, 35
Progestin, 36

Rape, and social status of women,
  63–65
Right-handedness, see Handedness

Self
  definition of, 15
  as perceiver, 29–31
  recognition of, 31–32
Sex differences
  cognitive-developmental theory of,
    39–40
  cultural determinants of, 43–47
  genetic determination of, 33–34
  in nonverbal communication,
    55–56
  psychoanalytic theory of, 40–41
  and social behavior, conclusions
    about, 194–195
  social-learning theory of, 39

in speech, 49–56
and submissiveness, 65–66
Sex roles
  controversies about, 192–193
  and submissiveness, 65–66
Sex-typed behavior
  acquisition of, theories about,
    39–41
  cultural influences on, 43–47
  see also Animal(s); Human(s)
Sexual identity, development of,
  39–40
Sinistrals, see Handedness, left
Social perception
  accuracy in, 111–112
  defined, 108–112
  emotion perception, 114–116
  in infants, 112–113
  and socialization, 122–124
Social psychology
  attitude measures in, 80–81
  conclusions about, 195
  fashions in, 81–84
  scope of, 71–72
  sociometric tests in, 80–81
  theories in, 79–80
  unit of study, 73–79
    dyad, 74, 76–77
    group, 74–75, 77–79
    individual, 74, 75–76
Speech
  cerebral dominance for, 23–25
  intonation, sex differences in,
    57–60
  sex differences in, 49–56
Split-brain(s)
  in animals, 25–26
  in humans, 26–29
Stereotyping, defined, 110
Sulcus, 17

Tachistoscope, 26
Territorialism, 168–171
Testicular feminizing syndrome, 38
Testosterone
  influence of, during critical period
    of gestation, 37–38

Testosterone—*continued*
 role of
  in aggressive behavior, 42
  in sex determination, 35–36
Turner's syndrome, 35

Vandalism, and environmental
 factors, 183–185
Visual field, defined, 26

Wada test, 23

Women
 attention to visual cues, 55–56
 preferences for correct speech,
  49–55
 role of, in marriage, 66–68
 social sensitivity of, 51–52, 55–56
 social status of
  future, 59–60
  and speech, 58
  and rape, 63–65
 see also Female; Sex differences;
  Sex roles; Sex-typed behavior

NOTES

NOTES

NOTES

NOTES

NOTES

NOTES

NOTES

NOTES